STAR-MAKING MACHINERY

STAR-MAKING MACHINERY:

INSIDE THE BUSINESS OF ROCK AND ROLL

GEOFFREY STOKES

VINTAGE BOOKS
A DIVISION OF RANDOM HOUSE, NEW YORK

Library of Congress Cataloging in Publication Data

Stokes, Geoffrey.
Star-making machinery.
Includes index.
1. Phonorecords—Industry and trade. 2. Rock musicians.
I. Title.
[ML3795.S856S7 1977]   338.4'7'789912   77-3061
ISBN 0-394-72432-1

Designed by Ingrid Beckman
Manufactured in the United States of America

For my mother. And the memory of my father.

ACKNOWLEDGMENTS

ANY BOOK COMES TRAILING its own network of indebtedness, and I suspect that first books carry a longer skein than most. The minimum list is long, but it is minimum. The most general debt, I suppose, is to the people who decided that my early attempts at learning to be a writer were not simply some awful manifestation of delayed adolescence, and who looked at my beginner's manuscripts without rolling around on the floor and giggling. Ross Wetzsteon and Diane Fisher, who first brought me to the *Voice,* were important, as were Jonathon Greene and Jerome Berne, who in London cheerfully accepted me as part of that city's free-lance fellowship. Similarly, in New York, I owe enormous debts to that shifting cluster of writers who meet at Dockery's to discuss agents, editors, the Knicks, the latest TV comedies, and other manifestations of the decline of the West. My thanks to them are general, but go especially to John Stickney, who helped me work on the initial proposal for this book and introduced me to his agent, Helen Brann, who is now mine as well. For support, love, and criticism in both cities—as well as in a half-dozen odd corners of my mind—I owe more to Karen Durbin than I can express without embarrassing both of us.

Once one starts this sort of thing, of course, there's no stopping the flow of thanks, and I could probably go on back to my kindergarten teacher with almost no effort, but it would be impossible for me not to mention my colleagues and editors at the *Voice.* Jack Newfield and Phil Tracy encouraged my natural skepticism; Alan Weitz and Judy Daniels taught me a great deal about expressing it coherently. Most important, because he has so far never let me get away with a lazy thought, is the ruthless editor of the music section, Bob Christgau.

In my early research for this book, I was aided by Susan Munao, then of Gibson and Stromberg; Tony Martell of Famous Music; and scores of music-business publicists. My obligations to the Cody entourage—especially to their long-suffering bookkeeper and fan, Susan Nadolna, who despite her fondness for ZZ Top is a sound and sensible woman—are manifest on every page. Joe and Bonnie Kerr put me up and put up with me; Rick and Rita Higginbotham were kind when I was dumb; Mary Hunt acted as though she thought I might actually write a book, and helped me through a dozen dark hours. But my greatest debt, obviously, is to the Airmen themselves and to their road crew, for letting me share so much of their lives. I had hoped, when I began this project, that I could hang around long enough to become invisible; instead—and better —I became a friend. I wish them the best of their dreams.

My prime debts at Warner Brothers are to Stan Cornyn, who took the time to introduce me to his colleagues and ease their natural nervousness; Ron Goldstein, who patiently led me from office to office in Burbank; and Bob Merlis of their East Coast office, who was a help in all my efforts, early and late. Most of all, I am grateful to Lew Feldstein, without whose intercession I would still be standing on a Burbank street corner, trying to get past the guard.

Between the record company and the performer, as always, stands the producer. John Boylan, who walked into a project without knowing that he was to be observed throughout it, accepted my presence with patience and grace; Paul Grupp went out of his way to clarify various knotty technical points so that even I could understand them. I was also sprung unawares on the staff and management of the Record Plant, who took me like the troupers they are.

Many of the people listed above read the manuscript as it was coming along, and I am particularly grateful to Paul Grupp and Barry Hessenius for their detailed technical comments. Others who read bits and pieces of it include Kit Rachlis, Bob Christgau, and Janet Beller. Their suggestions, when I followed them, turned out to be almost unfailingly useful, and they are surely not to be blamed for my stubbornly rejecting other, equally useful ones. I am also grateful to Robin Smith for taking time out of a Manhattan journey to track down an article that I had somehow lost.

David and Dinni Gordon also read the manuscript. Their criticisms improved it, of course, but that was really the least of their many contributions to this book and to my life. Without their generosity the book surely would have been different from what it is, and might not have been at all.

Diane Giddis of Bobbs-Merrill is a good editor. And I say that now, while I am busy hating her for all the rewriting she put me through. In a month I'll probably argue that she's better than good.

The people who bore the brunt of my own surly creativity are Liam and Timothy Stokes. Far more than any of us wished, they lived through a hundred variations of "I can't right now, I'm working." They took it better than I had any right to expect. For their patience, for their love—for them—I am eternally grateful.

And speaking of grateful, a word for the Dead, whose music kept reminding me why I was writing this book. And for the Joy of Cooking, Rod Stewart, Doc Watson, the Stones . . .

Shelter Island, New York
OCTOBER 1975

STAR-MAKING MACHINERY:

THE ODYSSEY OF AN ALBUM

1

THERE WAS a euphoric moment, not so long ago, when all the struggles in America came together, when veterans of civil rights marches, student demonstrations, and antiwar efforts coalesced into "the Movement." Hundreds, even thousands, of small victories had convinced its members that they could realize their dream for their country. The Movement marched to a different guitar—an electric one. For it was also a time when rock'n'roll was exploding into rock, the music that critic Robert Christgau has usefully defined as "all music deriving primarily from the energy and influence of the Beatles—and maybe Bob Dylan, and maybe you should stick pretensions in there someplace."

Rock'n'roll, among its other entertaining aspects, had created a wall of apparently unintelligible noise that separated the first consciously teenage generation from their parents. As that generation grew into the rock generation, the new music both reflected and shaped them. If the old music had distinguished young people from their parents, the new music—from "Fixin' to Die Rag" to "White Rabbit"—separated them from their country's conventional wisdom. It reminded them—and some of their elders—that even the President of the United States sometimes has to stand naked.

It was not only the consciously political writers and performers— Dylan, the Jefferson Airplane, Baez, Crosby, Stills—who informed the understanding of the generation that tried to save America from what it was becoming; Elvis Presley and Chuck Berry belonged to them as well. In 1968 a hundred thousand marchers sang "Blowin' in the Wind" on their way to the Pentagon, but the portable radios around the campfires in the Washington night played good old rock'n'roll, as did the radios in the New Hampshire storefronts where hundreds of young volunteers returned to report the votes they'd found for Eugene McCarthy. And when those votes were counted, they confirmed that the times *were* a-changin'.

Or so it seemed. Five years later the Osmond Brothers sang at one of the parties celebrating Richard Nixon's second inaugural. The political system had spewed forth an atrocity, and the corporate hegemony had provided him with its own predigested, unthreatening music. Clearly, the Movement had underestimated the resilience of the political system and overestimated the strength of its music.

Now, in the midst of the sometimes somnolent seventies, the facile optimism of the late sixties seems a little silly. It was perhaps too easy to confuse the musical and political revolutions, to wish into being the force that Ann Arbor political theorist and musician John Sinclair romantically termed a "Guitar Army." But as naïve as the theoreticians may have been, and as embarrassing as their apocalyptic visions may now seem, their theories were based on the undeniable confluence of radical impulses in music and politics. Though rock may not have made the revolution, it did define a sensibility. More important, especially in its more adventurous black branches, it still does. The popularity of the O'Jays' "Rich Get Richer," a song explicitly condemning the Gettys and the Rockefellers, denies the argument that rock has lost its political and countercultural impact.

If it sometimes appears to have done so, that is at least as much because the cultural mainstream has shifted in the direction of the music as the other way around. Yet the shift would probably not have taken place without the cooperation of the giant companies that were among the targets of rock's initial political impulse. Somewhere along the line, the commercial capital of the music industry, Los Angeles, captured and marketed the intellectual ferment of San Francisco; and, in the East, uptown conglomerates co-opted the sounds of downtown coffeehouses. Rock became a business, a part of the American economic base.

Though the outlines of the takeover and some of its implications are clear, the details are fuzzy, and even the most avid partisans of rock frequently have only the sketchiest idea of how their chosen music comes to them. Like city children who have never seen a cow—much less a dairy farm or a milk co-op's membership meeting—and therefore "know" that milk comes from cartons, most listeners choose simply to believe that rock comes from records.

And perhaps they are right. Connecting with a new piece of music is at least as much visceral as it is intellectual, and history may merely get in the way of the immediacy that has long been rock's strong suit. Nevertheless, the record we hear on the radio or on our own equipment is the end product of a long chain of events that shapes the nature of the music as surely as the commercial imperatives of the thirties' Hollywood dream factories changed their films—which in turn changed their audiences.

The rock chain may begin with a musician strumming his guitar in a tenement walk-up, but it includes a bewildering array of technology, armies of lawyers and accountants, and considerable wheeling and dealing in money and in drugs. All these elements are among the complicated mix that Joni Mitchell called "the star maker machinery/behind the popular song." This book is about the workings of that machinery.

To some extent, it is simply the biography of an album, the story of how one of the nearly five thousand albums produced in 1974 made its way from the practice hall to the pop charts. The band that recorded it, a San Francisco–based outfit known as Commander Cody and His Lost Planet Airmen, is not a supergroup of the "instant hit" variety. Their success depends at least partly on how hard their work is pushed. So the book is also—for the journey to the charts happens in no other way—a chronicle of the interplay between the giant corporations that invest in and profit from the music that a generation once considered genuinely revolutionary.

2

THE REVOLUTIONARY DREAM may have faded—or been stifled—but the commercial reality remains. For regardless of all that can be said about its political and social importance, rock music has become a commodity. Show business is like shoe business: it is subject to passing fads and fancies, some of which can be manipulated by the shoe manufacturers themselves, and it deals with a product that is packaged and sold to consumers. It is also a very big business.

Just how big can best be seen by comparing it to America's previous myth bearer, the film industry. In 1974 Americans paid $1.7 billion to exercise their fantasies at the movies. That's a full $500 million less than they spent on records and tapes (and 1974 was an exceptionally good year for films; a year earlier, the gap had been $700 million). To use another touchstone, the $2.2 billion that Americans spent on rock records was more than three times as much as they spent to see all the various national pastimes—football, hockey, basketball, and baseball, both college and professional—added together.

Impressive as these figures are, they don't include record sales in the rest of the world, which bring the total to $3.5 billion annually. Nor do they include the various ancillary developments that reflect the growth of the rock industry and its central place in our culture. Sales of musical instruments, sheet music, professional and home stereo equipment, and admissions to clubs and concert halls send the annual world-wide gross well up over $4 billion. (Even during the recession-plagued autumn of 1974, *Performance* magazine reported concert grosses averaging more than $10 million monthly, a figure which has held constant since then.)

Important as the ancillary segments of the industry are in their own right, they have increasingly become appendages of the record industry. Many bands now give concerts only during the time immediately after an album is released; groups on these promotional tours have largely supplanted the barnstorming bands that used to crisscross the country. And even those bands that tour year-round find it difficult to get bookings if they lack recordings, for record sales and airplay promote concert sales.

And concerts, in turn, promote record sales. Thus record companies seeking to introduce a new band will frequently "guarantee" a tour, promising the formerly independent concert promoters that the company will purchase enough tickets to make good any possible losses incurred in booking such groups. All this may seem fairly reasonable: how else is a new band to be introduced to concert audiences? But these guarantees give local promoters a way to avoid the risks formerly inherent in their chosen business. They allow the record companies to dictate which performers concertgoers will be allowed to hear.

Such control, of course, requires large amounts of concentrated capital, which provides one explanation for the marked acceleration in the industry's tendency toward centralization during the past few years. During the fifties a small number of major record companies dominated the American record industry (Charles Gillett's scholarly *The Sound of the City* defines "majors" as companies that "had their own distribution systems, which enabled them to ensure that each of their records would get to retailers in every retail market"), but those companies were initially hostile to rock'n'roll. They preferred instead to concentrate on their dependable Eddie Fishers and Perry Comos. As a result, the birth of rock'n'roll sparked the growth of scores of smaller companies that were willing to record the "jungle beat" music scorned by the majors. Many of these independents had already learned something about distributing records within the black "rhythm and blues" market, which the majors had abandoned during the Second World War because of material shortages. Occasionally the independents were able to move their unique product over into the larger pop market without being at a competitive disadvantage.

For the majors, the results were devastating. In 1955, of the fifty-one records that appeared on the *Billboard* top-ten charts, only eight were rock'n'roll records, and the majors beat out the independents by a score of forty to eleven. Within two years, when seventy records made the charts—forty-three of them rock'n'roll—the situation had nearly reversed, and the independents outscored the majors forty to thirty. Within a few years, many of the major companies were struggling for their lives; MGM and Mercury were lucky to achieve even occasional hits, and CBS, which had been the major company most resistant to rock'n'roll, had suffered a sales decline so precipitous that its parent corporation jettisoned the record division's management to bring in a team more sympathetic to the new music.

The majors fought back and began rerecording, or "covering," versions of songs recorded on the smaller independent labels. The Crewcuts covered the Chords' version of "Sh-Boom" and gave RCA a big hit. Georgia Gibbs attempted a note-for-note re-creation of LaVerne Baker's "Tweedlee-Dee," and Pat Boone covered a whole series of records by the inimitable Little Richard. With bland, formulaic, and (not-so-incidentally) white versions of black artists available to the majors, the independents no longer had a unique product and were forced to compete directly with the sophisticated marketing techniques of the majors. Predictably, the majors ate them alive and were firmly back in control of the pop charts by 1958. When rock, which was a bit more difficult to imitate than the earlier music had been, burst onto the scene during the early sixties, the majors were not about to repeat their earlier mistakes. Rock artists got contracts almost as fast as they could learn to play their instruments—and in at least some cases, it seemed, quite a bit faster.

Yet even if the majors had moved less rapidly to sign the new talent emerging from campuses and bars around the country, it is unlikely that they would have faced any severe challenge from independent recording companies. By the time rock arrived, the majors were more thoroughly in control of the market than ever, having used their money to achieve both horizontal and vertical integration. Though the horizontal process of mergers and acquisitions was more visible, vertical integration was more important; mergers and acquisitions merely prefaced it. For example, Warner Brothers Records' acquisition of Reprise and Atlantic Records, then, through mergers, of the Elektra label, gave the resulting firm enough wholesale volume to make establishing its own vertical distribution system economically feasible.

Other companies extended their vertical integration both into the pre-recording aspects of the business, by acquiring or forming music-publishing firms, and into the post-wholesale arena (both CBS and ABC operate retail record store chains). But for many independents, the urge to merge was fired directly by their inability to get control of the wholesale level. In the record industry, as in most other businesses, the level known as "the distributor" lies between the manufacturer and the retailer. Distributors buy records at one price from a manufacturer—in the range of $2.50 for a record carrying a retail price of $5.98—and sell them at a markup—generally for a price in the area of $3.00—to retail dealers. The smaller companies, which move into the national market less frequently than the majors, have no choice but to rely on a loose network of independent distributors to get their product into the stores and thus to the consumer. Only the largest companies can afford the costs of maintaining their own distribution systems.

The major advantage of such wholly owned distribution systems is that they allow the record companies to emphasize certain of their products—a key way to develop and expose the new talent that the companies hope will keep them on top of the corporate heap. Barring the kind of complicated special discount deals on which grand juries have looked with considerable skepticism, the smaller record companies have no comparable leverage on their distributors, for those distributors are by definition independent businessmen. Because their profits depend directly on their volume, it makes no sense for them to push the first few copies of a record that has only an outside chance of becoming a hit. In the same period of time they can instead move hundreds of units by an established performer. Thus not only does a lack of control over its distribution limit a company's potential for present profits; it hampers its ability to grow by developing new artists.

Vertical integration was not the only factor that contributed to the re-establishment of the majors' hegemony. Two other circumstances, each related to the rich getting richer, helped solidify their dominance during the sixties. The first was the increasing internationalization of rock music. It began with the Beatles and the "English invasion" and continued to expand through the emergence of other European artists as important figures in the American pop market. In the early seventies, well after the initial glut of English demi-Beatles had sorted itself out, bands like Focus (the Netherlands), Fusion (Poland), PFM (Italy), and a number of German acts began to make regular appearances on the American charts.

During the pre-Beatles years the large American companies which had held royalty/distribution agreements with their major European counterparts benefited almost willy-nilly from the global expansion of the rock market. For example, though EMI, the largest European music conglomerate, had the right to repackage Capitol's records in its native territories, and Capitol held American rights to EMI's home-grown products, the chief effect of such agreements was to increase the sales of American products abroad. In fact, most American companies rarely found it worthwhile to exercise their options on European records. As late as 1963, when the Beatles' first album appeared, EMI was unable to persuade Capitol to undertake an American release and had to turn instead to a tiny Chicago-based independent, Vee Jay. When the Beatles and their English followers began to take off, however, the large companies promptly called in their options. Vee Jay, which had run the major risk of handling the then-unknown Beatles, rapidly disappeared from the picture, and Capitol assumed the hugely profitable band at practically no risk at all. And the other major companies followed suit; of that first generation of English rockers, only the Rolling Stones survived despite independent distribution.

The second circumstance, partly technological and partly aesthetic, that helped ensure the majors' domination was the increase in the pop album market. When CBS brought out the first LP, the 33-rpm record, it was primarily conceived of as providing uninterrupted play for classical and jazz works whose natural flow had been interrupted by bothersome record changing. Pop albums were released, but they were largely collections of singles, packages of three-minute tunes similar to the familiar bulky boxes of 78s. But rock musicians saw other possibilities behind the technology and gradually began to take advantage of it. Almost all the Beatles' later work, as well as the Who's *Tommy* and even lengthy singles like Dylan's album-length "Sad Eyed Lady of the Lowlands," reflect conscious use of the new technology.

The LP revolution was felt most strongly in the rock and pop segments of the industry; both country and soul music continued to have a lively singles market that was notably more supportive to independent companies. Motown, a black-owned company that got its start in the singles market, eventually expanded to the point where it was secure enough to challenge the majors on their own terms. But many of the independents were one-hit companies that simply lacked the economic staying power to sustain a run of bad luck or bad judgment. For them, survival frequently meant accepting distribution or merger contracts with the majors.

The smaller independents that would have liked to move more actively into the album market were at an additional economic disadvantage: there was more money to be made in albums, but more to be lost as well. For the capital-poor independents, the downside risk often proved disastrous. The potential profit margin on an album far outweighed that of a comparable single, but its startup costs were approximately five times as high. An independent company with capital of $10,000 could easily turn out a single for $2,000 in production costs. If it became a hit, the label was of course instantly ahead of the game, but if not, the company's losses were still manageable. Besides, it had $8,000 remaining: four more chances to get even.

The same company could also bet its entire $10,000 on one album. If that album was a money-maker, all well and good, but if it missed, the company was out of business. Thus the advent of the LP changed the rules of the record game dramatically. Issuing an album was like a roulette player's throwing his entire pile of chips onto double zero instead of cautiously betting colors.

In any case, the day of the $10,000 album has long passed. Except for a few freakish examples, competition in the use of increasingly sophisticated studio techniques (as one producer put it, "Everybody's making perfect albums now") have escalated production costs for relatively modest albums into the $50,000 range. When one adds even minimal costs for packaging, distribution, and promotion, it becomes clear that only those with large amounts of capital can afford to sit down at the record-industry roulette table.

Though all these changes were gradual over the ten-year period from Elvis to the Beatles, their net effect was perceived by even the most obtuse artists and managers. Artists with real hopes for hits were better off surviving on barroom gigs while waiting to be discovered by the majors than they were signing with an independent. Not only could a major company advance enough money for studio costs so that the performers' work would not be at a disadvantage in technical quality; it could guarantee exposure and distribution.

As a result of all these forces, only one small independent company— Fantasy, with Creedence Clearwater Revival—had consistent rock-chart success during the late sixties and early seventies. Quasi-independent companies that signed distribution agreements with the majors did somewhat better, but in the mid-seventies the majors were as firmly in control of the industry as they had been in the days before rock'n'roll.

Though the exact figures are hidden behind various conglomerate screens, the best industry estimates are that two companies, Warner's and CBS, held over half of the domestic market during 1974. A handful of other majors divided all but 5 to 10 percent of the remaining share. The same drive for efficiency that gradually centralized the automobile industry into a "big three" had squeezed much of the competition from the record business. Like the automobile industry too, the record business was now so concentrated that it could defy conventional economic pieties. Faced with falling sales during the 1974 recession, both industries promptly *raised* their prices.

That sort of oligopoly is hardly the stuff revolutionary (or, for that matter, traditionally entrepreneurial) dreams are made of, but it is the reality of the only medium through which performers can reach the world. And reaching the world, of course, was what the Movement had been about.

The painful political paradox has not been successfully resolved. Some performers who have risen through the system have tried to shake it off by starting their own labels, but that path is economically open only to the hardiest of superstars. And for many of them, such moves may be dictated by a desire to exploit the economic system rather than to challenge it; one would hesitate to ascribe the explicitly political motivations of the Jefferson Starship to, say, Elton John or Led Zeppelin. And even the Starship's label, Grunt Records, is distributed exclusively by RCA.

Of the bands that started their own labels, only the Grateful Dead tried

—for reasons that they willingly admit were not of undiluted political purity—to break completely with the majors' system of distribution. Their brave beginning, however, soon faltered; the records they marketed on their own label failed to achieve the sales level of their Warner's efforts, which had enjoyed the services of WEA, the Warner-Elektra-Atlantic distribution system. Late in 1975 the Dead abandoned their attempt to build an alternative distribution system and signed a distribution agreement with United Artists Records. The first album released under that agreement climbed rapidly into the upper reaches of the sales charts, easily rivaling the band's best days at Warner Brothers.

Unless one subscribes to the theory that the Dead's recorded efforts on their own behalf were artistically inferior to those immediately preceding and following their company's brief life (which is of course possible, but difficult to support), their experience inescapably demonstrates the dominant role that the major corporations' distribution systems have given them in the music business. And if the hugely popular Grateful Dead could not make it on their own, it is clear that marginal artists' survival depends totally on the major record companies.

For a rock artist, survival means being heard. If an album falls in the forest and nobody hears it . . . The test of rock, as of any popular art, is finally its popularity in the marketplace. The giant corporations are therefore not extraneous to rock as a popular art; they are essential to it. Only against this background can we begin to understand the making and marketing of the fifth album by Commander Cody and His Lost Planet Airmen.

3

"AND NOW-OW-OW"—despite the best efforts of a team of audio specialists, the outdoor sound system in Central Park had a persistent echo— "WNEW-FM is proud to present . . . COMMANDER CODY AND HIS LOST PLANET AIRMEN!!" In a ritual made somewhat desultory by the heat of New York in July, fifty thousand people struggled to their feet as eight musicians shambled onto the makeshift stage. It was another in the series of free concerts that a local radio station was sponsoring in New York's parks during the summer of 1974. Of the half-dozen scheduled throughout the city's boroughs, this one—featuring both Cody and the New Riders of the Purple Sage—was the largest.

From the distant edges of the crowd spread over the Sheep Meadow, the band seemed miniaturized, too small to account for the sound that came booming from the strategically placed speakers. The lead singer, in a flurry of opening numbers which echoed rockabilly hits of the fifties, gestured energetically enough, but somehow meaninglessly. The personality of the band began to come clear only when one moved closer to the stage. There, where it was possible to see them sweating and struggling through the afternoon's mugginess, one got a sense of Commander Cody and His Lost Planet Airmen as more than just a bunch of noise-producing automatons.

George Frayne, a.k.a. Commander Cody, sat (or sometimes stood) exuberantly pounding on a grand piano to the left of the stage, sweat pouring down his shirtless back as he periodically downed one of a never-ending supply of cold beers placed on his amplifier by the road crew. Opposite him, at the other end of the stage, Ernie Hagar sat almost

motionless behind his pedal steel guitar. A veteran of more than twenty
years in country music (he once backed up Roy Rogers), Hagar looked
slightly out of place in the midst of a group of long-haired freaks. His own
hair was short and neatly groomed, and his flowered cowboy shirt was the
only outward indication that he was not still practicing the engineering
profession for which he had trained in his native Canada. Yet his soaring
steel guitar was very much part of the band, and occasionally, when some
especially complicated lick had ridden out over the other instruments, he
permitted himself a quiet smile.

Next to Hagar, looking like a cross between Fat Freddy, the Fabulous
Furry Freak Brother, and the-kid-who-was-always-smartest-in-physics,
was Andy Stein. Stein was capable of producing raucous, honking saxophone lines during the band's rock numbers, but he was most at home on
the fiddle—so much at home that it did no violence to his playing to refer
to his instrument as a violin. In the band's earliest days, Stein had divided
his time between the Airmen and the Toledo Symphony, once causing a
certain amount of consternation when he rushed onstage during the middle
of one of the band's appearances—in a particularly seedy bar—still
wearing tails from an early-evening concert engagement.

Standing center stage, clutching the microphone and bouncing with
manic energy, was Billy C. Farlow. The lead singer, and a man who would
have been most uncomfortable in tails, Farlow was born in Alabama and
moved to Detroit as part of the red-clay-to-auto-factory exodus. As a
teenager, Farlow had wanted to be Elvis Presley, and to some extent he
still did. The major difference between him and a thousand other Detroit
teenagers who dreamed of escaping the auto factories through rock'n'roll
was that Farlow could sing. Brandishing his guitar and flipping his mike
stand from side to side, he invariably brought audiences to their feet with
his closing set of rockabilly tunes.

His guitar, however, was not plugged in; audible and more dependable
guitarists flanked him. To his left was John Tichy, and to his right, Bill
Kirchen. Tichy, the most bookish of the Airmen, played a creditable
rhythm guitar and sang lead on the Airmen's straight country ballads.
Kirchen was like Tichy turned inside out: Tichy was slim, blond, and
conventionally handsome; Kirchen peered at the world through thin,
straggling hair and thick steel-rimmed glasses. Not only were their physical appearances different; their skills were complementary. Kirchen's
deep bass voice was adequate for country ballads, but he shone as the
band's lead guitarist. Perhaps the most genuinely witty member of the
band, he had a self-effacing stage manner that had delayed the recognition
for his lean, fluid guitar lines that a more flamboyant style might have won
him.

If Kirchen was self-effacing, however, the Airmen's rhythm section tended toward invisibility. Though Buffalo Bruce Barlow's shoulder-length blond hair, which had gained him his nickname, made him instantly recognizable, he generally worked toward the rear of the stage, coming forward with his bass guitar only to add his high harmonies to the vocal mikes, then retreating again into the background and standing near the drums.

Lance Dickerson, frequently hidden by the singers shifting from mike to mike, sat center stage rear and, with Barlow, provided the steady beat around which the more visible Airmen wove their instrumental and vocal lines. Dickerson's father, whom he described as a "Michigan hillbilly," was also a drummer, and Dickerson had entered the family trade via a series of Detroit rock'n'roll bands before hooking up with the Airmen.

Though the initial impression they made, reinforced by their frequent recourse to the bucket of iced Heinekens that stood center stage, was one of boozy casualness, the Airmen's playing refuted the image. The instrumental solos alternated in a pattern that featured each member of the band in turn, and even the fills—the instrumental phrases that appeared to be randomly tossed in behind the soloists—moved from instrument to instrument. At one moment there were rippling piano runs, at another the sweet, sustained soaring of the pedal steel, and at another the booming, echoing bass strings of the guitar. Even the alternation of styles, from purest country and western through tongue-in-cheek parodies (with stops along the rock'n'roll tradition), signaled careful preparation and implied a long history of playing together.

The history had begun almost ten years earlier, when George Frayne was starting college. Product of a middle-class Long Island upbringing, he was a model high-school student, or at least an acceptable student-athlete, county champion in shot put and fifth statewide in the high jump. In 1960, ostensibly to study art, Frayne headed for a typical jock-oriented school, the University of Michigan.

There, however, things athletic did not work out quite as planned, and though Frayne continued to paint, he wound up spending most of his time at the campus's wildest fraternity, from which he was eventually expelled for refusing to move from a tree house he'd built in their back yard. But before he was thrown out, he had struck up a friendship with some other mal-located freaks, among them musicians like guitarist John Tichy.

"There's no way of figuring out exactly how it happened," Tichy recalled twelve years later. "One night I ran into George, who had been talking a lot about being in a lifeguard band called the Fantastic Surfing Beavers [Tichy didn't blanch at the idea of a band made up of lifeguards or even at the name they'd adopted], and we started to play together—old songs mostly." Their country laments struck a responsive chord on campus, and other university musicians began coming over to jam with them. Among them was a nervous escapee from the music school, Andy Stein.

Stein did not actually regard himself as escaping from serious music— "It was just a goof, y'know. Besides, I like to play *everything*"—but he, Frayne, and Tichy found a handful of other middle-American misfits, formed a weekend band, and started playing at campus parties.

During the same mid-sixties period Billy C. Farlow was coming to maturity in Detroit. Farlow, his soft drawl a reminder of his southern heritage, remembers meeting Frayne: "I always knew that I wasn't gonna work makin' cars, that I was gonna be some kind of musician instead. I knew I could play, guitar and harmonica mostly, and I sure thought I could sing. So I was in a whole bunch of high-school rock'n'roll bands and eventually put my own together. It was called Billy C. and the Sunshine, and I guess we must've played every rock'n'roll bar in Detroit. After a while we began getting gigs in the colleges around, and that's when we met up with George and those guys down at the university."

Largely through Tichy's influence, Frayne's group was playing a lot of straight country music, but they and Farlow shared a root fondness for fifties rock, and eventually the two bands merged into the first version of Commander Cody and His Lost Planet Airmen. The name had come to Frayne one afternoon when he was watching an old sci-fi movie on television: "There were all these outasight cowboys floating through space, and that seemed to me to be just right for the kind of band we were turning out to be." As leader of the combined venture, Frayne became Commander Cody.

There is something of a contradiction inherent in the idea of a "Commander" merely accepting, rather than directing, "the kind of band we were turning out to be," but it is a contradiction that was very much part of the times and setting in which the Airmen got together. As a band, they embodied the intellectual/working-class synthesis that was central to the radical theorists who envisioned a bridge between Ann Arbor and Detroit. The "rock as revolution" thinking of John Sinclair was very much part of the Ann Arbor environment, and the Airmen—with varying degrees of self-consciousness—were playing "the people's music."

"George never talked about it much," said a veteran of the Movement years, "and I don't know if he was even conscious of it, but he seemed to me to be almost deliberately suppressing his leadership role. I mean, you couldn't go out and play touch football without George getting involved in diagramming every play, but he really stood back and let that band take its own natural shape. I like to think that it was all the stuff that we'd been talking about, about our own need to learn from the workers, but I really don't know. It's probably just as likely that he took touch football more seriously than he took the band. Whatever it was, they certainly did manage to actually put together a whole lot of things that the rest of us were still only thinking about."

A layer of romantic memory has spread over those early days by now, but the truth seems to be that Frayne took the band more seriously than he admitted, perhaps even to himself. Even though graduations, academic mishaps, and economic pressures caused a certain amount of shuffling about among its personnel, the band stayed together. Eventually, when Dickerson and Barlow were recruited from Charlie Musselwhite's Detroit blues band, the Airmen numbered eight. "But we weren't really a band yet," said Frayne. "I mean, we played together and all, but none of us really thought we were going to make a commitment to being in this band —or maybe any band—for the rest of our lives." Stein, for instance, was doing more concert work, and both Frayne and Tichy were set to go to graduate school, Tichy to study engineering in Georgia and Frayne to continue his painting at the University of Wisconsin. But as Frayne put it, "There was a whole social scene in Ann Arbor that went beyond the college thing, and I used to go back there on weekends and sit in with what was left of the band. We all kind of kept on doing that for a couple of years and finally said, 'Wow, I guess we're a band after all. It's time to go to California and make a million bucks playing rock'n'roll.' So we did." Pause. "At least, we went to California."

Children of their times, the Airmen arrived in Berkeley in 1967, at the height of the Bay Area's chemical and political ferment. "We were all living together," Kirchen remembered, "in this seemingly abandoned house, and playing for dinner money at any bar that would have us."

"We worked in some pretty scuzzy places," Frayne agreed, "including one place that was a big Samoan hangout. I don't know what the Samoans saw in us, but they used to dig us pretty good for about half the night, until it got to be time for them to start their regular killer bar fights. After a while we got used to it and developed this whole fire drill thing about clearing the stage and protecting our axes." It was during this rather unpropitious time that Tichy reappeared. The ink was barely dry on his Ph.D. in fluid engineering, but he had decided that singing in a rock band would undoubtedly be more fun than being an engineer, and perhaps more profitable as well.

With both Frayne and Tichy armed with graduate degrees, the Airmen might have been expected to fall into the San Francisco intellectual melting pot and disappear among the welter of vaguely artsy rock bands, but nothing could have been further from their collective mind. Inspired by Farlow's flair for straightforward rockabilly, they remained a long-haired country-rock band. They also began to find regular work, opening for touring attractions as well as for such San Francisco mainstays as the Jefferson Airplane and the Grateful Dead.

"They were always their own band," said a *Rolling Stone* editor who remembers their earliest days in California. "There was just never any way you were going to confuse them with anyone else. Like when everybody else was into acid rock—whatever that was—with all those interminable, self-indulgent solos, Cody would get up there and do a set of three-minute thirties swing, or maybe a half-hour of Jerry Lee Lewis. But whatever they were doing, you always got the feeling that it was supposed to be fun. And it was."

Eventually, however, when the record companies began to discover San Francisco, the Airmen's versatility proved to be something of a handicap. At least one company executive passed up the chance to sign them after hearing them do a program of country tear-jerkers and western swing. It wasn't until well after he'd returned to his Los Angeles headquarters that he discovered they'd been saving all their rock tunes for a second set. But they persevered, and in 1969 they found a manager: Joe Kerr, who'd known them in Ann Arbor. Through him two years later, they signed a record contract with Famous Music, a New York independent that promised them country distribution on its Dot label as well as regular distribution on the company's Paramount label.

To their own amazement, their first album became a hit. Fed by the success of a novelty single, "Hot Rod Lincoln," which featured Frayne growling his way through the fast-talking verses, the album spent thirty-three weeks on the best-seller charts and sold some 225,000 copies. Three years and three more albums after that initial success, however, they were still struggling for survival. Though the subsequent albums had sold respectably, and though they had astounded their Berkeley fans by being voted the Best New Band of 1972 at the country music disc jockeys' convention, they remained a middle-level rock band.

They were hard workers, professionals who lugged tons of equipment across countries and oceans in a grueling two-hundred-night-a-year endurance contest, but they were not superstars. In 1974, when Crosby, Stills, Nash and Young grossed more than $9.3 million on a tour of only twenty-four cities, the Airmen were lucky to gross $5,000 a night. And though they occasionally hit bigger paydays, two-show nights at $2,500 (usually added to bridge otherwise empty nights between better stops on a tour) were not nearly as uncommon as they would have liked.

More painfully, the absence of any single hits since "Hot Rod Lincoln" had made higher-paying dates increasingly hard to come by. During the first eight months of 1974 (including the slow summer season), their books showed gross concert earnings—with their booking agent's 10 percent fee deducted—of $171,935. Though earnings from recordings and publishing royalties pushed the total slightly over the $200,000 mark, the band was scratching to hold on. Twenty-five thousand a month in gross earnings simply didn't go very far when matched against expenses for six staff members (four roadies who traveled with them and handled their equipment, lighting, sound, and on-tour business, and a secretary and a bookkeeper located in Kerr's office); management fees; legal and accounting costs; payments for their office in San Rafael, a practice hall, and vehicles (a decrepit Econoline van and an ancient Greyhound bus fitted out with bunks); and meals and accommodations on the road. In purest financial terms, an observer might have wondered whether it wasn't time for them to start filling out those matchbook covers that promise high-paying careers in accounting.

That they hadn't broken up—in a business in which bands disappear and re-form under new names with the same rapidity as advertising agencies—was due both to Frayne's peculiar leadership and to the music they played. Leaving aside crossovers from straight country or soul music, the pop music of the early seventies fell into three broadly defined categories: hard rock, stretching in its further reaches to the decibel assault of heavy-metal music; LA-country, featuring intricate vocal harmonies floated over acoustic instrumentals; and the singer-songwriters, who employed a variety of styles, but for whom the lyrics were paramount. In that context, the Airmen were *sui generis*.

They were in some senses a typical bar band, coming up on stage to provide alternative versions of jukebox tunes when the jukebox was turned off. The only difference was that the jukebox they carried around in their heads was programmed rather weirdly. It included country, but usually in the western swing style that hadn't been popular since the disappearance of Bob Wills and his Texas Playboys twenty years before; rock tunes that had disappeared from jukeboxes—and just about from the collective unconscious—during the late fifties; and a smattering of boogie-woogie piano tunes. The few original songs they regularly included in their sets were of a doper-truckdriver-macho variety that did indeed reflect a synthesis of town and gown, but were hardly in tune with the developing political ethos of the seventies; titles like "Mama Hated Diesels" and "Everybody's Doin' It (Truckin'n'Fuckin')" provide some indication of their thematic range.

Yet despite the politics of their remarkable repertoire, or perhaps because of it, the Airmen had developed a significant following. Promoters —who generally found the Port Huron statement less relevant than their own bank statements—didn't regard the Airmen as a headline attraction in major markets, but they did regularly seek them out as an opening act. And the Airmen equally regularly sold out college auditoriums on their own. They were, as John Rockwell of the *New York Times* summed it up, "a cult band."

Though their recording success had certainly been limited to those cult members who dutifully bought even their most ill-produced albums, they were widely regarded as one of the best live acts in the country. And by the end of their Central Park set, the audience, many of whom had not heard of the Airmen but had come to the concert because it was a free event, were crowding up to the barriers in front of the stage. On their feet and clapping their hands rhythmically above their heads, they looked as if Central Casting had sent them over for a remake of *Woodstock*. When the Airmen finished their set and went backstage to find a shady spot to cool off, the crowd was calling for an encore.

Watching them backstage was a Paramount executive. "I just don't understand it," he said. "Everywhere these guys play, they knock people out. But they haven't been able to get the sound down on records at all. We think they're capable of so much more than they've done so far. . . . That's why we talked them into going with an outside producer on the next album. They've always produced themselves, and it just hasn't worked. So we got together with Kerr and told him that we'd pay for someone to come in and kind of help them on the next one. They're picking him now, and we'll get the new album out in time for Christmas. Eventually, just because of how hard they work on the road, they're gonna hit it big—and maybe another set of ears in the studio will make it happen quicker. I mean, just *listen* to that."

For a moment his voice was inaudible, lost in the roar that greeted the Airmen as they came back onstage for the encore. Hot and sweating, they gathered up their instruments and waited for Farlow to count off the rhythm. "Okay," said Farlow, punching the air with his fist, "uh-one, two; uh-one-two-three-four," and with a crash of cymbals, they were off on a rockabilly medley. When they finally stormed through the last coda, fifty thousand people were standing and shouting their approval. "They've gotta make it," said the record executive. "How can they miss?"

4

IN ROOTING for the Airmen's success, the executive was also rooting for his own, and by the summer of 1974 it had become apparent that Famous needed all the hits it could get. Not that the company was a struggling studio-in-a-suburban-garage operation; it was simply that Famous was the wrong-sized company in the wrong place. It was too small to maintain its own distribution system, but too large to manage with a back-pocket overhead. The company had in fact opted for the opposite approach. Like a lot of "creative" enterprises, the record industry is marked by an intuitive understanding of the links between style and substance. And Famous Music *looked* like a major company. Their offices, looking out over Central Park from two floors of the Gulf and Western skyscraper, were self-consciously flashy, but "tasteful" in the bastardized Bauhaus style that almost passes for class.

Still, plastic décor and the difficulties of independent distribution notwithstanding, Famous Music was a money-making corporation. Gross sales had gradually increased to slightly more than $40 million annually, and pretax earnings approached a satisfactory if unspectacular 10 percent. But Famous Music was in the wrong place: it was a piece of a growth-oriented conglomerate.

The Gulf and Western financial empire had begun in 1957, when a commodities dealer named Charles Bluhdorn used some of his accumulated capital to purchase control of a troubled auto parts company. Within a decade, it had become Gulf and Western, a rising star of the Fortune 500, with net *earnings* almost ten times what its gross sales had been when Bluhdorn purchased it. With sales totaling over a billion dollars, its interests ranged from zinc to cigars to sugar to television sitcoms, and included, as a result of a 1966 acquisition, Paramount Pictures. Almost as an accident of the motion-picture acquisition, Gulf and Western found itself in the record business, for Famous Music had grown from the firm that held publishing rights to Paramount's film scores to the company that issued its original soundtrack recordings. From there it had expanded into other segments of the record market and was active in rock, jazz, and country music at the same time that it maintained its MOR (middle-of-the-road) base in film soundtracks.

Although Gulf and Western's annual internal growth—exclusive of acquisitions—had averaged close to 20 percent during the sixties, it too suffered when the conglomerate bubble burst. Like most of the newer conglomerates, it was heavily burdened by long- and short-term debts. When the stock market ran into severe battering during the recession of the early seventies, Gulf and Western was in Alice's unattractive position: it had to run as fast as it could merely to stay in one place. Its subsidiaries not only had to earn money; they had to grow.

Growth, even at the rate required by Gulf and Western, was not an impossibility in the record industry's boom years. CBS Records had increased sales almost tenfold under the canny and aggressive leadership of Clive Davis, and Warner Brothers had gone from the edges of a $400,000 industry to a dominant position in an industry six times that size. Famous Music had grown, but at a slower rate than the rest of the industry: in the first four years of the seventies, when overall industry growth averaged nearly 20 percent annually, Famous' annual 7 percent growth barely kept pace with inflation. And because the company lacked the superstars whose spectacular sales balance the much larger number of marginal hits and near misses, sales as a percentage of profit remained constant. It was profitable, but not profitable enough.

The company was strongest in the country market—Famous' purchase of the Dot label had given it an important position in country sales—but its attempts to break through into the rock market had been less than satisfactory. Its largest-selling rock group, the Dutch-based Focus, had left Famous for Atlantic Records (and its WEA distribution system) when its contract expired. Famous was down to two dependable sales producers: the Climax Blues Band and Commander Cody and His Lost Planet Airmen. And Famous had not succeeded in making the most of the Airmen.

The company had had its chance a few years earlier but had somehow blown it. It had admittedly been something of a surprise to all concerned when "Hot Rod Lincoln," the Airmen's second single, took off for the top ten. Although it had been a staple of the country-novelty repertoire for years, the Airmen's was the first version to break into the pop market.

In fourteen weeks on the charts, it rose to number nine and sold almost 900,000 copies, but the album from which it was drawn sold only slightly more than 200,000 copies. Though a sale of 200,000 was spectacular for a debut album, it was nonetheless disappointing in relation to the single.

"You've got to figure," said a promotion man for another company, "that when you get a single hitting top ten, you're going to sell at least one album for every three singles. And that's true even for the kind of one-hit band that pads its album out with a lot of filler. You just sticker the front of the package with 'Contains their big hit Whatever-It-Is,' and the people who buy albums instead of singles will buy it. But with a band like Cody, where they've been out on the road awhile and where they've got other cuts that pick up FM play, a three-to-one ratio is low. There was no excuse for the sales figures on that album. The only way you can explain it is bad distribution. It just couldn't have been in the stores when people went to look for it."

Famous' distribution problems, coupled with its difficulties in the rock market, left it in a weak position within the industry, and the resultant low growth rate left it shaky within the Gulf and Western empire. Its problems within the parent conglomerate reached their peak in 1973, during which Famous' sales rose hardly at all from the previous year's base. By the spring of 1974, Gulf and Western had decided to get out of the record business and was seeking buyers for Paramount and the other Famous labels. They found one in ABC Records.

If the fate of Famous Music illustrates the drawbacks of independent distribution, ABC's situation during the early seventies represents some of the problems that accompany vertical integration. First, of course, a company has to have sufficient capital to begin setting up a nationwide network of distribution. Then it must have a flow of product that sells well enough so that the distribution branches can turn a profit, for each branch can lose money as well as make it. It may be more profitable in the long run for a company such as Famous to sell 250,000 copies of an album through independent distributors than to sell twice that number through its own chain, especially if the company must then wait several months for another hit album. For the manufacturing arm to increase sales at the cost of continued losses in a wholly owned distribution system is obviously not good business, but the advantages of such a network are so tempting that many companies have fallen into that trap.

ABC-Dunhill Records, as it was originally called, came into existence in 1966, when producer Lou Adler sold Dunhill Records to ABC for three million dollars. Next to Adler's production wizardry, Dunhill's chief asset at that time was the Mamas and the Papas, a group that served for a while as America's answer to the Beatles. Their hits, a solid half-dozen during the period from 1965 to 1968, added to ABC's original product flow to produce sufficient volume for the company-owned distributors. But when internal problems led to that band's breakup, the company's growth was severely cramped. The label's strong soul division produced moderate overall growth, but product distribution was geographically spotty, and several of the local distribution branches were relatively unprofitable. ABC had no choice; late in 1972, the company began shopping around for other acquisitions.

Its first purchase, in November of that year, was a small company called Cartwheel Records, whose major artist was Billy "Crash" Craddock. What was most significant about that purchase, in retrospect, was that it represented ABC's initial move into the country music market. Country performers have long careers, and because their sales are relatively impervious to the mercurial swings of taste that send pop and soul performers spiraling into obscurity, a strong country division is a godsend to a distribution system. It provides a consistent flow of product to sustain the system if the parent company hits a fallow period in the pop market.

A few months later, in February of 1973, ABC bought up Duke-Peacock Records, labels with considerable strength in the perennially hardy area of blues and gospel, another ABC weak spot. A year later, when Gulf and Western began letting it be known that it wouldn't mind getting out of the record business, ABC was ready to move. It had more than a passing interest in picking up pop acts like the Airmen, but its prime reason for interest in Famous was the strength of its country label, Dot. Although other bidders were involved in the negotiations with Gulf and Western, among them Warner's, Motown, and a group headed by Famous president Tony Martell, they were bidding only for the performers' contracts and their catalogs of already released records; ABC was buying more. Since it was also purchasing security for its distribution branches, ABC could afford to outbid its rivals, and for $5.5 million (of which the Dot acquisition was valued at about 65 percent), ABC took over Famous' assets.

Among the assets, of course, was Commander Cody and His Lost Planet Airmen. And the band undeniably was one, despite Tony Martell's presale declaration that they were "$60,000 in the hole to us." Martell was technically correct. Although the precise size of the debt was in question, and the Airmen's accountant eventually won an agreement that Famous had underpaid the band by some $16,000, the band was undoubtedly "in the hole" for a significant amount of money. Yet the terminology is misleading, for the Airmen had actually been a consistent money-maker for the label.

The apparent anomaly is not unusual in the record business. It results partly from a number of complicated accounting practices, but primarily from the hard fact that the company itself grosses a great deal more from the sale of a record than its performers do. The Beach Boys, for instance, have always had outstanding sales figures, but according to the company's David Berson, their distribution arrangement with Warner Brothers had left them almost $800,000 in debt by the summer of 1974. "But," Berson pointed out, "we're making money. Sometimes, *sometimes*"—he grinned ironically—"the record company recoups before the artist does."

Understanding how such things can happen requires some knowledge of the typical recording company contract. The one the Airmen had signed with Famous in June of 1971 contained the standard features. It obligated the band—and each of its members separately, should the band break up —to produce two albums a year for Famous. For each album sold, the band was to be paid a royalty of 14 percent of the wholesale cost of $3.01, minus a percentage allowance for packaging costs. The contract with Famous was a "one-and-three" document, providing for three successive option years after the first year of the contract. The option could be exercised only by the company, not by the artist, and the agreement required the band to supply two albums during each year the option was exercised. Famous in turn was required to increase by specified amounts the royalty percentage and the advance paid against royalties during those years.

These plans, however, had been thrown off when, after a slow start, the Airmen's first album went on to spend more than six months on the charts. Famous clearly didn't want to introduce a competing product while the first album was still riding high, and so wanted to delay the second album. The Airmen were of course delighted by the success of their initial album, but they realized that any delay in the subsequent release schedule would also mean a consequent delay in reaching the higher royalty percentages specified during their contract's option years. Capitalizing on the situation, Kerr negotiated an agreement whereby the option clauses would take effect by the calendar, rather than at the time the band actually delivered new recordings to Famous. "It was an easy deal," he said, "because it benefited both of us. We just shook hands, and that was it."

At the time of the ABC sale, the Airmen were just beginning to record their fifth album, although they were actually entering their final option year. Famous had avoided the potential losses involved in cutting short one album's sales life by releasing another too quickly, and the Airmen had moved up to 18 percent from the initial royalty figure of 14 percent. Similarly, their advances, from which they were required to pay all recording costs, had increased from the initial figure of $32,500 to $55,000. The contract specified that the Airmen's advances were nonreturnable if

an album failed to sell well enough to earn any royalties beyond the recording costs, but they nevertheless stood as a loss on the company's
books.

If a band with this kind of contract, which is fairly standard in the
industry, should try to switch labels at the end of its final option period,
the word that it "hasn't even made back its advance" could be leaked to
all possible purchasers. And that, of course, is the sort of rumor that
makes it difficult for a band to negotiate a new contract. Yet a band that
is in that sort of "debt" to its record label may well have turned a tidy
profit for the company. During the period in which the Airmen built up
their debt to Famous, the retail album price was $5.98 (subsequently it
rose by a dollar, and wholesale prices rose proportionately). The wholesale cost was $3.01, and the price to distributors $2.51. In addition to
covering the Airmen's royalties, that $2.51 included the costs of manufac-
turing and packaging the record, shipping it to the distributors, royalties
to the publishers of its various songs, and a pension contribution to the
Musicians' Union Trust Fund. Manufacturing and distribution costs depend on the total number of albums pressed and shipped, but royalty costs
reflect only the number actually sold. Such costs are mathematically
relatable to the number of albums pressed or sold, but there are variable
costs as well. Famous, for instance, promoted the albums through its sales
and advertising budgets, and through the distribution of free records to
reviewers and radio stations. But even when all these costs are deducted,
the record companies have a significant cushion.

Fixed costs included the actual manufacture of the record at roughly
35 cents (a 10 percent increase in this price that occurred during the
plastics shortage and oil boycott contributed to the subsequent retail price
increase), packaging at an average cost of 15 cents per album, and a little
less than 3 cents per album for shipping from the manufacturing plant to
the distributors. In addition to the costs it bore for each record manufactured, the company absorbed costs for each record actually sold: 2 cents
per cut to the music publisher (a total never exceeding 24 cents and generally running much lower), approximately 8 cents to the union's pension
fund, and royalties, which were 38 cents for the Airmen's first album. At
the 14 percent royalty figure, the maximum fixed cost to Famous for
manufacturing and selling each copy of the first album was $1.23.

To this figure are added the costs for promotion and overhead—costs
that are not necessarily related to the number of records ultimately sold.
These figures are obviously more difficult to calculate than those for the
fixed costs, and most record companies are skittish about releasing them.
A 1974 *Business Week* article cited Warner Brothers' promotion and
overhead figures as 43 cents per album. There is a possibility that this

figure is overstated, because during the same year Atlantic Records, one of Warner's sister companies, held its promotional and overhead costs to about 24 cents. Nevertheless, taking the Warner's statement at face value brings the cost per album sold at the 14 percent royalty figure up to $1.66. It was generally accepted in the industry that Warner's spent more on promotion than Famous did, but even granting Famous the 43-cent figure, its profit picture was quite rosy.

Consider the case after the manufacture of 60,000 albums. Assuming a difference of 25 percent between the number of albums manufactured and those sold (another profit-reducing assumption; Warner's actual figure during 1974 was only 16 percent), Famous would at that point have sold 45,000 albums. The gross revenues from such sales would have been $122,950. Against that total, we can set off the following:

Manufacturing, packaging, and shipping: 60,000 units		$31,800
Publishers' and trust fund fees: 45,000 units		$14,400
Advance against royalties/recording costs		$32,500
	Total	$78,700
Add the generous estimate of 43 cents per unit in promotion and overhead		$19,350
	Total costs	$98,050

In other words, even with costs overstated to reflect the least profitable position for the record company, the sale of 45,000 albums (with an inventory of 15,000 already manufactured) yielded a pretax profit to the company of $24,900.

At that same time the band would have earned $17,100 in royalties (14 percent times $3.01 minus packaging). At such a point in the history of the Airmen's first album, though the record company was already ahead by nearly $25,000, the band was still almost $15,000 away from earning back its advance. The company was in the black, but the Airmen's break-even point wouldn't be reached until the album sold some 85,000 units. The record company would be able to sell the next 40,000 albums essentially royalty-free. By the time Famous was actually obligated to pay the band any royalties at all, the company would have earned a net profit of $70,100.

But as the radio disc jockeys tirelessly insist, "The hits just keep on coming." That profit picture doesn't include earnings from single records pulled from the album. For singles, because promotion and recording costs were already absorbed in accounting for the album, Famous needed to pay only the fixed costs associated with manufacturing, shipping, and royalties. For each single sold to distributors at 40 cents, Famous thus earned 20 cents. At that rate, even assuming an inefficient marketing operation yielding an ultimate return of 40 percent of the singles manufactured and shipped, the sale of 500,000 singles represented a clear profit to the record company of $85,000.

And, in fact, the Airmen's first album—and its single, "Hot Rod Lincoln"—did considerably better than that for the company. Which might lead one to ask: If profits from the first album more than equaled the advances to be paid against the next three, how could the Airmen have been in debt to Famous? Which in turn brings up yet another element in record company accounting: each album is figured separately. For the band to move out of the company's debt, not only did each album have to sell the approximately 30,000 copies that allowed the company to break even; it had to sell well enough to recoup the band's advance. Partly because the band's advance increased, the next three albums' sales of about a hundred thousand each did not do that.

At the time of the sale to ABC, then, not only had the Airmen failed to earn any royalties beyond those advanced to cover recording costs; they had also incurred bookkeeping debts to the company. In the real-world language the record companies used in negotiating the sale, however, they had been counted as one of Famous' biggest attractions. And ABC had high hopes that the band could do even better with the new company.

5

To THE AIRMEN, the news of the transfer to ABC was a little disorienting
—Barlow said it was "like playing all your life for the A's and discovering
that you've been traded to the Dodgers"—but they adjusted to it readily
enough. Despite their personal fondness for some of the Paramount
people, they decided that ABC would probably be able to do more for
them than the frequently disorganized Paramount team had been able to.
"Let's face it," said Frayne. "We need a hit, and those guys can get it for
us."

Though all the Airmen would surely have agreed that the band needed
a hit, their reasons were as varied as their backgrounds. For Frayne, it
probably came down to pride as much as anything. "It's one thing kinda
knockin' around and playin' in bars and gettin' loaded every night when
you're a kid," he said during an uncharacteristically morose conversation
one night. "Which is what we all were when we started this trip, right?
Eighteen, nineteen? What the hell, when you're nineteen, you can do
anything, man, and it's cool. But I'm thirty now—I'm the oldest guy in
the band next to Ernie, and he's different, 'cause he's new with the band
—and how long does this stuff make sense?

"You know, this is really the first time since we started that I've begun
to think, 'Okay, what do we do when the trip is over?' I don't know if I
want to paint again. I don't even know if I *can.*" After a minute's pause,
he brightened. "I mean, I know I could if I worked at it and got my chops
down, but that's not the point. The point is that I've been doing the same
thing now for a long time, and something's gonna happen soon or it won't
be worth the hassle."

Did he think he'd made a wrong choice, thrown away a career as a painter? "No, it's not that at all; I still paint when we get home. It's that when you put so much time—your whole life, really—into something, and it gets as good as you want it to be, then you want everyone else to know it. We've been playing together for years now, and we've really gotten *good*. But no one's gonna know that unless they hear us. And the only way they're gonna hear us is if we get another hit. And then they'll be knocked out.

"Listen, I gotta tell you, one of the things that went wrong with 'Hot Rod Lincoln' was that it came too soon. We were good, all right, but we weren't anything like the way we are now. So when people came out to see us, we were okay, but we weren't killer. If we got a hit and brought 'em out now, it'd be all over. And that's what I want, I guess. Before I stop this thing, I just want to hear everybody saying, 'Oh, yeah. Commander Cody, they're the best band I've ever *heard*.' "

Fame, or at least the subtle subspecies that involves recognition from one's professional peers, was at the heart of most of the Airmen's ambitions—for after all, acclaim is a central part of the rock'n'roll dream. "I remember goin' to shows when I was a kid," said Billy C. Farlow, "and I just *knew* that I was gonna be up there someday myself." For Frayne, the musician's life had been a way out of the conventional American dream; for Farlow, it was the only way into it. The most likely alternative for him would have been a life in the Detroit factories. Farlow was perhaps the only Airman who wished for stardom in its traditional sense. "Billy's the only one who really gets off on life on the road," said a member of the Airmen's road crew. "It's not even just the groupies and stuff, though he's surely into that; it's just standing up there and getting hold of a crowd. For that minute, man, he *is* whoever he always wanted to be."

Frayne's and Farlow's need for outside validation was shared by all the Airmen, except possibly Andy Stein. "I don't know what makes Andy tick," said the Airmen's roadie. "He's just . . . Andy, that's all." Certainly Stein seemed to be an anomaly among the Airmen. The rest of them generally wore western-style clothes and lived in the mountains north of San Francisco. Stein, who alone among the Airmen chose to live in the city, wore shapeless, ageless pants, short-sleeved sport shirts, and ragged sneakers, and the road crew occasionally had to remind him to change after he'd spent a week or so in the same clothes. Stein's indifference to what he had on seemed a good metaphor for his relationship with the rest of the world. It was a reality that needed to be dealt with, but it wasn't the *important* reality.

One of the Airmen's wives said that whenever she answered the telephone and heard a voice saying, "Um, er, uh . . . ," she called her husband and told him Andy was on the phone. Certainly, to anyone steeped in the cliché of Jewish verbosity and wisdom, Stein, much as he looked like a veteran of Bronx Science, seemed surprisingly inarticulate—except about music. Faced with the opportunity to discuss a theoretical or practical music problem, Stein leaped into the middle of any available discussion. But the rest of the time a pleasant, stoned smile was his normal mode of communication. Asked about his hopes for the record, he paused reflectively. "Uhhhhh . . . well, I hope, uh, like it's good, right? Why wouldn't I?"

Other Airmen, especially John Tichy, had their feet more firmly rooted in practicality. In regard to money Tichy was the opposite of Frayne, who saw monetary success primarily as a side effect of the recognition he craved: "Money is just the way they keep score." Tichy, on the other hand, though he basked in the spotlight during his vocal turns, matter-of-factly called his stint with the Airmen "another kind of job. It's fun and all that, but it's not the kind of thing you could do if the money wasn't there."

The money was equally important to the other Airmen, although the rest of them seemed to be more serious about their musicianship than Tichy. Kirchen, particularly, drove himself hard in practice sessions. Occasionally he and Barlow talked about classical music with a breadth that would have surprised many of the Airmen's fans.

Of all the Airmen, Kirchen most embodied their Ann Arbor–Detroit axis. Though he spoke self-deprecatingly of his academic career as "a hot two weeks at Western Michigan," even his most casual conversations revealed a restless curiosity that was equally at ease with the abstract and the concrete. With Frayne he discussed the mysteries of psychokinesis; with Farlow, the mysteries of malfunctioning carburetors. Most important, he was capable of unifying his divided loyalties in his music. His "Seeds and Stems (Again)" so perfectly captured the down-and-out loneliness of country music that several straightforward country performers included it in their repertoires; yet, as its title implied, it expressed an attitude toward marijuana that might well have been anathema to any self-respecting Okie from Muskogee.

Barlow, whose "Buffalo Bruce" nickname had been universally shortened to "Buff," was the Airmen's only native Californian and had begun his musical career playing what he called "stand-up bass" in the state high-school orchestra. Somewhere along the line, though, he had transferred his allegiance to the electric version of the instrument and had fallen in love with the blues. Tapes of his pre-Airmen performance with Magic Sam at an early Ann Arbor Blues Festival, though unreleased, decorate the bootleg collections of blues fans across the country. If Kirchen stood as a middle ground reflecting the Airmen's history, Barlow played the same role in their present. Easygoing and open, he had a personality as solidly dependable as his sense of rhythm. "Especially when we're on the road," said one of the roadies. "Buff is the guy that everybody counts on. If anybody is feeling fucked up at all—anybody except George, and with him you just have to get out of the way until it's all over—they kind of automatically have dinner with Buff. He's so steady that he's like a human tranquilizer. He'll talk about his farm, or about kids, or about being married. . . . Whatever it is, people just end up feeling better after they've talked to him."

Barlow too wanted a hit record, but his attitude toward it was as relaxed as his attitude toward any of the disasters or delights that the other Airmen brought to him on the road. He would clearly have welcomed the recognition and the money, especially to keep up with his wife's expensive habits, but one had the feeling that he could accept whatever came along with the same unvarying equanimity that made his bass playing the rhythmic anchor of the band.

Ernie Hagar expressed a similar attitude toward the Airmen's future: "It would be nice—more than nice, I guess—if this one turned out to be a hit. But there's no way you can plan on that. You just do your best and hope it will work out." He thought a moment. "I don't want to sound too fatalistic or anything, because that's not the way I feel, but I think if we just keep playing the way we have been, eventually things will work out all right. I can't even be worried about what will happen. I already decided I couldn't do that when I joined the band."

Hagar had joined the Airmen at the age of thirty-five, having given up his full-time position with an engineering firm to follow his avocation. "I'd been playing for years at night and on weekends," he said, "and suddenly I got to be thirty-five years old. I was happy enough doing what I was doing, but I really wanted to give it one shot, you know? And I figured if I didn't do it now, when was I going to do it?"

The full-time musical career that Hagar had had in mind was that of studio musician, but he was unexpectedly offered a chance to join the Airmen when their pedal steel player, Bobby Black, whom they'd acquired after they arrived in California, himself decided to leave the band for studio work. Stein, who restlessly haunted country music bars, had heard Hagar playing and asked him to come up to the San Rafael practice hall for an audition.

"We talked it over," said Hagar's wife, Yopi, an administrative nurse, "and I said I really wanted him to do what he'd always wanted. I knew that there were chances we'd be taking, and that he'd be away a lot more than he used to be, but I knew I would rather be with him part-time when he was happy than full-time when he wasn't. I certainly wouldn't expect him to stand in the way of my career, after all, and it was clear that he'd been waiting for a chance like this for years."

After one audition, during which it turned out that he knew most of the Airmen's repertoire, Hagar became an Airman. "There comes a time in your life, " he said, "when you know you'll either make your move now or it will pass you by forever. I came to that time, decided to make my move, and wound up in this band. Sometimes I think it might have made more sense to go down to LA and look for studio work, but there's something about performing all over the country that makes me feel—" He paused, embarrassed, then shrugged. "Alive, I guess."

Yet for Hagar the demands of the road were hard. A hit would enable the band to earn enough per concert so that the sheer number of days on tour could be reduced somewhat. A hit would also provide some practical justification for his over-thirty leap into the relentlessly young world of pop music.

Dickerson, whose wife was pregnant with their first child, had perhaps the strongest immediate cause to want the money that would come with a hit, because the couple wanted to move closer to the city before the baby was born. "It's real cheap living as far out in the country as we do, and it's nice living too. But it's awful far from anyplace else, and with the baby coming, Ditka just won't be able to get around as much. It'd be better for her and better for the baby if we were someplace where there were a few neighbors around."

But neither Dickerson nor any of the others were willing to trade the Airmen's self-respect for a hit. Except for Farlow and Frayne, whose personalities seemed too large for comfortable anonymity, any of them could easily have found a place in a more commercial band, but they all felt that the Airmen were special. "We know we're getting better," said Dickerson. "It's one of those things that you can really feel when you get some distance on yourself. Right now we can open a show for almost any band in the country and get through to their audience. And that's without any compromise at all. I really like some of the LA bands—I'm sure I listen to the Eagles a lot more than any of the other guys do, for instance—but I don't want us to be the Eagles. I want us to keep being *us*. Eventually people will start paying attention."

Like self-taught tennis players who have struggled to weekend success, the Airmen were reluctant to abandon their idiosyncratic strokes in favor of a more conventional approach that might make them tournament players. And they were aware that, unlike championship tennis, popular music is not played in any one "right" way. There have been many manufactured and formulaic hits, but there have been nearly as many unpredictable successes. Well within the Airmen's memory, for instance, Bob Dylan had demolished the boundaries within which singers were expected to operate. Perhaps, if only they persevered, they could do the same thing for bands.

Yet they did dream of winning their metaphorical Wimbledons. And time was not on their side. For three years their career had been at a near standstill, and though they all felt that they had grown better during that time, no one else had seemed to notice. As they hit milestones in their lives—children, marriages, birthdays—they had begun to be haunted by the unstated fear that they just might not have it in them to become important rock musicians. The next album, with a new producer and a new company, had a large basket of hopes riding on it.

So they were doubly disturbed when they learned that ABC had refused to advance the money for recording it.

6

ABC's ACTION was obviously affecting the Airmen directly, but it was not up to them to do anything about it. That responsibility rested with their manager, Joe Kerr. When there were problems with record companies, travel agencies, concert promoters, IRS auditors, or any of the legion of creditors who trail in the wake of marginal bands like the Airmen, solving them was up to Kerr. On the face of it, he was an unlikely candidate for such a task.

Like Frayne and the other Airmen, he was a product of Ann Arbor in the sixties. Unlike them, he was not a musician, and had actually been a high-school teacher and football coach when he met them. But his mildly unorthodox views on sex, dope, and politics had so excited his local school board that he had been summarily dismissed, and had preceded the Airmen to California by a year or so. There he had drifted comfortably into the relaxed Marin County ethos, unselfconsciously adopting cowboy boots and hats that obscured his background in Eastern prep schools, and appeared at first glance to be simply another aging hippie. As his former school board unhappily discovered when he sustained a successful suit against them, he wasn't. Like Frayne, he eschewed confronting his friends; but with anyone else he had a will of iron.

That tenacity, combined with his easy tolerance for the foibles of both musicians and corporate executives, made him nearly the perfect manager for the Airmen. His tolerance did not, however, make him happy about ABC. Even with his breath held so as not to lose the effects of an early-morning toke, Kerr nevertheless communicated his feelings about the company.

"Well, let me tell you," he said with uncharacteristic anger, "they don't know what they're getting into. We'll fucking bust 'em for antitrust, then we'll sue them for breach of contract, and *then*—after they're totally fucked—we'll get 'em for drugola. One of their promotion guys came to the Port Chester gig and packed George's nose for him. They're *dead*."

Kerr may actually have thought that ABC was dead at the time, but it is more likely that his restless enthusiasm led him to exaggerate his case considerably, for the actual situation was perilous. The Airmen were heavily in debt already and were facing a long income-less period when their recording work would keep them off the concert circuit. Unfortunately, not all the band's debts were of the bookkeeping variety; they involved missed payments for travel, bus, insurance, and rent. More painfully, the Airmen were already three weeks behind on salaries, and each of them carried individual additions to the debts they owed as an organization. "You know," said Kerr, "these guys all have responsibilities now, and there's a limit to how long you can ask them to go without getting paid. I don't know what the hell ABC is doing, but they're likely to find themselves with no band left to record if they go on for too long."

A few weeks earlier, when he accompanied the New Riders—whom he also managed—and the Airmen to the Central Park concert, Kerr had first heard the rumors about Famous' being sold. At that time he'd been excited about going to a new company, almost any company. Standing backstage, he'd gestured disdainfully toward the Gulf and Western headquarters towering to the west: "It's gonna be so good to get with a company that can sell some records for us. . . . Famous is all right to deal with—they're good guys, and all—but when it comes to promoting product, they're chumps." He had, in fact, been delighted when he learned that ABC had won the bidding—"Can you imagine us on *Motown?*" he asked. But all his good feelings had rapidly dissipated in the unanticipated quarrel with the new company.

What triggered the fight was ABC's realization that the contract they'd purchased from Famous had less than a year to run. The final option year had begun less than two months before the sale, and when the band turned two albums over to ABC, it would be free to negotiate elsewhere. Kerr and Barry Hessenius, the young San Francisco lawyer who handled the band's day-to-day legal business, had made it clear that other companies were indeed interested in signing the band.

ABC, naturally enough, was not eager to sink money into promoting a band that would shortly be leaving its label and began negotiations for a new contract. Kerr expressed interest but suggested that if ABC was really interested in signing a new long-term deal, the new contract should not start from the conclusion of the option period but immediately, and that the advance and royalty figures for the two albums still required under the old contract should be renegotiated. He suggested an advance of $75,000 plus producer's fee rather than the $55,000 required by the current contract. While these negotiations were under way, the ABC legal department began researching Famous' records and discovered that—despite the handshake deal with Famous—the band had technically failed to deliver the required two albums during the second option period. They decided that it was legally possible to invoke the contract's extension clause.

Behind its complicated legal terminology, the standard extension clause simply says that if a band fails to deliver the required number of albums during an option period, the company may extend the length of that period until the band has complied with its terms. ABC's legal department thus argued that Kerr's band was not actually in its final option year, but only in an extension of the previous year's option. That judgment was contained in a letter which ABC's chief counsel, Lee Young, Jr., sent to Cody's attorneys on August 30.

The letter was terse and its contents unpleasant. Its key message was:

> ABC Records, Inc., as assignee of the contract between you, as Producer, and Famous Music Incorporated, dated June 6, 1971 (hereinafter the "Agreement"), as amended, supplemented and extended, herewith notifies you that according to records furnished it by Famous Music Corporation, you have failed to deliver product required under said Agreement, to wit: two (2) long playing albums for the period June 6, 1973, to June 5, 1974. As a result of delivery failure, you are herewith notified that pursuant to Paragraph 3(c) of the Agreement, the term of the Agreement shall be and hereby is extended for a period of time equal to the length of time it takes you to satisfy the deficiencies in delivery of product.

If that was indeed the case, Cody did not owe ABC one more album after the one they were ready to record, but two (plus a "greatest hits" compilation that ABC had the right to assemble from previously recorded albums). ABC, if its contention was true, was under no real pressure to renegotiate the Cody contract at all. If the legal point held, ABC had the band, at the by now nominal cost of $55,000 per album, for four more records.

But the point was dubious. "We didn't even take it that seriously," said Barry Hessenius. "Famous might have been able to do something like that when the option actually came due, but they didn't. We'd agreed with them to slow it down. They knew what the situation was—in fact, they were still trying to promote the fourth album—and they didn't extend. What they did instead was waive their rights to extend by picking up the new option."

On that basis, and considering ABC's letter merely another, rather heavy-handed negotiating tool, the band continued preparations for the new album. On September 4, the same day that Hessenius's senior associate, Dick Hodge, responded to Lee Young's letter, Kerr wrote to ABC executive vice president Howard Stark, sending him an estimate for the costs of album art work and notifying him that the band was to enter the studio on September 9. He also asked ABC to advance $30,000 in production costs, as had been Famous' practice on previous albums, and requested confirmation that ABC would honor Famous' agreement to pay John Boylan the outside producer's fee of 3 percent royalty (with an advance of $5,000). Two days later, ABC said no.

Though ABC executives were privately contemptuous of Famous' business practices (ABC's president once turned down a request with a curt "This ain't no candy store, and I ain't no Tony Martell"), Famous' reliance on oral agreements stood ABC in good stead in this dispute. By the terms of the written contract, ABC was bound neither to advance production monies nor to pay the outside producer. Stark wrote Kerr that "our policy is to comply under normal circumstances with the specific terms of written contractual agreements." Cody appeared to be out of luck.

"Appeared to be" is the crucial phrase, for Hessenius's and Hodge's weekend researches had yielded some critical information. The Famous contract required the record company to exercise its options, if it chose to do so, in "timely fashion," by written notice at least thirty days before the conclusion of the prior option period. For the first two option years Famous had notified the band of its option intentions some forty-five days in advance. For the third, Famous had been a day late.

"Don't you see what this means?" said Hessenius, pacing restlessly around Kerr's cluttered office. "They've been saying we owe them four fucking records, and we've been saying it's only two. Now it turns out we don't owe them shit. We can go sign with Warner's today and they can't touch us. It's clear, absolutely clear under the laws for personal service contracts, that you've got to exercise an option in timely fashion. If you don't do it on time, you haven't done it at all. They're fucked."

Hessenius's excitement was contagious, and both Kerr and Rick Higginbotham—the Cody road manager, who was sitting in Kerr's office when Hessenius burst in—responded to it. Within minutes they had mentally signed a half-dozen high-dollar contracts for the band with other record companies. All they had to do was start negotiating and the pot of gold would appear. In the meantime, though ABC would probably fight them, they really didn't have to worry at all. "Let 'em try," chortled Hessenius. "I want to put those motherfuckers up against the wall."

It was not going to be quite that easy, of course. While Hessenius was rummaging through Kerr's files to find the proper dope for a celebratory joint, ABC was making plans of its own. Hessenius may have had personal motives for fighting the company, but ABC had solid economic reasons for holding on to the Airmen.

Much of ABC's motivation, according to a source who wishes to remain nameless because he still holds a high-ranking position with the company, had little to do with Cody at all, but with the Blue Thumb record label. Blue Thumb, though it had been sold to ABC along with the other Famous labels, had always been idiosyncratic. It had contributed its share (rather more than its share, actually, since it had high-riding artists like the Pointer Sisters and the Crusaders) to Famous' profits, but it had always maintained separate corporate offices and had worked at arm's length from the parent corporation. It had been rumored in the trade papers that the Blue Thumb staff was very unhappy about the sale, and that a legal challenge was in the works.

"What they were challenging—or at least planning to challenge, from what we heard—was the whole legitimacy of the sale," said the ABC executive. "We weren't really very worried about their winning the suit, because our counsel was very clear on it, but we were worried about getting into a court fight that could cost us a couple of million dollars—not just in legal costs but in product we couldn't release. They had the money to tie us up for months, even years.

"So we were sort of looking for a chance to set some quick court precedent that would validate the sale. When Cody came along flexing their muscles, it looked perfect. Hell, we had their royalty statements for the last three years; we knew they couldn't put up much of a fight. We really did want to deal with them, and we would have been happy to negotiate a new contract, but they came in with just enough of a chip on their shoulder that it made it look worthwhile to fight."

Finally, Hessenius himself had been added to ABC's internal reasons for making the case. "Kerr is a good guy," said ABC artist relations director Corb Donahue, "and we always felt—I always felt, anyway—that Cody was one of the really exciting reasons for making the Paramount deal. But the guys in the legal department had enormous trouble with their lawyer. He just came down and started throwing his weight around, making all kinds of impossible demands. They really don't like him."

An ABC lawyer, speaking not for attribution, was even more blunt: "He's a chickenshit punk. He doesn't know the law, and he doesn't know music. Every time he opens up his loud mouth, he hurts the band." Yet perhaps because the music business has become as litigious as the garment industry, almost every band, regardless of who else is on its personal management staff, is co-managed by a lawyer. Except on those special occasions when a "name" lawyer was required, Hessenius did that job for the Airmen.

Unlike most of the band's semiofficial family, Hessenius had no Mich-

igan roots. He was a native Californian, a graduate of Boalt Hall, probably
the West Coast's finest law school, and had been a part of the music
business for most of his adult life. He obviously lacked the experience of
the best-known music-business attorneys, but the chances are that the
ABC lawyer was wrong, and that Hessenius knew both the law and the
music business. Still, there was no denying that he was combative by nature,
and the prospect of courtroom conflict excited him. The problem, as far
as his function within the Cody organization was concerned, was the
disquieting possibility that Hessenius might be over-optimistic about the
band's chances of winning.

One looks to a lawyer for dispassion, for a cold view of the legal
implications of any business decision. But Hessenius was a true believer, a
zealot whose personal fondness for the band quickly led him to the conclusion that they could do no wrong. It was a role that Kerr and the band
appreciated, especially in times when they needed the kind of emotional
support that Hessenius freely gave, but it was a role not without its risks.

Frederic B. Gershon, an expert on entertainment law and a lecturer in
his specialty at New York's Practicing Law Institute, put the lawyer's
position in perspective in a *Variety* interview during which he talked
about the need for reasonableness: "In the entertainment business, to
lose a record deal because you have overnegotiated can mean the difference between the artist ever recording or never recording. It can mean
the difference between the artist being a $10,000-per-night act or being
destined to work forever in discotheques at $1,500 a week. If he lasts
forever."

And now, with the Airmen's life hanging in the balance, Hessenius was
preparing to do contract battle. Regardless of the legal merits of his
arguments (which Hodge, too, felt were strong), the real-life position of
the Cody organization was tenuous. Although Kerr felt personally be-
trayed when he read Stark's statement that "we have contacted Tony
Martell directly and he advised us that he never made any commitment
to pay the costs of an outside producer," the real problem lay in ABC's
refusal to advance recording costs.

Kerr had been planning to pay overdue bills and back salaries with that
money, as well as to pay salaries during the period when the band would be
in the studio and unable to earn money by performing. Though a phone
call before the weekend had made Kerr fairly sure what ABC's answer
would be, the arrival of the certified letter in Monday afternoon's mail
sealed it. Already in debt to itself and to outside creditors, the band was
now about to absorb a five-thousand-dollar obligation to producer John
Boylan as well. Kerr put down the letter and cradled his face in his hands.
"I'm sick," he said, "I'm fucking sick." Just then his intercom buzzed.
Boylan was at the heliport—could someone come down and pick him up?

7

JOHN BOYLAN ENTERED Kerr's office late on the afternoon of September 9. He'd actually been due the day before, and his lateness had pushed the band's schedule back a day, but his excuse was so fascinatingly implausible that no one much minded. Kerr, at least, was not about to press a five-thousand-dollar creditor. And all three of the people waiting in the office—Kerr, Hessenius, and Higginbotham—were so glad to see him at all that they asked for no apologies. They were glad to see him because he was their hope to lead Commander Cody and His Lost Planet Airmen out of the commercial wilderness into which they'd drifted.

Boylan did not look much like a leader. If anything, in a pleasant coincidence of nomenclature, he looked boyish. He was then thirty-three, and though his hair was prematurely gray, its carefully floppy shag cut and his clothes—on this occasion an Eagles T-shirt, faded jeans, and clogs—combined to give him the air of a Greenwich Village bartender: older and wiser than his customers, perhaps, but still comfortably weird. Only the expensively tooled leather briefcase in his hand indicated that he was not only John Boylan but also John Boylan, Incorporated.

John Boylan, Incorporated, was Los Angeles come to San Francisco, the man chosen to process the Airmen's music into commercially palatable form. To the extent that the Airmen actually sought such success, he was a potential friend and ally; to the extent that they were willing to accept success only on their own terms, he was a potential enemy—or, at very best, an imperial emissary sent out to cajole the colonials into showing a little sense. For their own good, of course. And for the greater profit of the record company.

Neither the corporate nor the personal Boylan, however, belonged to any record company. He was an independent producer, working at least as much for the performer as for the company, and, as a rule, paid by both. For this project, at least as it had been set up between Kerr and Famous Music, the company was to pay his advance and the Airmen any royalties beyond that advance. Given the Airmen's ambivalence about "selling out," the financial arrangement symbolized his ambiguous role. In a business in which tensions between art and commerce are the norm, the independent producer stands in the middle, balanced between accountancy and aesthetics.

There are, of course, many excellent producers who work directly for record companies (the Warner Brothers production staff is generally regarded as the strongest artistically), but many performers feel that such producers are more likely than not to come down on the side of the accountants. And many producers—artists themselves, in their own way —want the freedom to work with performers under contract to a variety of companies. As a result, the rock years had seen a growth in both the numbers and the importance of independent producers like Boylan.

The pioneer independent was Phil Spector, the energetic young Brooklynite whom Tom Wolfe celebrated as "the first tycoon of teen." Spector began work as a producer with Atlantic Records in the late fifties, then moved out to Los Angeles to start his string of record companies, which had a series of hits with groups like the Ronettes. But Spector, though he was growing increasingly wealthy and successful, was also increasingly unsatisfied, for he was an artist as well as an entrepreneur. Creator of the "wall of sound" technique, Spector dreamed of producing a kind of record that his own labels' artists simply could not deliver. So he put his record companies aside and began hiring himself out as a one-man production company. For a sizable advance plus a share of the royalties, Phil Spector was for sale on a single-project basis. Quite soon there were more potential buyers than he could handle.

Other producers soon followed Spector's example and fulfilled their hopes of working with particular artists regardless of what company held the performer's contract. At the same time, hearing the results that some of the successful independent producers were able to achieve, established artists began to negotiate for the right to choose their producers from the independent ranks, rather than from the limited pool of producers on their record company's staff. For such artists, whose huge sales more than subsidized the development of younger performers, record companies were willing to cooperate. By the mid-seventies the field of independent producers had grown large, with producers like Richard Perry able to demand and receive front-cover billing on the albums they chose to do, and electronic wizards like Todd Rundgren (himself a Warner's/Bears-ville recording artist) receiving a flat fee of $50,000 per album.

John Boylan, though he was hardly successful on the Rundgren level (a $50,000 producer's advance would have eaten up 90 percent of the Airmen's recording budget), was a respected independent producer, just beginning, at the time of the Airmen's fifth album, to be so much in demand that he had difficulty meeting his commitments. Originally a New Yorker, a graduate of Bard College and the Greenwich Village folkie scene, Boylan had moved West stylistically as well as geographically. Socially, he was very much part of the LA music scene: he had a house in "the Canyon" and had formerly lived for several years with Linda Ronstadt. Musically, he specialized in "LA country," a sound in which the electrified rock beat blended with traditionally influenced country instrumentation and vocal harmony.

At the time he began working with Cody, Boylan had already earned a gold record for producing a now-defunct pop group called the Associa-tion, but his greatest commercial success had, rather ironically, been the Eagles, a band he hadn't produced but had assembled to play behind Linda Ronstadt. Still, he was well regarded, and his association with the new Cody project had sparked a small flurry of interest within the music business. ABC's Corb Donahue talked about the company's hopes for the album chiefly in terms of Boylan: "They've always been one of my favorite bands, but their records have really been, well, pretty awful. Boylan is a professional, and if there's any way to get a sound out of them in the studio, he'll get it."

The LA country sound, though it provides the illusion of relaxation, is actually a meticulously constructed artifice. It may feature lyrics about "takin' it easy," but it is, as the Airmen were to discover in working with Boylan, a highly disciplined and technically polished creation. When critics fault it, it is likely to be because they find it, if anything, too per-fect; as Robert Christgau once wrote about the Eagles: "The music, the lyrics, and the distribution machine are all suave and synthetic. Brilliant stuff—but false."

The Airmen, on the other hand, were a lengendarily undisciplined band. Like a lot of touring acts, they substituted the sheer energy of per-formance for the polish of the studio. When Frayne had made attempts to capture their style on tape, however, the results had been consistently disappointing. One critic had noted that one of their earlier outings sounded "as though it had been recorded in the La Brea tar pits," and Frayne himself described their standard studio procedure as "playing a song until we can't stand it any more and then saying 'okay, we got that one.'" So when he entered Kerr's office to meet with Boylan, Frayne was both nervous and a little defensive. Boylan's presence, though welcome in some ways, was an implied criticism of him.

Like any talented producer, Boylan was a part-time psychologist. He had already anticipated some problems and had told Kerr that he would first work with the band on the four or five numbers he felt were nearest to being ready for recording: "Once they get a sense of what they can do with material that's almost there—and once they get a sense of confidence about what I can do to help them—then we can go to the harder stuff." But that was for later. Frayne was their leader, and his cooperation was critical. Boylan and Frayne hadn't seen each other since Boylan had made a trip to one of the band's concerts some months earlier; no matter what ploys and stratagems Boylan might later adopt, the first meeting in their new relationship would go a long way toward determining how the album would be made.

To describe Frayne as having a commanding physical presence would be to understate. He was physically large—and strong enough to have worked for years as a lifeguard in the Jones Beach surf—but the impression of barely controlled energy inside the body made him seem even bigger than he was; one photographer who had been assigned to do backstage shots of the band simply said that she'd "never seen anyone take up so much room." Certainly he filled Kerr's diminutive office, but once past the opening pleasantries (including Boylan's ritualistic shedding of his Eagles T-shirt for a duplicate of Frayne's Lone Star Beer number), Boylan quietly controlled the conversation. Within a half-hour of Frayne's arrival, Boylan had made three key points: he unequivocally regarded Frayne as the leader of the band; he liked and respected the band as professional musicians; and he, Boylan, was running the recording project.

With all that clear, Frayne's initial growled apology ("Listen, we may be a little rusty, because we haven't practiced together for a week or so") rapidly gave way to a relieved partnership as they began considering material for the album. They started by picking their way through the demo records (minimally produced renditions of possible songs) and the sheet music that had been sent to the band by several publishing companies.

8

IN THE MUSIC INDUSTRY the term "publisher" is by now an anachronism left over from the days when a song's popularity was measured largely by the sale of its sheet music. In those days the publishers *were* the music industry. Aspiring songwriters worked their way from floor to floor of Tin Pan Alley's Brill Building, hoping desperately to sign a contract with one of the giant firms like Chappell or Leeds—firms which, like today's giants among the record companies, had their own distribution systems. But all that began to change with the advent of the phonograph record.

The nature of the change was first legally recognized in Congress' 1909 revision of the copyright laws. In those revisions, for the first time the question of "mechanical reproduction" of copyrighted musical compositions came up. Largely because the copyright revisions had been spurred by trust busters, Congress dealt with the fear—and the frequently realized fact—that the holder of a copyright on a popular song could essentially create a monopoly pricing system on it. It could, for instance, be sold to one record company at a low rate—in return, say, for the company's purchase of a guaranteed number of other songs from the publisher— and offered at arbitrarily high rates to other prospective purchasers.

As a result, the 1909 law required that once a publisher granted any-one the right to make a commercial recording of one of its properties, anyone else could legally record it simply by filing the basic informational forms required by the law. This "compulsory licensing" regulation estab-lished a statutory royalty fee of two cents per song to be paid to the publisher for every recording sold. In the succeeding sixty-six years neither the compulsory licensing provision nor the two-cent fee has been altered.

At first there was not much reason to change it. Two cents a copy was a rather generous figure in 1909. Beyond that, the royalty combined with the burgeoning of the record industry to create a significant new source of income for publishers. It also, at the general rate of 50 percent of the royalties received by the publisher, created a number of wealthy songwriters. Thus for a long time the shared interest of the record companies in getting the right to record whatever they wanted and of the publishers and songwriters in getting a guaranteed royalty on every record sold kept either of the parties from seeking changes in the law. Only when sheet music sales plummeted alarmingly during the Depression did the publishers finally begin agitating for a larger share of the profits made by recordings of their songs. By then they were too late.

In the first place, to have any leverage in Washington the publishers would have had to present a united front. But a number of large publishing firms were quite content with the flat two-cent royalty because they had become subsidiaries of the record companies. Recording executives, being sensible businessmen, had rather rapidly figured out that if they were themselves in the publishing business they could halve their royalty costs, paying one cent per copy to the songwriters and the other penny back to themselves. In the days when mechanical royalties amounted to more than 10 percent of a record's 39-cent retail price, there was obviously a great deal of incentive for them to do so.

There was even more reason later, as the record companies, whose profits are geared to the wholesale price of their product, grew far more rapidly than the old-line publishing firms. The swollen record companies could simply go into the open market and buy up even the largest of publishers. Chappell, for instance, was purchased by Mercury/Phonogram, and Leeds by MCA (which had previously bought up Decca). In doing so, the record companies profited in two ways: first, they increased income by becoming legally entitled to collect performance royalties (when a song is played on the radio, neither the performer nor the record company receives a royalty, although the publisher does), and second, they cut their recording costs.

If, for instance, a record company had publishing rights to sell twelve songs on the hypothetical album we used as an illustration earlier, its net profits on each album sold would increase by the approximately 12 cents it would retain in publisher's royalties. In the case of hugely successful albums that sell more than 5,000,000 copies, the profit potential is clearly enormous, but it also makes an important difference for marginal albums that sell 20,000 to 30,000 copies. For these albums, the increase (equal to 15–20 percent of the company's net profit per unit) is the difference between red ink and black.

Another factor that contributed to the record companies' takeover of music publishing was their control over performer-songwriters. This control dated back to the fifties, when the less scrupulous companies signed performers to their publishing companies by inserting restrictive clauses into their recording contracts. Unless a performer signed over his publishing rights to the company, he didn't get to record. And frequently— especially in the rhythm-and-blues field—a semiliterate performer would sign an agreement that not only gave the record company rights to publish a song but also saddled the performer with mysterious "co-authors" whose presence further diluted his claims to songwriting royalties.

This practice came to light during the rock'n'roll era, when popular singers made gigantic hits of songs copied from old 78s, while original authors of the songs received almost nothing. One of the more notorious cases involved Arthur "Big Boy" Crudup, who both influenced Elvis Presley stylistically and wrote one of Presley's early successes, "That's All Right, Mama." Because of the almost routine exploitation of blues performers, Crudup didn't even know that he'd written the country's number-one song until he heard it played on a tavern jukebox one evening. When he heard Presley's version of the song that he'd recorded for Victor (now RCA) a generation earlier, Crudup promptly wrote to his former manager, to whom royalties were being paid. He never got a response, and over the next fifteen years received only a few hundred dollars in royalties, even though that song and his "My Baby Left Me" were recorded by dozens of artists ranging from B. B. King to Elton John.

By now, sophisticated managers have pretty well put an end to that sort of rampant exploitation, but it is still common practice for a performer who writes his own material to sign a publishing agreement with his record company's publishing subsidiary. Frequently the contract provides that advances paid to the recording artist will be cross-collateralized against publishing receipts. If, in other words, a record does not sell enough copies for the performer's royalties to repay the advance, royalties which the publishing subsidiary would normally pay to the performer as songwriter will be applied instead to the debt—a debt that, as noted earlier, is frequently spurious.

Thus the pile of music and records Boylan and Frayne were looking at bore the names of dozens of publishing firms, but they were exclusively compositions by performers under contract to CBS or Warner's. The variety of fanciful company names resulted from the need for writers to protect their early work by copyrighting it through publication companies they formed themselves. Because of the antitrust impulses behind the copyright law, forming a publication company was relatively easy, and during the singer-songwriter boom of the early sixties publishers multiplied with great rapidity. But there was a great deal of difference between "publishers" consisting only of the songwriter himself and the giant firms with which they eventually became associated.

One of the differences was that no one-person publishing company could hope to keep up with which artists were looking for new material at any given time. The publishing divisions of Warner's, CBS, and other firms kept routine tabs on which performers were going into the studio and shipped them batches of appropriate material ahead of time. For a songwriter who hoped to make money at his trade—or who hoped to capitalize on the singer/songwriter boom and be discovered as a performer through his songwriting—it made very good sense to sign a co-publishing agreement with one of the large companies. In making such an agreement he would lose the bulk of the publisher's share of the mechanical royalties, but a percentage of something is worth more than 100 percent of nothing. The different names on the demo records therefore meant next to nothing, except perhaps as a measure of the various record companies' aggressiveness. To all intents and purposes, record companies had become the publishers of the seventies.

From the consumer's point of view, however, the problem is the enormous temptation for such combines to channel their artists into works whose copyright the company holds. Gene Lees, longtime critic for *High Fidelity Magazine,* put it this way: "The average record company would rather record a bad song it can publish than a good song it can't."

To some extent the same thing was true of the Airmen. They tended, of course, to cull much of their repertoire from old 45s and 78s, but they also had their own subsidiary, Ozone Music, which published their self-written material. And because they occasionally used songs by Kevin "Blackie" Farrell, Kerr had prudently signed him to Ozone Music as well. Like the record companies, the Airmen too favored self-published songs; the band had learned their economic value through unhappy experience. "We were so dumb when we started out," said Kerr, "that we didn't put one of our own songs on the back of 'Hot Rod Lincoln.' It doesn't even *matter* what you put on the back of a single, right? Nobody listens to B sides. But we fucked up, and cost ourselves about $9,000. You do that once, and you learn. We're always going to have enough Ozone material on any album that we'll be able to pull something for a single."

But even without considering economics, Frayne and Boylan found nothing in the pile that interested them except an early Dylan tune, with the early Dylan shouting and strumming his way through it. Boylan mentioned that he had a couple of ideas, Frayne tossed in a quick plug for his own

version of "That's What I Like About the South," and their meeting was
over. With Frayne gone, Boylan turned quickly to Kerr and asked about
the situation with ABC.

Kerr hesitated for a moment, then began to pick his way delicately
around the subject. Though he understated the depth of the conflict, he
finally came to the bottom line: he didn't have $5,000 to pay Boylan.
"I just don't understand it," Kerr concluded. "I mean, record companies
always fuck with bands, and you kind of get to expect it. But when they
start fucking with producers and studios, which is what they're doing
here, they've got to lose." With that, he paused and waited for Boylan
to respond.

He had to wait awhile: Boylan sat silent, mulling things over, before
he spoke. It was not an easy decision, for Kerr was asking him to trust
the Airmen's nearly bankrupt organization more than he trusted a multimillion-dollar record company, a company that was obviously in a position to give him a lot more business than Kerr ever could. If he walked
out of Kerr's office and took a plane directly home to Los Angeles, no
one would blame him. On the other hand, walking out would mean not
an uncertain payday, but no payday; it was too late for him to find another
project for this time slot. More than that, he knew enough about the
record business to suspect that someone was eventually going to release
this album, and that when they did he would be paid. Furthermore, he
wanted to produce the Airmen; he had chosen them from among the
other performers seeking his services precisely because he thought he
could do for them what they'd been unable to do for themselves. In
addition, his walking out would precipitate some sort of confrontation,
and though Kerr didn't know it at the time, Boylan tended to side-step
confrontations whenever possible. And so he finally said: "I think you're
going to come out of this all right. . . . Of course, I'll have to protect
myself the best way I can." It was a signal that he was ready to negotiate.

Within ten minutes he and Kerr had worked out an agreement that
increased Boylan's partnership in the project. If anyone other than ABC
released the record, Boylan's share of the royalties would rise to 4 percent,
and his advance would increase to a maximum of two-ninths of the
$55,000 recording budget (if there was that much left when the record
was finished) or a minimum of $5,000. Hessenius went into a tempo-
rarily empty office down the corridor to prepare the agreement, and
Kerr added one more point: "You understand that if we make the deal
with ABC, I don't want word of our arrangement getting around . . ."

Boylan said nothing, but mimed a gesture of tearing up a piece of
paper. He then rose and headed for the practice hall to meet the band.

9

THE PRACTICE HALL, like everything else in the Cody operation, was a low-budget item. Its chief advantages were its huge size (large enough to accommodate both the Airmen and the New Riders, with whom it was shared, as well as trucks and equipment when the bands were not on the road) and its location in a dingy industrial district on the outskirts of San Rafael, far from any residential areas that might be upset by high-volume practice sessions at two o'clock in the morning. Even more to the point, it cost about as much to rent the practice hall for a month as to use a recording studio for two hours.

For the past couple of months on the road, the band had been playing the songs they hoped to use in the album, but this was the first night they were to work on them in the producer's presence. The Airmen, of course, wanted to impress him, and he wanted to get them used to taking directions from him. Both of them wanted to get some numbers polished enough so that they could be recorded with minimal use of the studio. The first step, necessary though not sufficient, was for Boylan to win the band's confidence.

That process was complicated not only by the strangeness of the Airmen's working with a producer, any producer, for the first time, but by their ambivalence about the smooth Los Angeles style that was Boylan's forte. Though they were not native Californians, they had identified completely with the typical San Franciscan's conviction that everything in Los Angeles is made of plastic, and cheap plastic at that. Their objections went beyond geographical chauvinism, however, and extended to the heart of their craft. They had worked for years to achieve their unique style, and had been through hundreds of grim motel nights together. They wanted a hit, certainly, but they wanted it on their terms.

Unfortunately, their own terms had produced no hits except the freakish "Hot Rod Lincoln." Equally unfortunately, from the point of view of anyone who might want to change their style, the same terms had produced some unqualified successes; they had been watching their audiences, and with thousands of concerts behind them, the Airmen knew they were a good band. Getting them to adapt their style to the realities of the recording market would be as difficult as getting a neurotic —who after all clings to his neurosis because it works—to abandon his usual way of dealing with the world.

That the Airmen to some degree welcomed a producer, just as the neurotic may welcome a psychiatrist, made them no less defensive. They valued their distinctive style, and they had visions of a slick Los Angeles type coming in and blanding out what they had achieved only after six years of struggle on the road.

Farlow, who was skeptical about what Boylan could do for the Airmen, was particularly so about what any producer could do for him. "Shit," he drawled, "I've been singing this stuff for as long as I can remember. I already know what the people like to hear. I'm a rock'n'roll singer anyway, not one of them LA dudes. I'm gonna sing the same no matter what any producer says." Boylan, aware of their mixed feelings toward him, began working with them not as a producer but as a musician.

When Boylan arrived, only Ernie Hagar was there, sitting at his steel guitar and noodling aimlessly while tuning it to the strobe. (Like most rock bands, the Airmen used an electronically calibrated tuning device that relieved them from having to rely on their ears in the midst of the invariable backstage din; the habit had carried over into the practice hall.) Hagar had brought the band some promotional T-shirts from the Santa Cruz music store where he bought his equipment. Just as he had previously replaced his Eagles T-shirt with one of the Airmen's Lone Star numbers, Boylan now discarded that shirt in favor of one that matched Hagar's, then sat down at the piano to improvise a country-tinged blues.

Hagar, who had been a little tentative during the greetings, sat at his steel and started to eat a brown-bag sandwich, but soon responded to the riffs Boylan was playing. After a few minutes, as Hagar began to construct harmonies around the basic tune, Boylan looked over at him and offered an enthusiastic, "All right!" Hagar grinned appreciatively. One down.

The jam continued as other band members drifted in, eventually growing to include Rick Higginbotham on guitar and Paul Grupp, Boylan's regular engineer, who had flown up from Los Angeles to work on the project, on drums. Within twenty minutes of the appointed starting time, all the musicians had assembled, and Boylan rose from the piano to say, for the first of what would be at least a hundred times during the two months they were to spend together, "All right, let's cut this turkey."

A few more minutes of serious warming up, and they kicked off with "Four or Five Times," rapidly encountering the evening's first problem. The practice hall was inexpensive, but also, to be charitable, acoustically imperfect. The only vaguely sound-absorbent material on the walls was a lone fuchsia-and-black banner reading "It's Movietime, U.S.A." arbitrarily located in a corner behind the band, and the combination of low ceilings and an unbaffled, cavernous cinderblock room produced an ungodly echo. Boylan tried to deal with it by suggesting that they play "supersoft," but pianissimo was not part of the Airmen's musical lexicon. He soon abandoned any hope of working with the ensemble sound and moved into the center of the circle of musicians, focusing on Lance Dickerson's drums. Boylan wore a somewhat worried expression but made no comments, simply jotting down notes in a small spiral notebook until they'd finished the fifteen songs they'd practiced on the road.

Boylan then called a beer break, for which the band had to take up a collection, there being nothing in the collective kitty. After a few minutes during which other Airmen watched uneasily as Frayne batted crumpled beer cans around the room with a broomstick, Boylan called the Airmen back together and began to speak: "Okay, everybody get back to their instruments now. There are a few songs that I'd like to work on tonight. I'm not ruling out any of the others in any way at all, but these are the ones that struck me as being closest to ready." He listed a half-dozen, starting with "Keep on Lovin' Her," a hard-rocking number featuring Billy C. Farlow on vocal.

As they played it, Boylan returned to the center of the circle; after the first time through, he simply said, "Do it again." A few bars into the second pass, he cut it off: "Let me hear it now without the lead instrument, no licks at all." After they'd finished, he spoke again: "When I take the lead away, I like it a lot less well. The band has got to be a lot tougher all along. The solos are ready, but the drum part's light. Lance, you might try pronouncing the back beat a little more."

After the next run-through, with the rhythm section playing more strongly, Boylan eased up and offered some guarded praise: "That sounds a whole lot better already, mostly because you're just playing it harder. That's what recording is all about: you've got to concentrate, got to focus on every part." He was then ready to add the other instruments, but as soon as the band started, he cut them off: "Okay, let's start clean now . . ."

There was another half-hour's work on the song, during which Boylan shifted the order of the solos and adjusted their flow from one to another. Through it all, he stood near the drums, taking punches at the air to emphasize the rhythm. Finally he seemed satisfied: "That really sounds about twice as good already. I could cut it exactly as it stands except for the background vocals. Only one thing bothers me, and that's a tendency to rush."

Kirchen, perhaps the first to relax, laughed. "That's because we used to be able to count on Lance to be laid back." But they were all pleased, and Boylan's strategy of taking something they were already good at and building on it had increased their confidence in themselves and in him. The pattern repeated itself during each of the next five songs.

As they played, Boylan continued to concentrate on the rhythm section, trying to get Dickerson and Barlow to establish an absolutely unvarying tempo. To some extent, the technology of the recording studio forced him in that direction, for although a self-contained band like Cody will generally play together when it records, each of the instruments is recorded on a separate track. If there is a mistake on an instrumental solo, it is a relatively simple matter to erase the error and record the solo again. But if the basic tempo wavers, everything—including solos that may be perfect—has to be thrown out.

By the time they finished the grueling repetition of the last number, they were all a little groggy—even a little cranky, for Boylan's assumption of leadership had superseded their traditional method of working together. Over the years, the Airmen had developed an unspoken détente that was an important factor in their having stayed together. Basically, everybody got a piece of the action: solos, vocal leads, songwriting credits were all divided so that every member of the band got a share of the spotlight (and of the royalties).

Now, however, someone else was deciding which vocalists would be used and whose songs would be included on the album. As the evening wore on, the Airmen became increasingly nervous at the lack of clues to what Boylan was thinking. Finally, when Kirchen's second vocal solo had slid by without receiving any approving comment, he turned to Boylan and burst out: "You don't like *this* one either, do you?"

But after a quickly called break, during which Boylan took Kirchen aside to assure him that he liked all the songs they'd worked on that night, they were back in good spirits and ready to run through them all "just one more time." By then they'd been working for more than six intense hours, but Boylan's exuberance combined with their realization that they were almost finished to produce a spirited set.

When it was over, though, Hagar was still a little unhappy: "All this live work we do, and then practicing in this place . . . It's so sloppy. We never really hear ourselves, and it hurts the band. When we get into the studio, it's going to be different. Everything is going to be heard." The next night they would begin work in the studio.

10

THE AIRMEN'S PLANS to go into the studio were complicated, however, by ABC's continued refusal to advance them money for recording costs. Hoping to pressure the band into signing a long-term contract, ABC would not even certify to the recording studio that the company would be willing to pay for the tapes once they were completed and delivered. "I don't get it," Kerr complained. "They say we owe them four albums; we say we don't owe anything. But to stop the hassle, we're willing to give them two at the old rate. That's been our negotiating position all along. What they're doing now is making it impossible for us to begin recording an album they say we owe them." And indeed, unless Kerr could somehow arrange a line of credit with the recording studio on his own, the band was going to be unable to record. For recording studios, like the other aspects of the music business, exist to make money.

The $200,000 album is no longer the unthinkable freak that it was a few years ago, and even modest albums now cost in the range of $50,000. With some five thousand pop albums released annually, the studios where they are recorded have an annual gross of approximately $250 million— making them a hidden industry with income comfortably matching that of the National Football League.

One reason they need to make money is that the capital costs in setting up a serious recording studio are very high. The time has long since passed when any records (except perhaps "field" recordings made by ethnomusicologists for documentary purposes) contain the kind of straightforward single-mike reproduction of a singer and his instrument that was prevalent as recently as twenty years ago. There are still entrepreneurs traveling the country seeking unrecorded artists, but their first step is no longer to bring the performers into a hotel room and put them in front of a mike, but rather to bring them into a studio to cut a demo tape.

More than a thousand recording studios are listed in *Billboard*'s annual directory, but most of these are very basic outlets that do not share in the rock largess. Instead, they make their money by such tasks as preparing demonstration tapes of commercial jingles for ad agencies. The bulk of pop albums are recorded in fewer than 10 percent of the studios —the fully equipped locations concentrated in New York, Nashville, and Los Angeles, with strong satellite centers in another dozen cities. About half of these studios are operated as separate profit-and-loss centers by record companies, but the other half are independent ventures like the Record Plant in Sausalito, where the Airmen were scheduled to record.

If its three studios are booked for an average of only seven hours a day (a modest enough goal), the Record Plant's hourly rental of $130 will yield an annual gross of $1.1 million. If tighter scheduling produces an additional two hours in average daily usage per studio, the annual gross will increase—with no comparable rise in costs—by more than a quarter of a million dollars.

The busier the Record Plant or any studio is, the more profitable. But no one is going to go there unless the studio's recording equipment is technically competitive. Because technical innovations that increase a recording studio's capabilities are constantly being developed, the process of becoming and staying competitive is expensive.

The capital costs for even a modest studio like the Blue Door, in the Soho district of New York, go well beyond $50,000. More elaborate facilities, like the midtown–New York Media Sound, where the high-vaulted ceiling of a former church provides room and resonance for a full string section, are capitalized at more than a million dollars.

One reason for the extraordinary expense is that a first-line recording studio's equipment must combine the sensitivity of a delicate violin with the durability of a Mack truck. If it's not delicate, it won't capture the musicians' nuances. And if it's not durable enough to run at full capacity for eighteen or twenty hours a day, malfunctions will cost the studio in both money and reputation. It's bad enough when musicians are kept idle by equipment breakdowns, for they are likely to begin bouncing off the walls in short order. But if a flaw is not immediately apparent during the recording process and is, for instance, discovered only when an ineradicable tape hum disfigures the perfection achieved on a band's fortieth version of a song, there are few remedies short of suicide. Naturally, musicians who have had such an experience are unlikely to return to that studio in the future, and they are all too likely to tell their friends what happened.

Yet state-of-the-art technology is only a part of what recording studios sell. The first-line studios are also competitively distinguished by the quality of their engineering and housekeeping staffs, and by their general ambience. For some artists, the search for the perfect combination of set and setting is never-ending, but others roost comfortably in one place. Sly Stone's erratic concert habits have become legendary, but he has become so completely at home in the Sausalito Record Plant that he has set up a permanent office in one of its rooms.

Conversely, the liner credits on Stephen Stills's first Columbia album read "Recorded at Record Plant in Los Angeles and Sausalito, Caribou Ranch in Colorado, Criteria Studios in Miami, Fla., and Island Studios in London, England." It is hard to guess what Stills was seeking (and there is always the possibility that it was merely a vacation), but there are reasons for choosing one studio over another. Some are known for their isolation—Caribou Ranch is an enclosed compound of several hundred acres—and others for the musicians who work in the area. The Nashville studios, for instance, flourish because of the first-rank country musicians available for hire, and the rhythm section based at the Muscle Shoals Studio in Alabama is its *raison d'être*. Studios outside the United States, particularly in English-speaking areas like Jamaica and Britain, are frequently sought out as economy measures when recording involves a lot of extra musicians. The union minimums for session work there are so much lower than in the United States that the costs of travel are more than made up.

There are other economic motivations as well, some of them more complicated. For instance, Boylan had come to the Airmen's project from Seattle, where he'd been mixing an album in the brand-new Kaye-Smith Studios. As a new studio, it was both up to date technologically and disquietingly empty. Kaye-Smith was therefore eager to make deals with independent producers who might bring them artists to fill their vacant hours. The standard deal involves a producer's committing himself to a certain number of hours during the year. The rate he is charged, as a contract customer, is 15 to 20 percent lower than the official list price that is billed to the performer's record company, and the difference goes to the producer. Boylan, who was then considering such an arrangement with Kaye-Smith, called it a "finder's fee" and argued that no fee could be high enough to make him take an artist into an inadequate studio. That was believable, but it would be very hard to argue that all producers are models of scrupulousness; certainly in other businesses the finder's fee would be called a kickback.

Such arrangements are most common in newer, out-of-the-way studios; the established ones have a reputation for producing hits that frequently puts them into a seller's market. The Sausalito Record Plant is in such a position. Though it too occasionally offers discounts to regular clients, most performers pay a flat rate—which at the time of the Airmen's session was $130 per hour plus $100 per reel of tape. That hourly rate is somewhat high by industry standards, but owner Chris Stone is quick to point out that the Sausalito Record Plant is a special place and that no "extras" sneak onto its bills; that rate buys everything it has to offer. And its everything is quite a lot.

What it offers is a combination of technology and emotion that makes it as easy as possible for artists to work at the outer limits of their capabilities. Inside its natural redwood walls are three studios: two of them conventionally designed, with the producer and engineer separated from the musicians by a soundproof glass booth that houses all the recording equipment except the microphones, and one—under construction during the Cody sessions—an unconventional space where musicians can be placed around the room while the producer and engineer work with recording equipment set up in the middle of the circle. In all three studios every facility exists for the accurate recording and blending of what the musicians produce.

And sometimes, of course, of what they don't produce. John Herald, an acoustic guitarist now working as a session musician in Los Angeles, recalled his first recording with a bluegrass group known as the Greenbriar Boys. "We had been working for hours on 'Sally Ann,' and we couldn't get the instrumental breaks down—particularly the one where I was flat-picking. Lots of times I screwed it up, and when I didn't, someone else missed it. Finally we took a break, and when we came back, the engineers played us a version of what we'd done. It was great. Everything was really perfect, and I just couldn't believe it. I looked over at one of the other guys and said, 'Wow, I didn't know we could play like that.' And the engineer just grinned and said, 'You can't.' He'd spliced a couple of different takes together."

The studio experience that Herald remembers is more than ten years past; techniques have become so much more sophisticated since then that almost no sound makes its way to the tape without being in some way electronically modified. The Record Plant has every conceivable piece of equipment required to achieve those modifications.

The process starts out simply enough: a sound is picked up and transformed into electrical impulses by a microphone; the impulses are channeled through a control board, then put onto magnetic tape. When the tape is played back, the electronic patterns are retranslated into sound. Because of the way the sounds are altered during recording, and because of the changes of emphasis that may be made long after the musicians have gone home, the final version is generally something different—and, ideally, better—than what the musicians actually played.

The equipment in the Record Plant's Studio A, which Kerr had reserved for the Airmen, is capable of doing as much as can be done to an
individual sound. It can make it louder, add echo, position it in various
places along the left-to-right stereo spectrum, modify its timbre, and correct it so that volume remains consistent across its various frequencies.
Finally, even when an entire band is performing together, it can put each
musician's part onto a separate channel of the tape, allowing one instrument's errors to be erased without affecting satisfactory work recorded by
others. The last feature is crucial to modern recording; it allows instrumentalists and vocalists to add solos to basic tracks that the rest of the
band may have recorded days or weeks earlier.

The console on which the engineer and the producer control the input to
each of the tape's channels has a bewildering array of dials, gauges,
switches, push buttons, and a somewhat anachronistic tangle of patch
cords similar to those on old-fashioned switchboards. The patch cords,
however, are the only such element in the control booth, for the console
itself, stretching perhaps twelve feet across the front of the booth, is as
modern as the dashboard of a jumbo jet. For $130 an hour, the Record
Plant provides the studio and an assistant engineer capable both of operating the console and tape recorder and of setting up the microphones
and other equipment in the recording room.

In addition to the studios inside the building, the Record Plant keeps
a full studio in its parking lot. This one, filling nearly the entire interior
of a straight-body truck, is a mobile unit used to record "live" in concert
settings all over the country. Sometimes bands hire it to follow them
through a national tour; at other times radio stations arrange to tape
an act appearing in a neighborhood club for later broadcast. The rolling
studio's equipment is fully as elaborate as that used inside the Record
Plant, because live recordings require the same kind of separation and
fidelity as studio albums. If anything, live recording is more expensive on
an hourly basis than studio work, since mileage costs for the van and
travel expenses for the Record Plant personnel must be included, and the
amount of time in mixing is the same. Whatever savings occur are the
result of a reduction in the amount of recording time. (The Airmen's
previous album, recorded live during a series of performances at the
Armadillo Hall in Austin, Texas, had been recorded by a traveling crew
from Wally Heider's San Francisco Studio in only four days; a typical
studio album requires at least four weeks.) The mobile unit is more a
service than a money-maker for Chris Stone's operation, but it pays for
itself in contracts and relationships that lead to future studio work.

The truck does not, however, have all the amenities of the Record
Plant proper: the understated luxury, unparalleled in the record business,
that reflects the Marin County setting in which Stone decreed his stately

pleasure dome. Though hard, serious work regularly goes on at the Sausalito studio, it is a true pleasure dome when compared to most other studios—including Stone's Los Angeles Record Plant—which generally run to stark functionalism. Its specialness—which is its unique selling point, since Marin County boasts neither the studio musicians nor the night life of other recording centers—begins with its location, a half-minute walk from the edges of upper San Francisco Bay.

From the outside it is nearly indistinguishable from the other more-or-less hip businesses that dot the Sausalito waterfront. Its angled planking of natural redwood, though striking to an East Coast visitor, is almost a commonplace of West Coast construction. But a second glance reveals a rich attentiveness to detail that is typical of the entire operation. The mammoth doors from the parking lot are hand-carved hardwood, wide enough to accommodate any imaginable equipment, and are reached by an easily negotiable ramp rather than stairs. Around the corner, its regular entrance is marked by no sign, and is discreetly fitted with a one-way mirror for spotting uninvited visitors.

Throughout the building the walls are paneled with varying tones and grains of polished wood. The soft background blend of umbers and tans in the corridor walls is picked up by the matching floors and enhanced by wood mosaics set into the panels. In addition to the studios, a visitor wandering the corridors will find a lounge with a foam-padded floor, a well-stocked bar and refrigerator, and a stereo system. Outside its sliding glass doors is a flagstone patio, and adjoining is an enormous Jacuzzi in which tired musicians who have failed to be rejuvenated by the bar can refresh themselves. There is also, of course, a pong machine to help temporarily idle musicians fill their waiting periods, and the soda machine by the door responds to twenty cents with a nondiscriminatory offering of Coca-Cola, mineral water, or Coors beer.

For those whose batteries need recharging by travel, the Record Plant speedboat is docked nearby and is available at any time of day for trips across the bay to waterside restaurants in Tiburon and Belvedere. The Record Plant's assistant engineers are equally adept as nighttime harbor pilots. And for artists who don't live in the area, the Record Plant house high in the hills near Muir Wood provides a secluded off-hours retreat.

To an observer, it all seems a little bit overdone, a parody of the American Dream, until the resident manager, Michelle Zarin, places it in perspective: "Listen, we've got all kinds of people coming in here, from guys who've made dozens of records and live around the corner to kids from Brooklyn who've never been in the studio before. But no matter who they are, along about the fortieth time of playing the same part of the same song, they begin to get a little crazy. That's when it's good for them to be in this place. We try to make it feel like home."

For many rock musicians, of course, home is where the drugs are, and operating a business in that context can be a little tricky. Legally, Stone cannot afford to tolerate drug use; practically, he has no other choice. "We certainly don't condone sales," he said flatly. "It's illegal, and it's a bad vibe." But he was also reasonable: "If a client who has rented one of our studios comes in and has something with him, there's not much we can do. As long as the door is locked, it's like a motel room, and we can't control what goes on in there."

Stone also felt that social drug use can be preferable to other chemical abuses: "We just had"—he named a prominent southern rock band—"in the LA studios, and they're notorious drinkers. It was a mess. They broke up things, and they were"—he paused to seek a polite description— "rowdy."

One cannot be really sure how serious Stone was (except about heroin, which he rigidly rejects, at least partially because of "the bad karma that comes with it"), for the prevailing attitude inside the pleasure dome is genially relaxed. There are absolutely inflexible limits about interfering with someone else's work, but within them the attitude is one of nearly Summerhillian permissiveness. Any recording studio will necessarily have a plentiful supply of single-edged razor blades that can be appropriated to prepare cocaine, but at the Record Plant dope smokers (or, one supposes, tobacco heads) who run out of rolling papers can always replenish their supply from a carton in the supply closet. And though the staff scrupulously avoids the legally dodgy business of helping out-of-town clients who are away from their regular suppliers, area musicians have been known to drop by and use the lounge to deal a little coke to temporarily embarrassed travelers.

None of this, as far as Stone can manage, goes on with the connivance of the Record Plant staff, but it would be hard for any business which caters to rock musicians to operate without the kind of tolerant friendliness that is the Sausalito studio's key selling point.

Much of the friendliness comes from the Record Plant staff; if one were to go to God's Central Casting for a person who could make strangers feel at home in an alien environment, it would be hard to do better than Michelle Zarin. A softly zaftig woman in her early thirties, she got her job when Chris Stone selected her from among a bevy of employment agency nominations for the manager's position. Though totally inexperienced in the music business, Zarin has become very much a Jewish mother to the Record Plant's clients. That means making sure that the Record Plant maintains its friendliness twenty-four hours a day, seven days a week, 365 days a year. "Listen, we're here to help people make the best records they can. If someone really thinks that he's going to get a special sound by coming in on Christmas afternoon, we're here." But most actual recording goes on at night. There may be local bands coming in to cut demo tapes during the day, but most touring musicians have adjusted their body clocks to a work day that begins no earlier than eight or nine P.M. and stretches out until three or four in the morning. Given the demands of album making, it is physiological as well as emotional common sense for performers' recording routines to approximate those they normally follow, and studios that charge varying hourly rates collect a premium for the hours after midnight or ten P.M. The cheapest rates, conversely, generally begin at eight or nine in the morning, when the people who make the record industry's business decisions are leaving Beverly Hills or Greenwich to begin the commute to their downtown offices.

Zarin herself usually leaves the studio soon after the bands arrive to begin their working nights, returning the next day to wrestle with scheduling, the Record Plant's most serious problem. An empty studio, of course, brings in no income; what's worse, it loses money, for maintaining a first-rate staff requires paying their salaries whether or not the studios are in use. Thus there is always a tendency to overbook, but that has to be balanced by the need to preserve the relaxed, unhurried feeling that is the Record Plant's stock in trade. "There's a lot of juggling involved in trying to keep the studios filled without overbooking," Zarin says. "After a while, you get to know who means he's going to take a week when he says he needs a studio for a week, and who really means two months.

"And of course there's all the personal stuff. Some people have a lucky studio, and they won't work in any other one. So that complicates things. And sometimes there are people you don't really know. I mean, what do you do when someone you don't know swears up and down that they'll be out by the fourteenth of July—and on the thirteenth, when you've already given their studio to someone else, they come in to ask you for another week to mix?

"There's really nothing you can do about it, and most people are flexible enough to make some room for it. What we'll try to do is kind of juggle three bands back and forth between two studios for a week or so. We may also ask the band that's run over on its schedule to switch to afternoon hours, particularly if they're just overdubbing or mixing, but if the other people are really adamant about wanting to work only in a specific studio, we just have to help the first band find space somewhere else. Generally, of course, the first place we look is the LA Record Plant, but there are a lot of people who are happy here who just don't like the feel down there. It *is* very LA."

The scheduling that occupies most of Zarin's time is important, but it is only part of the Record Plant's day-to-day operations. Zarin's most important duty is to make sure that the Plant is regularly paid for the services it provides. It was this last element that made for trouble in the Airmen's project.

"I called ABC to get an approval for this," Zarin recalled, "and they just started giving me a runaround. I couldn't quite figure out what was going on, because getting that kind of sign-off is really just a routine thing. At any rate, all they did was say they'd call back. Only they never did.

"Finally I got a little worried and put one of the girls on it full time. I told her I didn't care if she had to call them every five minutes, she couldn't give up until we got someone to confirm that they were going to pay for it. She finally had to stay on them for nearly a whole day, but eventually she got an answer. Only it wasn't what we expected: they said they wouldn't pay.

"At that point, I really didn't know what to do. I mean, I have the right to make deals with people and stuff like that, but I wouldn't feel right about letting someone—even a regular client like Joe Kerr—come in and run up a fifty-thousand-dollar bill without any kind of guarantee at all. If I let him in, we might wind up with a bill that no one could pay—I know that Joe doesn't have that kind of money lying around. But if we keep him out, we've got an empty studio for a month, because it's probably too late to fill it on such short notice. Besides, we make an enemy. So I finally just called Chris and asked him what he wanted to do."

For Stone, the problem was old-hat: "We're *always* in the middle. The artist is our client, but the label pays the bills, and we always have friends on both sides of any dispute. There are times when something like this happens in mid-project, and then we just lock up the tapes and don't release them to *anybody* until they all agree. This one just happened earlier, that's all." And so he tossed the ball back to Zarin. Did she think Kerr was good for it?

"Chris knows Joe too, though maybe not as well as I do, and besides, he really wants me to run this place as much without him as I can. That leaves him free to work the LA end and handle all the business things like building the new studio up here. So when I said 'Yes,' he just said, 'Then let 'em have it.' I guess I'm feeling a little nervous about that now, and maybe I should have said something like 'He's good for it if he's got it,' but it's settled now. They're coming in on credit."

Though she might have been having second thoughts, the Airmen's road crew had already installed their equipment in the studio. Kerr's reputation had held things together, and ABC's attempt to use the Record Plant to force the Airmen into signing a long-term contract (or perhaps—remembering the Blue Thumb story—to precipitate a lawsuit) had failed. Of course it was only an early round in the band's struggle with the company, but at least the recording could begin.

11

LIKE ALMOST EVERYTHING the Airmen did, the recording process began with the road crew sweating and heaving heavy instrument cases into the back of their van. On subsequent nights things would be a little easier for the roadies, because the huge amplifiers would remain in the studio for the duration of the recording and only the instruments would have to be lugged back and forth from the practice hall. But the first night was as demanding as setting up for a concert. Setting up the equipment was also complicated, ironically, by Kerr's other band, which had fallen well behind schedule on its own recording and needed to use the studio for mixing until late in the afternoon. By the time the road crew was actually able to begin setting up the band's instruments, there was only an hour before six o'clock, when the first Airman was scheduled to arrive.

But the crew was experienced and professional, and within forty-five minutes the basic setup was done and only tuning remained. When Neil Fink, the band's traveling sound man (who first met them in Ann Arbor when he was playing junior high school football under Coach Joe Kerr), had adjusted the electronic tuning device so that it was in tune with the piano, the crew's setup job was complete, and the pong game began its never-ending nightly workout.

After a few games, Fink drifted away to examine the giant console in the control booth. "Examine" is too neutral a word; actually, he was gaping at it. "It's amazing. This stuff is all new within the last two years . . . even the last eighteen months. It's quad, too, with thirty-two in and twenty-four out," which meant that it could accept sound impulses from as many as thirty-two different sources, grouping them, as the producer desired, into twenty-four separate bundles on the tape. But when Boylan and his engineer, Paul Grupp, arrived a few minutes later, they seemed noticeably unimpressed.

What they were complaining about, in arcane language that involved a lot of phrases like "70 cycles . . . that's a 15-12 . . . we're elevated plus three," was that the Record Plant lacked the absolutely latest device in sound control: a parametric equalizer. Each input channel had an equalizer, but it was of the comparatively old-fashioned type that had first been used about five years earlier (Those at the Record Plant were, Grupp admitted later, the best available on-console equipment; it was merely that the parametric version had been developed so recently that it was not yet available on consoles and had to be plugged in off-board). Equalizers are necessary because each instrument has certain frequency ranges in which its tone and timbre shift. The low notes on a particular steel guitar, for instance, may be warmer and less edgy than the same instrument's high notes. Such natural variation is not much of a problem in live performance, where there are visual distractions and other elements of excitement, but it can pose real difficulties in recording, where a crucially important bit of low harmony from the steel may be lost behind the other instruments.

The problem in such a passage might be solved by boosting the steel's amplification, but it would then in turn overwhelm the other instruments when played in its higher frequencies. One could also, of course, have the engineer furiously adjust the volume and tone controls for each instrument as it moved from range to range, but he would inevitably end up as frantic as Charlie Chaplin on the assembly line in *Modern Times*. The equalizer is the answer.

The kind associated with each input channel at the Record Plant was activated by three separate dials per channel, nearly a hundred in all. The dials divided the range of audible frequencies into low, middle, and high ranges, and allowed the engineer to establish an automatic tone equalization for each segment—adding, for instance, a little edge to the steel's lower ranges. Coupled with the use of limiters, which have the same sort of function for volume that the equalizers do for tone, the tri-pole equalizers at the Record Plant were adequate to ninety-nine out of a hundred recording situations.

Grupp, however, was something of a fussbudget. Then only twenty-two years old, he already had almost five years of engineering experience behind him and had developed very clear ideas about how he wanted things to sound. The three-part division was simply not fine enough to do the kind of things that he aimed for. The problem with the steel, for instance, might exist within only a part of the lowest frequency range;

adjusting that entire range would simply shift its locus. And because Grupp was a perfectionist, the gap between what he wanted and what was technically possible was often unbridgeable. Which didn't, of course, stop him from trying. Beginning, on the first night, with the drums.

The road crew had set up Lance Dickerson's drums in an alcove to the far left of the studio. Boylan had arranged for Dickerson to come in earlier than any of the other Airmen, and when he arrived Grupp went out and joined him in the studio. Together they began tuning the drums. Though the tom-toms (which are analogous to tympani) are not usually tuned to a specific pitch, each one does have its own initial note, a variety of overtones, and a concluding tone that may or may not be the same as the initial one. "These were tuned," said Grupp, "so that the note would bend down to another note. What we worked on originally was the length of the initial note, the distance of the bend, and how long it was gonna take to get there—and of course rattles and buzzes." All this was necessary because the key to a drummer's sound lies as much in his tuning as in his technique.

With the toms in tune, Grupp and Dickerson then went to work on the snares and the kick (or bass) drum, which were adjusted less for pitch than for percussive power and punch. With each drum finally satisfactory individually, it was time to begin balancing them, for each time a drum was hit, it sent sound waves out from its vibrating head. Some of these waves would go directly to the microphones that Tom Anderson, the Record Plant assistant engineer assigned to the Cody project, had previously set up, but others would "bump into" the remaining drums, creating a range of sympathetic vibrations echoing a millisecond behind the first note. Though that time lag is almost unmeasurably small (sound does travel at the speed of sound, after all, and the drums are only inches from each other), the peaks and troughs from the sympathetic vibrations will not be precisely aligned with those of the first note. The resulting effect, called "phasing," means that a drum will have a richer, more complex sound when it is part of a properly tuned kit than it will if it is set off by itself. But the same phasing that is almost unnoticed when it contributes to making drums a delight for an audience is not at all unperceived by the delicate recording equipment. The drum sound is a hellish problem for a producer.

It was only the first measure of the differences between the Airmen's previous happy-go-lucky studio work and the regimen that Boylan and Grupp would impose on them, but the drum tuning took more than an hour. When it was over and Grupp had returned to the booth, Dickerson joined him for a brief break. "Jesus," he said, "I've never been through anything like that before."

"Yeah," Boylan responded, "Grupp thinks you're Nigel Olsson." Dickerson raised an eyebrow questioningly, and Boylan explained: "He's Elton John's drummer."

"Oh," said Dickerson, less impressed than exhausted. "Who's Elton John?"

"He's the man who just signed an eight-million-dollar recording contract. Is that worth getting your drums in tune?"

Though Dickerson's question had made clear that he, like the other Airmen, had little use for Elton John, he nevertheless agreed that it was. And he soon returned to the studio to begin the second part of establishing the album's drum sound.

During this phase, Boylan and Grupp stayed in the booth, listening to the drums over the studio monitors, two huge speakers above the glass panel that allowed them to view the studio. "Okay, Lance," Boylan began, "start to hit one stroke at a time on the snare." The monotonous tone filled the booth regularly every three or four seconds as Grupp carefully adjusted dials. After a few minutes he cut the volume and matter-of-factly turned to Boylan. "This sounds like shit."

Boylan nodded glumly and punched the talk-back device so that Dickerson could hear his voice in the soundproof studio. "Lance," he said, interrupting the drumming which had continued in pantomime after Grupp had cut the sound from the monitors, "do you have another snare?" Dickerson did, and Grupp went out to the studio to help install it in the kit—after, of course, another quarter-hour of tuning. Grupp then returned to the booth, and when he had completed his adjustments on the board, the drum sounded noticeably different from the first one, but no better. They decided to try changing microphones.

Microphones, like other electronic equipment, have certain peculiarities; the sensitivity and tonal quality differ significantly from model to model. One that narrowly pinches overtones in upper ranges, making it perfect for a producer who wants an early-fifties sound on guitar, will completely sap the warmth and emotion from a female singer. And beyond those differences as to purpose among types of microphones, there are also marginal differences among manufacturers' versions of a specific type. Because producers, for reasons that no doubt seem arbitrary to studio owners, tend to have pets among manufacturers, a first-line studio has to maintain a large inventory of mikes if it is to hold its competitive position. The Record Plant's consisted of almost a hundred different microphones (along with duplicate copies of the more versatile and popular models), and cost as much as the full range of equipment in a complete but more modest recording studio. At $130 per hour, the Airmen were paying not only for the mikes they did use, but for those they *might* use.

Still, they did use a lot of microphones. Dickerson, for example, had two overhead mikes on booms, plus a smaller mike located just above each of his drums, for a total of seven. Miking the drummer is especially difficult, because each microphone must be sensitive enough to pick up the sympathetic overtones that provide the phasing, but not so sensitive as to produce an undifferentiated blur instead of cleanly defined rhythms. A microphone capable of picking up the overtones bouncing off an unstruck drum is all too likely to keep picking them up on the second and third rebound from the walls, producing a certain mushiness. But a mike whose sensitivity is too low will leave even the best of drummers sounding as if he were merely pounding out rhythms on a kitchen table. One way of handling the problem is to cut down the number of vibrations bouncing around the walls. The carpeting and panels of the Airmen's assigned studio were absorbent enough for most instruments, but they were too bouncy for the Airmen's drums and piano: a portable, highly sound-absorbent wall was the answer. As Grupp tested different microphones, Tom Anderson began to build a wall of baffles around Dickerson's alcove. The wooden frames were approximately four by six feet, their four-inch depth packed with cotton and—a typical Record Plant touch—covered with tie-dyed crushed velvet. When they were in place, Dickerson's isolation from the rest of the band was broken only by an area deliberately left open so that the Airmen could see each other play.

As they were working on the kick, Boylan sensed that it was ringing too much and sent Neil Fink out for extra material to pack behind the drumhead. When Fink arrived with an armful of fabric, Grupp spoke to the booth through one of the mikes: "It sounds perfect out here." To which Boylan responded, "I don't give a shit what it sounds like out there. It's ringing in here, and in here is where it counts."

Seduced by reality, Grupp—who knew better, since he had worked on dozens of albums—had forgotten that what the listener will eventually hear is the sound as modified, not the sound as played. For the perfectionist, it was an unusual mistake. And the Airmen, whose previous studio experience had been blissfully free of anything like Grupp's compulsiveness, were becoming more than a little frustrated by it. They had been arriving, as scheduled, at half-hour intervals, but had so far done little besides sit and watch Grupp fiddle alternately with the drums and with the board. They were growing restless. More than that, the fussiness seemed to them pointless; they wanted simply to go out into the studio and make their music. Boylan, sensing that a perfect drum sound would make no difference if it was surrounded by a group of disgruntled musicians, called Grupp in to begin setting proper sound levels for each of the other instrumentalists.

As Boylan and Grupp concentrated on the levels, another Record

Plant assistant eventually appeared with a set of smaller speakers that Boylan had been asking for and set them on top of the console. After some muttering about how long it had taken—mostly to himself, for there was no one from the Record Plant in the booth at the time—Boylan cut the monitors and began listening through the smaller speakers: "I think that too many people in the record business listen to the monitors. These are much more like what people will listen to at home."

Compared to the time it had taken to get the drums even close to Grupp's finicky standards, setting the levels for the other instruments went fairly quickly, perhaps fifteen or twenty minutes for each. Only the piano took longer, for Grupp tried a few microphone changes, and as they waited for Frayne to finish, the other Airmen wandered into the booth and tried various styles of relaxing. Tichy sat off in a corner reading *The Sotweed Factor;* Stein rolled and offered several joints of some remarkable dope recently provided to him by a touring Texas band; Barlow laboriously peeled duck eggs which he had gathered and hard-boiled at his farm earlier in the afternoon; Kirchen and Dickerson undertook a complicated doubles game on the pong machine with some of the road crew; Hagar sipped a beer and minutely observed Boylan's performance; and Farlow, the last scheduled to arrive, eased over next to Stein, saying that he needed a few tokes to relax him from the road.

Six hours after the road crew had begun setting up the equipment, Boylan pronounced himself satisfied, and they were ready to play together for the first time that night. Dickerson and Frayne retired behind their baffles, Stein brought his fiddle into a soundproof, glass-fronted isolation room next to the control booth, and the other Airmen took up their instruments and put on their headphones. Farlow, who would not be called upon to sing for a while, rolled a little more of Stein's dope and remained in the booth with Grupp and Boylan as the band kicked off with "Armadillo Stomp."

The song is one that the Airmen could probably have played in their sleep, for it is the standard opening number in their concerts. It had also been featured in their previous album, and their playing it merely gave Boylan and Grupp another chance to work on sound quality. Still, as the fiddle opened up with insistent jig licks, Boylan couldn't help grinning and rhythmically stomping his foot. At the end of the song, however, the booth was filled by complaining cries from the Airmen—primarily, it seemed amid the cacophony, because they couldn't hear themselves.

That they had played well without being able to hear themselves properly was a tribute to their years on the road, but it also illustrated another difficulty of life in the studio. To minimize the cross-microphone leakage that a rock band at full blast would inevitably produce, the electrified instruments are frequently plugged directly into the recording panel. When it is not possible to do this, and when, as in the case of the Airmen, acous-

tic and electronic instruments are combined, the more sensitive microphones of the acoustic instruments have to be shielded. Thus Stein had
to play his fiddle in the isolation booth, where none of the other musicians
could actually hear him. His notes, and all those captured through the
console, were relayed back to the musicians instantaneously, through
headphones. These headphones, called "cues," are the way the musician
hears not only himself but the rest of the band as well. Because the cues
don't have to contain the same mix as the one in use on the board itself,
any group of eight musicians is likely to want eight different mixes on the
headphones. Generally, they will all want the rhythm tracks (bass, drums,
and sometimes second guitar) boosted so that they have a clear sense of
the piece's timing, and some like the level for their own instrument and
for the vocal (so they can keep track of where they are in the song) raised
as well.

"OK," said Boylan, "that's one of the reasons we do run-throughs.
Let's everybody go 'round one at a time and tell the Grupper what you
want on the cues. Then we'll do it again and see if it works." When they'd
finished going around the room, Boylan hit the talk-back again. His voice
was transmitted through both the studio speakers and the cues, so that it
could be heard whether or not the musicians were wearing their headphones. " 'Armadillo Stomp,' take two," he called, and they were off
again. Something was still wrong, though. Stein, perhaps because of the
psychological distance imposed by the isolation room, had been adamant
about raising the fiddle track to full volume, but now he was practically
inaudible.

"Android," Boylan said gently as the song ended, "I'm willing to give
you anything you want in the cans, but let me explain a certain psychological fact to you. You wanted the fiddle boosted way up, right? That
means it sounds *very* loud to you. So what happens is that you play quieter
and quieter. By the end of that take, you were falling off the bottom of
the meters in here. I want you to play louder with your fingers, not with
your ears. If you're playing so quietly that the tape can't find you, we're
in trouble. I'll leave the cans the way they are for now, and let's try it
once more and then we'll have a playback. If you still have trouble hearing yourself play, just take off one of the phones. That way you'll have
the band in one ear and your fiddle in the other. OK?" A bowed acknowl-
edgment from Stein and then, "Anybody else got cue troubles? No? OK,
'Armadillo Stomp' rolling on three."

As they played, Grupp continued to adjust the levels on the drums and
bass, which he had moved to a graphic equalizer. Though not as sensitive
as a parametric, it divided the sound spectrum into considerably finer
divisions than the three-tiered EQs on the board allowed. But as they
trooped in for a playback, Grupp still looked unhappy.

The playback, unlike those which would occur when they actually got down to the business of serious recording, was fairly relaxed; everyone was listening more to the general quality of the sound than to specific performances. Still, Kirchen complained that Stein was playing over one of his solos (Stein, without objection, agreed), and Barlow asked whether Dickerson had been able to hear the fiddle solo over his cues, telling him that he had rushed the ending by coming in a half-beat before the solo finished. Because they knew it didn't really count, however, the conversation was all good-humored, and revolved mostly around the snare sound. The consensus was that even after all Grupp's and Boylan's efforts, it still felt, in Boylan's words, "too much like a toy." Boylan suggested that the problem might simply be that the drum had been out on the road too long and assigned one of the road crew to scare up another drum before the next night's session.

They then returned to the studio for a half-dozen passes at "Don't Let Go," a Farlow vocal they planned to record for this album, after which Boylan finally called it a night, saying, "I want everybody here *and ready to play* at seven o'clock sharp tomorrow night." By then it was approaching two A.M., and the exhausted Airmen, in a night that had passed without a single serious attempt at recording, had run up a studio bill of more than a thousand dollars.

12

BY TEN the next morning, when the Airmen—with the exception of Barlow, who was presumably hard at his farm chores—were still recuperating from their first night at the studio, Joe Kerr was already well into his work on their behalf. Kerr had briefly appeared at the studio the night before, but only long enough to drop off a properly typed version of the new contract with Boylan, a document that Boylan read *very* carefully before signing. Kerr tried to stay as much as possible out of his bands' musical business because, as he cheerfully admitted, he didn't understand rock'n'roll. Instead, he concentrated on getting his acts as much money as possible.

The office from which Kerr operated could hardly have been more different from the quarters that Famous Music had occupied. It was actually not an office at all, but an aging two-story house near the center of San Rafael, itself an aging city whose most recent, and perhaps only, distinction was that its main street had been used in the "cruising" scenes from *American Graffiti*. Near it stood a secondhand bookstore, a laundromat, several gas stations, an automatic car wash, a brightly lit derelicts' bar, and a Mexican restaurant from which the pervasive smell of nacho cheese wafted regularly. It was not a prepossessing setting for a business that grossed a million dollars a year, but what was saved on frills showed up on the profit side of the ledger. Famous Music had been more impressive, but Famous Music was no more.

The offices didn't need to be impressive, for Kerr's natural instrument was the telephone, and the bulk of his business was conducted long-distance. The day after the Airmen's first night in the studio, he began with a phone call to Magna Artists, the band's booking agent in Los Angeles. The West Coast office of Magna (a subsidiary of General Electric) was headed by Ron Rainey, who had been booking the band since it first made the trek from Michigan. The call began with a review of the Cody-ABC situation during which Kerr seemed perfectly willing to appreciate the company's position. At one point, when Rainey urged him on to a harder line, Kerr pointed out that he didn't have the leverage: "You gotta understand, Ron. This ain't the Mamas and the Papas; this is a sixty-thousand-dollar liability. Which they're about to go to a hundred and fifteen thousand on with this album. Now you know, and I know, and *they* know, that they could do that on the catalog of old albums alone if they got even one good new one out of us, so I really don't know what they're after. I mean, after what they've put us through, they know they're not gonna keep us."

After more talk along the same lines, including Kerr's observation that he was "sitting here with money in my pocket from Mo Ostin [of Warner Brothers] for future product," he got down to the business of the call. The band was planning an eastern swing during the Thanksgiving and pre-Christmas period, and Kerr wanted to find out how the bookings were going. There still remained a dozen or so dates to be filled, and as the two went over the possibilities, Kerr picked up his phone and stood near a highway map that dominated one of the office walls. Rainey, who received a flat 10 percent off the top of any of the band's concerts that he booked, mentioned a few offers he'd had, but Kerr was not happy with them. "Ron, that gets us traveling around in a circle. If you can switch those two around, then we've got a couple of four-hundred-mile days in a row, which isn't too bad. But if we do it the way you want, then we've got to go eight hundred miles one day, *back* almost four hundred the next, and then *another* eight hundred the day after that. What kind of shit is that?"

That part of their conversation—together with subsequent questions about the nature of the acts that might open for the Airmen in other areas —dramatized the difference between Kerr's and Rainey's attitudes toward the Airmen. Rainey had been with them a long time and liked them both as people and as musicians, but—like any other agent—he couldn't afford to be concerned with their long-term development. He had other acts to worry about—the New Riders, Kris Kristofferson, and Waylon Jennings among them—and was more concerned with the number of dates than with their quality. He would of course benefit if the band's career flourished, but he was not responsible for that flourishing. As their manager, Kerr was.

There are a couple of stereotypes of rock managers floating around. One features a hondeling, minor-league Las Vegas mafioso in double-knit slacks, a shirt open to his navel and a flashy medallion nestling among his exposed chest hairs; the other—a class act—is some variation of Albert Grossman. Grossman is now the owner of a small, successful Warner

Brothers affiliate, but his importance as a manager—of Dylan, the Band, Peter, Paul and Mary, and Janis Joplin, among others—was so great that his current position is thought of as a sort of semiretirement. The style with which he carried off his role is revealed by the fact that audiences and critics spontaneously recognized him as the real star of *Don't Look Back,* D. A. Pennebacker's documentary of Dylan's 1965 British tour. Grossman, in that film, epitomized the kind of brooding presence that Sax Rohmer used to describe as "evil incarnate." There was never a letup in his intensity, never a sign of wavering from the goal of more and more money for the performers in whom he dealt as unemotionally as though they were commodity futures. His relentless practicality is perhaps best indicated by his naming himself as beneficiary on life insurance policies he took out on his stars, a tactic that netted him a tidy settlement after Janis Joplin died of a heroin overdose. The insurance company at first refused to pay the claim, arguing that Joplin's death had not been accidental, and a trial brought the policies to public light. Any number of other managers used the occasion to condemn Grossman's cynicism, but neither they nor anyone else ever claimed that he had taken one penny more of his artists' earnings than he was entitled to. And in a business where penniless performers with surpassingly wealthy managers are a commonplace, that's not a bad tribute.

Kerr, neither a mafioso nor a Grossman, violated both stereotypes. He dressed in jeans and T-shirts (and for formal occasions a black Stetson and a denim windbreaker), and would probably not have known a double-knit from second base. Certainly he shared the Airmen's feelings about slickness, and the strongest term of opprobrium in his vocabulary was that something or someone was "too LA." He often seemed uncomfortable in dealing with the chest-medallion lads who base their operations there. His aim, he said, was "simply to keep the bands from worrying about anything but their music.

"My job," he continued, "is pretty much like any other businessman's job; it's just that my clients are a little weirder than theirs. But it's all the same thing. I pay the bills, make sure the checkbooks are balanced, and handle any hassles with the record companies. None of it," he said with engaging modesty, "is any big deal."

Of course it could be argued that Kerr had a great deal to be modest about; neither the New Riders nor, of course, the Airmen were of a stature that would have allowed him the cold-eyed practicality that made Grossman such a successful manager. Kerr's job, regardless of his personality, simply didn't permit him the luxury of arrogance, for the manager of an act like the Airmen is generally not in the position of deciding among equally fabulous offers facing his band. He is far more likely to use his time trying to create adequate ones.

Thus Kerr spent the bulk of his days attached to the telephone, talking endlessly in an attempt to win friends and influence music-business people throughout the country. If he had been managing only the Riders, who were already clearly established as a headline act in most of the country, or managing a band whose career was just beginning, his business day would have been different. But the Airmen were in a difficult spot in the musical spectrum: their cadre of hard-core fans made them a superb opening act, because they could build up a headliner significantly, but they were themselves weak headliners. Except for the band's home bases in Michigan and the Bay Area, they could safely headline only in New York and Texas. And even there they required a strong second act to sell out large houses.

Kerr's problem with Magna was that it was to bookers as Cody was to bands: respectable, certainly, but hardly spectacular. There was no one at Magna who could go to a promoter and say, "You want X for a week at the Garden? You can have them if you take Commander Cody as the opening act." And opening for an attraction capable of filling a large hall like Madison Square Garden or the Philadelphia Spectrum would clearly benefit the band. The money would not be better than they could earn from their own tours of smaller halls—it might even be worse, since any bonuses from sold-out houses would go to the headliners rather than to the Airmen—but the number of people who heard them would escalate geometrically. Such a tour could introduce them to regions where they were not enough of a draw to headline in anything but halls so small that the bookings would hardly pay for touring expenses. And Magna couldn't help them that way, for it had no artists who could fill the huge arenas.

Magna's biggest act was Kerr's New Riders, and Kerr was already capable of putting Cody on any of the Riders' bills without going through an agency. Magna had plenty of acts that could benefit by opening for Cody, but none that the Airmen could use to pyramid toward a larger audience; none except the Riders, at any rate, and as they were Magna's trump, the company tried to use them to help all its artists.

Unable to gain any leverage for Cody from Magna's other acts, Kerr therefore had no choice but to use the Riders—which did not necessarily make the Riders all that happy. They shared managers—not bank accounts —with the Airmen, and there was no economic reason for them to sacrifice a lucrative booking, or travel to an out-of-the-way one, to help the Airmen. Kerr might be richer if the Airmen became stars, but the Riders would not. They might even be less well off, for if the Airmen became headline attractions in their own right, they would no longer be available to boost the Riders in chancy billings.

One result of all this was that a recurring conversation took place in Kerr's office almost every time he got off the phone with Rainey. It always involved leaving Magna. The question came pointedly from Rick Higginbotham, the Airmen's road manager, who was responsible for shuttling them through the nearly impossible schedules imposed on them by what he viewed as Magna's weakness. Kerr's answer generally went something like, "Well, remember what he did for us *when*." It was certainly true that Rainey had been uncommonly helpful during the years when the Airmen were first getting established, but it was becoming increasingly clear that he could do little for them in their current position. Each year made the question a little sharper. Not only had Rainey's favors fallen further into the past; the Airmen had also spent another year convinced by the enthusiasm of their concert audiences that they were a first-rate band and stuck in a second-rate rut. They wanted out.

Performers in more arcane arenas than rock can get along reasonably well without popularity. They find affirmation from critics, government grants, the progress of their craft—a hundred different sources. Most of those sources of affirmation were open to the Airmen, but neither they nor any other popular artist can survive without mass audience recognition. One reason the mortality rate for rock bands is so high—aside from the frustrations and pains of touring—is that they constantly splinter and regroup in search of ever expanding audiences. A casual glance at the genealogical charts of rock groups that Pete Frame lovingly prepares for his British fan magazine *ZigZag* shows an almost endless shuffle of members back and forth among a widening pyramid of LA-based bands. The Byrds, Buffalo Springfield, Crosby, Stills, Nash and Young, Poco, Grin, the Flying Burrito Brothers, Loggins and Messina, and the Eagles are only some of the better-known names; dozens of others have disappeared altogether. The Airmen had somehow maintained their confidence, but it was becoming palpably more difficult every time they climbed aboard Honeysuckle Rose, their decaying bus, for yet another trip to twenty places they didn't want to go.

And though Kerr's association with the New Riders had probably helped them to get even as far as they had, being Kerr's *second* band rankled. They believed that they were better performers (as did most of the critics who had written about the two bands). Certainly they often received the more enthusiastic crowd reaction when the two bands played together. But the Riders wrote strong material and worked hard in the studio; they had sold a lot more records. The record sales generated concert grosses, so that the Riders made more money in a hundred and fifty nights on the road than the Airmen did in more than two hundred. And the Riders traveled by air.

Kerr's job, perhaps especially because he had first been the Airmen's manager and had only recently taken on the Riders, was complicated by the rivalry between the two bands. Sometimes it took irrational forms, as when Kerr's continuing attempt to get the Riders to purchase their own customized bus repeatedly fell on deaf ears. "It doesn't make any sense," he said. "You can only go as fast on a tour as your equipment can travel, and it has to go by truck. What's wrong with flying across the country and having your bus meet you for the length of time you're on tour in a region? There's no advantage to all those dinky little flights from Ithaca to Albany. It just costs money." In the previous year, for the four Riders and their road manager, air fare had cost about $60,000. Had they been able to halve that, each musician's income would have increased by more than $7,000. But they wouldn't do it. Why? "It's easy," said Dale Franklin, their road manager. "Bands like Cody travel by bus. Bands like the Riders travel by air."

Despite their airborne status, the Riders were not without their own jealousies. If the Airmen resented the success of their managerial sibling, the Riders were the perpetual younger brothers. Their success couldn't change the fact that the Airmen had got to Kerr first, and it sometimes seemed that no amount of Kerr's efforts on their behalf could ever convince them that he didn't do more for the Airmen. And now, with his first loves fighting for survival, he was indeed lavishing his attentions on them. The Riders staff felt neglected and angry, and a meeting with them had nearly blown up in Kerr's face the day before. This morning Kerr was determined to work his way through a batch of Riders business before returning to the Airmen.

He began with a call to the West Coast offices of Wartoke, the Riders' independent publicists, to report progress on the album being mixed at the Record Plant. "Listen, we just got the art work in, Marv, and it's really great. The whole southwestern thing . . . The album's called *Brujo,* which means sorcerer, like in Don Juan . . . No, like in *The Teachings of Don Juan* . . . Yeah, that's right, a whole magic and drugs thing . . . The album's ready . . ." As Kerr was talking with Wartoke's LA representative, Franklin came in to say that she had Columbia Records on the phone wondering where the album was and threatening to postpone the release date, but Kerr didn't waver in the slightest from his optimistic barrage to the publicists. After he'd hung up, he said, "You can't *ever* let those guys know that anything isn't perfect. You're paying them to talk for a living, and you don't want them to have anything but good in their heads."

He then called the CBS corporate headquarters in New York. The Riders were under contract to CBS, whose West Coast office had learned a few days earlier that the new album was behind schedule when Kerr had called to push back the "mastering" date for a week (mastering is the cutting of a perfect copy of a record from which the others will be manufactured). The East Coast offices had just learned, however, and were disturbed. They had promised their salesmen the record by a given time, and had scheduled it at their factories and printing plants. There was some elasticity built into the schedule, but not much. If they were going to have to change their plans, they wanted to know it now.

Kerr was in a particularly difficult position because he really had no idea when the record would be finished. Ed Freeman, the producer, was having an extraordinarily difficult time with the mixing, frequently tearing up whole songs and starting all over again. The recording proper was completed, and the musicians were resting before the start of a short tour, but there was no telling how long it would take Freeman to get the thousands of recorded bits and pieces put together to his satisfaction—and then, of course, no telling whether the band would like what he had done. Still, Kerr didn't want to delay the record beyond the start of their next long tour. If it was in the stores by then, the tour could help sell it (and company-sponsored support ads could help sell the tour). Besides, he had to tell CBS something.

After a brief consultation with Franklin, he decided to guarantee that it would be ready for mastering on the date that he had rescheduled with the West Coast office. "Listen," he cajoled, "we're really on the same side here. Neither one of us wants to sacrifice the quality of an album to gain a week. We know you don't want that. And we certainly understand your scheduling problems enough so that we won't mess you up on that. We want product just as much as you do, and we're going to meet the new mastering date for sure." He also found time to slip in a reminder that the Airmen's option was soon going to be up, that he'd always enjoyed working with CBS and had always found them very reasonable and understanding.

The last bit may have seemed to Franklin to be a gratuitous intrusion of Cody business on a Riders phone call, but it was actually Kerr's strongest argument in his attempt to get CBS to accept the new mastering date without pushing back the scheduled release. The Airmen were a proven quantity in the record business. At worst, unless a record company had gone hog-wild with advances, they were dependable money-makers, with the possibility of becoming big money-makers. Almost every record executive in the business had watched Paramount's bobbling them and thought, "Oh boy, what *we* could do with these guys." At least partly by prudent dangling of the Airmen before CBS's corporate eye, Kerr got his way for the Riders. Then, of course, he had somehow to make sure that the record was actually ready for mastering on time.

He needed to do this for the Riders, but it would also help the Airmen. When record companies consider their contract offer to a new band, one of the things at which they look hardest is the band's management. The manager is their link to the band, and he or she has to be absolutely dependable. A trustworthy manager can save money for a band all year round, but because record companies will risk more on a reliable manager than on an unknown, he can *make* the band money by simply being there at contract-signing time. And so, after more consultation with Franklin, Kerr's next call was to Tom Flye at the Record Plant; the schedule was too tight for them to rely on Freeman any longer.

The conversation with Flye was a little oblique but relatively easy. Flye, after all, was being offered more responsibility, which would be reflected on the album credits that are an engineer's résumé: "Do you think you can arrange to get your hands on the dial a little more in the next few days . . . give the producer a little break . . . I'll talk with Ed and let him know what's happening . . . I'm really not trying to put any pressure on him. I'm trying to take it off . . . Oh, and listen, if you can't do the mixing yourself or be contributory in the way we need, get in touch with me . . ."

The call to Freeman was considerably more difficult. Kerr opened with some unconvincing small talk and then began to ease Freeman off the project. "I just talked to Ellen at CBS and she's slightly freaked . . ." It was all as gentle as it could be, given the circumstances, and with a some- what exaggerated account of how tough he'd been on CBS: "I told 'em, 'Fuck you guys. You want to sacrifice the quality of an album for one week?' Listen," he continued, perhaps unconsciously echoing his earlier words to CBS, "we're both on the same side here; we want to make the best record possible. We just all have to do our jobs. Mine is to fight the record company end of it, and yours is to work with Flye on getting this thing finished."

When he'd hung up, he shook his head rapidly from side to side, as though trying to shake off something vaguely disgusting. "I hate that," he said, "but he really sounded *relieved*. I think it will work out OK." At any rate, he had done what he could, and it was time to get back to work for the Airmen.

13

MANY MANAGERS ARE more musically aggressive than Kerr, choosing songs
for future records, recommending changes in lyrics, and so on. Kerr's concentration on his bands' business lives had obvious advantages, in that the
Airmen's finances were managed with the attentiveness that their pre-
carious position demanded, but it did leave them somewhat rudderless as
performers.

Though the Commander himself was the band's acknowledged leader,
Frayne's take-charge instincts simply did not extend to their music. At
worst, he was lazy (he had no piano at home and didn't practice between
performances) and, at best, terminally democratic. Some of the band's
longevity could no doubt be ascribed to Frayne's refusal to assert his
titular leader's role, for certainly no Airman ever felt pushed around, but
the band's participatory decision making had its drawbacks. As its previous
records proved, the raucous interplay that worked brilliantly on stage was
almost wholly unsuited to the highly structured world of the recording
studio. It was Boylan's job to bring some sort of order out of the Airmen's
casual chaos.

At the time Boylan's role was announced, music-business gossip had it
that Paramount had foisted him on the Airmen; it seemed inconceivable
that they had freely chosen to work with him. To the extent that such
rumors were current, they demonstrated a greater grip on the band's image
than on reality. The record company had indeed wanted a producer, but
it was the band—prompted by Dickerson's appreciation of a record that
Boylan had produced for Rick Nelson—that decided on Boylan. Perhaps
more significantly, Boylan had been the Airmen's second choice. They had

decided on him only after they'd learned that a somewhat better-known
but equally "commercial" producer, Bill Szymczyk, was unavailable during
the time they'd set aside for recording. They were ambivalent about
"selling out," but they did not intend to sabotage their tentative commercial foray by saddling themselves with a producer who was not at
least as good at what he did as they were at what they did.

The band's iconoclastic image was somewhat exaggerated anyway (a
Rolling Stone article flew cheerfully in the face of their rejection by
Warner Brothers to assert that they had signed with Famous-Paramount
solely as a populist attempt to use the Famous-Dot connection to bridge
the gap between long-haired politics and redneck music), but their reputation was not without a basis in fact. They had been influenced by radical
politics during their Ann Arbor days, and they were still well known for
their willingness both to perform without charge in prisons and to raise
money in benefit concerts for political prisoners. It is at least arguable,
moreover, that Frayne's refusal to exert leadership stemmed less from his
personality—he was more than capable of organizing the Airmen's pick-up
volleyball team into a strikingly cohesive unit—than from his Sinclairite
anarchism. Whatever its cause, the final musical personality of the Airmen
evolved more from the complicated interplay of equally strong and
talented personalities than from following any one leader. Neither Frayne
nor Kerr had ever even attempted to fill the role that had been assigned to
Boylan, and as the Airmen gathered for the second night in the studio,
they were a little unsure about whether the attempt was going to succeed.

Perhaps the most apprehensive was Billy C. Farlow. Though the Airmen were very much an ensemble, and their one hit had featured Frayne
on the vocal, Farlow was their "star." His vocals regularly opened and
closed their shows; his energy drew the inevitable encores. Certainly the
contrast between the self-consciously artless country boy and the sophisticated Boylan represented the extreme of Boylan's relationship with the
band. Perhaps that—and a shrewd guess that Farlow might be somewhat
more amenable to authority than the more middle-class Airmen—was
what led Boylan to come down hard on him early in the second session.
Farlow, knowing that he would not cut his final vocal until all the instrumentals had been completed, hoped that one of the previous night's
vocals had been good enough so that it could simply be replayed while
the other musicians worked on their parts, leaving him free to go home.
Soon after Boylan arrived, Farlow rather tentatively asked, "John, was that
a scratch vocal laid down last night on 'Don't Let Go,' or do you, er, want
to . . ."

Boylan responded sharply. "Are you kidding? I didn't even record that,
just put it on some old tape I had lying around here." He then continued
in an aside to the booth at large: "Can you believe it? That's the second

guy thinks I'd accept that." Farlow flushed angrily, but Boylan's point had been made: this was going to be different from the Airmen's previous studio experiences.

Still, Boylan's muscle-flexing gesture didn't quite ring true. Though Boylan had agreed to take on a producer's responsibility, he was no more at ease with direct confrontation than the Airmen. He preferred to get what he wanted by manipulation and persuasion rather than orders, and he quickly moved to make peace with Farlow by reaching out to include him in a conversation that Kirchen and Stein had begun about the ending of "Keep on Lovin' Her," a Farlow vocal. Kirchen wanted to fade out gradually and Stein favored ending with a series of strong chords. The conversation, which included Stein's brilliant pantomime of a vibrating cymbal, ended with Boylan's accepting Farlow's suggestion of a big-band-style ending.

The decision, though quite defensible musically, seemed also to be directed at easing the tension that Boylan's brief burst of authoritarianism had created. Farlow had clearly not liked it, and at least in the initial stages of this project, it was probably important to Boylan that the band feel comfortable with him. It was also, however, to become clear that Boylan himself valued his own image as a "good guy," and maintaining that image meant defusing tensions before they had a chance to build. In the long run, it could even mean smoothing them over rather than actually resolving them.

In the short run, however, the technique worked. Farlow grinned and, after a final toke, moved out to the studio with the rest of the band. Taking the mike, he announced, "Hey, everybody, we're going to use like a big strong ending." Boylan confirmed the decision over the talkback and called for a run-through to check their cues.

During the run-through he and Grupp busied themselves at the board, moving from instrument to instrument to isolate each as they rechecked the levels. They were quickly satisfied by the new snare which Tom Flye had borrowed from Tower of Power, the band in studio B, but continued, after a tour of the other instruments, to focus on the rhythm section. They were interrupted by Stein's pantomimed request for more fiddle on his cues, and Boylan, grinning wickedly, set the track at top volume. When Stein played on without flinching, Boylan looked over at Grupp in wonderment. "Jesus, he's crazed." Then, still shaking his head, he returned to the interaction of the bass, drums, and rhythm guitar.

The technical problems seemed fairly well resolved, though Boylan was unhappy at the amount of audible finger noise from Hagar's steel, when an insistent hum began to fill the booth. "Cut!" he yelled, and then, to Anderson, "What the hell is *that?*" After much frantic rooting around among the patch cords, they isolated the hum as coming from Tichy's guitar, and one of the roadies was dispatched to ground it directly to an AC outlet. Despite their apparent concentration on the hum, Boylan and Grupp had also been rethinking the problem of finger noises on the steel. As soon as the hum had been located Grupp asked Anderson to get a direct box, which would bypass the mike, for Hagar's instrument. "Sure," he said, and vanished from the booth, only to return in classic double-take style a minute later: "For the *steel?*"

"Of course," said Boylan calmly, not even noticing that the level of communication he and Grupp had developed over their many shared projects was extraordinary. Yet even more important than their effortless sharing of thoughts and tasks was Boylan's apparent ability to concentrate on everything at once. Solving the problem of the steel while ostensibly searching for the cause of an electronic hum was only one example of the kind of rapid and complete shift of focus that is more generally character-istic of time-sharing computers than of humans. At any given moment in the playing of a song, Boylan was listening for problems in tempo, attacks and releases, the arrangement and execution of solos, and the quality of the sound itself, simultaneously sensing what was wrong, and considering various psychological or technical ways to fix it. Even this early in the night, it was clearly exhausting work, and occasional lapses in concentration seemed almost inevitable. The inevitable arrived during the next take, when he didn't hear Grupp's shouted warning and absent-mindedly plugged his own headphones into the mix being used by Stein. Reeling back in his chair, he ripped his headphones off and freed himself from the fiddle assault: "Jesus, he really *is* crazed."

But with that exception, his attention never flagged, and at the end of the next run-through he was ready to record. "OK, let's do it. 'Keep on Lovin' Her,' take one." After a second take, he called them in for a playback: "I want to listen to that, then we'll get to work on it."

When one of the roadies had taken a round of hamburger orders and gone up the road to a restaurant, Boylan signaled Anderson to roll the tape. The Airmen listened attentively, but without high hopes; they knew that a good take this early in the evening would be a fluke. As the tape rolled, Kirchen and Stein, who traded solos throughout the song, talked quietly about their timing. Toward the end, they checked a point with Farlow and conversation became more general, with everyone but compul-sive reader Tichy joining in. Then they listened to Boylan.

"OK, the places that were in trouble are the two fives [studio conven-tion identifies chords by number rather than letter], and we're also out of tune with the piano. So during the break either everybody walk over to the piano and tune or we re-spec the strobe." There were a few groans and accusing looks at Fink as Boylan continued, "I'm sure you guys could hear that. Also we're slowing down a little before the chorus."

They had obediently trooped out to the piano and begun retuning during the wait for the hamburgers, when Frayne reentered the booth to announce that the piano was out of tune with itself. Anderson was instantly apologetic, saying that the tuner came three times a week, but that he would be sure to get him in the next day. After listening to it himself, Boylan concluded that it would do for the night, suggesting that Frayne's part could always be recut later if necessary. He then talked quietly to Anderson. "It's really not too bad, but the way George plays, you gotta get it tuned every day." The remark prompted a few anecdotes about Frayne's legendary maltreatment of pianos from the listening Airmen, who reminded Boylan that in live performances Frayne would frequently dance on the keyboard, and that even in the studio he eschewed the pedals, preferring to achieve dynamics by pounding at the keys either hard or harder.

They finally abandoned their ribbing when the hamburgers arrived, and there was a barely decent munching interval. Then Boylan called, "Places," and went out on the floor to work through the song with the bass, drums, and guitars. He gradually adjusted what they were doing, tending always to simplify as he went ("Bill, I think that fill just adds to the clutter. Go back to the old one, why don't you?"), then brought Frayne out to do the piano line. By then he had the basic rhythm track assembled, ignoring the solos that would be added later by the steel and the fiddle. Finally satisfied—and secure in the knowledge that whatever went wrong with the solos could be corrected later—he returned to the booth. "Ecch," he said. "French fries!" and promptly began picking up the booth floor. Despite protestations from Anderson that the lingering presence of French fries on the carpet certified that they were indeed in a recording studio, Boylan went around the booth on his hands and knees gathering detritus. Finally, a little embarrassed, he looked up: "It's just that I can't think in the middle of a mess. All of a sudden my brain gets cluttered too."

The French fries patrol at an end, he began take three. He quickly interrupted it with a call for take four, suggesting a moderately slower tempo. Take four went all the way through, but the big-band ending sounded painfully weak: "Listen, everybody," he called over the talkback, "watch Billy C. at the end and really build it. If you're going to show it, show it hard. Either that or keep it in your pants. Now let's get back to it. Couple of more times and we'll have something worth listening to."

By this time Billy C. had been toking steadily for three hours, but his timing and sense of dynamics seemed absolutely unimpaired. Though Boylan was running the entire project from his perch within the booth, Farlow, as lead vocalist, was so thoroughly in charge of things in the studio that Boylan was free to use the next take primarily to change the sound of Stein's fiddle. "It's too hi-fi," he told Grupp. "Make it funkier." Which, with a few twists of his dials, Grupp obligingly did.

With the end of take five, Boylan began feeling better about the basics and started pushing at the margins of the Airmen's capabilities: "Again, it's getting better, but I've got a couple of things. Billy C., can you manage to keep the extraneous finger-popping noises down? We're picking them up. And, George, start doing your licks on the chorus as well as on the verses. Now it's really going good, and everybody should keep concentrating. The only overall problem is still on the ending." Taking advantage of Farlow's leadership role, he challenged him. "Billy C., are you going to show it hard on this one or should I just fade it?" After a brief interruption for a pep talk from Farlow, Boylan spoke over the talkback: "This is six. Let's cut this turkey. I've got a party to go to." Midway through it, the drums missed a beat; Boylan slumped suddenly, then turned to Grupp: "Dammit, I hate that. One mistake."

By the time they'd finished take six, however, he'd recovered his ebullience: "Okay, this is seven, lucky seven, and this is the one we're all going to write home to mother about. And this is all intercuttable, by the way. The times are really grooving in, so any time you make a mistake, even if *you* know it's just awful, don't stop. Keep right on playing. Nobody stops unless you hear a cut from us, all right?" The seventh take seemed to be going all right, but there was another clinker and Boylan turned to check with Grupp ("I could intercut the ending of that, right?"), then sighed to the rest of the booth: "They're really gonna puke when they hear their mistakes. George . . . oh, George . . . he went to the two chord when everybody else went to the six." Nevertheless, when it ended he called for a playback of the last two takes.

Boylan waited until the Airmen had arrived to begin speaking: "I can probably get away with intercutting. There was a drum mistake in six, and—"

Frayne, who had stopped to get a beer from the soda machine, cut in, "And I blew the chorus in Andy's solo on seven."

"And George's mistake," Boylan continued. "The way it's going on times, we could really just put the two of those together and they'd be about as good as anything you've ever recorded. But there are a couple of things I want to try, so let's just listen quickly to these and go on out and get it right." During the following playback, Boylan raised a fist affectionately toward Farlow as the band hit the big ending on take six: "Watch out, Count Basie," he said, grinning. "That was really *good*." After telling Anderson to take the hold off three and put it on six, he sent them quickly out to the studio for a few more tries.

This time his instructions were a little more detailed, and he worked with Dickerson on a series of drum fills that he had suggested were "too busy." As Dickerson experimented with half a dozen patterns, Boylan continued to opt for the simplest of them. "All those others are too eighth-notey, Lance. You can get a lot more drive out of a quarter-tone pattern on the toms." After a brief pause to work again on the fiddle sound, they began take eight.

This take was better, with the rhythm section crunching along in an absolutely solid pattern through which the soloists interwove, but the ending fell curiously flat. Boylan, who appeared to have had his eyes closed throughout the take and to have been focusing only on the sound, interrupted the studio crosstalk: "I think the problem is in the way you're standing. C., if you turn around when you finish the vocal and face Lance, you can give him the cue for the cut. And, Andy, if you then move up to the front of your booth, you can get your cue directly from Lance. That should just about do it, so let's try another. And"—he repeated the reminder to Frayne—"George, will you play what you're supposed to behind the chorus?" Frayne obediently began playing several bars; Boylan, unable to resist a guaranteed laugh, let him go on for a while before speaking: "Right, now this time could you play it *when* you're supposed to?" Amid the laughter, Frayne claimed that he had figured out what Boylan meant about halfway through his little solo, but that he didn't know how to stop. And then they were off on take nine.

As it ended, Boylan looked over to Anderson for a judgment on how much time was left on the reel of tape. Assured that there was enough room for one more version, he quickly interrupted the crosstalk: "OK, everybody, that was a real good cut. There's one more on the tape, and that's the last one. We're rolling on ten. C'mon now, Billy"—miming an exaggerated series of masturbatory gestures—"Whip 'em up!"

Farlow, though he knew that his vocal was merely a reference for the other musicians and that the final version would not be cut for weeks, responded with an impassioned, virgorous lead, pulling the rest of the band along with him. As they soared into the final series of solos, the excitement built as Boylan had wanted it to, from the layered structure of the instrumental phrases rather than from the uncontrolled acceleration of the tempo. But on the last chorus, as Boylan stood up and began to dance in a circle behind the console, Stein snapped a fiddle string. "Son of a bitch," said Boylan, then quickly to Grupp, "Did they keep playing all right? I didn't hear them slow down." He paused reflectively. "Do you suppose they really kept playing? These guys may be better in the studio than I thought." With the final cymbal crash, take ten ended, and he called them into the booth to hear it.

The playback may be unique to the recording industry. Though film directors regularly view the day's takes when shooting is over, cinema technology doesn't allow for the instant replay, and instant criticism, as does the recording studio. The ritual combines the disinterested expertise of a wine tasting, the openness of evangelical public confession, and the collective responsibility of a Maoist cadre practicing revolutionary discipline. The most familiar American analogue is probably a football team's gathering on Monday morning to watch the films of Saturday's game.

To begin with, the tape doesn't lie. The same technology that allows musicians and producers to struggle toward perfection inescapably captures their imperfections. In the excitement of live performance, or even in the exhilaration of ensemble work in the studio, a slightly dropped tempo or mistimed note may go unheard. Under the playback's intense scrutiny, the same mistakes leap out to embarrass the malefactor. Even in cases when the musicians knew that *something* was wrong—as football players can hardly doubt that someone's mistake led to a back's being thrown for a long loss—it may be impossible to pinpoint responsibility until the tape is played. Then, just as the coach's pointer zeros in on a blocker's missed assignment, the producer can isolate channels until a musician's error becomes excruciatingly apparent.

Some producers, particularly those working with session musicians (the hired paragons who are simply not supposed to make any mistakes), exploit the tape's unfeeling fidelity to humiliate the offending musician and goad him into a better performance. But the Vince Lombardi approach was alien to Boylan, and during playback he was—though unsparing—solicitous. Recognizing the importance of keeping the band relaxed enough to play with spontaneity, he also limited his sharpest criticisms to the musicians he was sure could take them without retreating into a shell of boring safety (Frayne and Farlow were often singled out for this reason rather than for any inordinate amount of musicianly gaffes), and structured them according to the band's general mood. As a usual pattern, he began working on a song by casually pointing out odd errors and offering suggestions, which were gradually toughened up as they grew nearer to getting the song down the way he wanted it, then relaxed the pressure once they had found the groove he was seeking.

By the eighth or ninth time through, the Airmen had established that groove, and the real question on this playback was whether the tenth take was good enough to keep. Beyond that, their unquestionable exhaustion precluded any harsh criticisms; Hagar, in fact, was so drained that he tipped over in his chair while reaching back for a pack of cigarettes. They were aware of their own exhaustion as well, and though Farlow and Stein continued regularly passing a joint back and forth, most of the others let it go by.

Still, the excitement of getting close to finishing the first of the dozen or so songs they wanted to record transcended their tiredness. As the playback started, Frayne lit up his Red Auerbach cigar and delightedly elbowed Boylan. "Finally found a fill," he said, and even Tichy momentarily put aside his copy of *Time*. Midway through take eight, Frayne's new piano fill appeared for the first time. "That's it," he said, "that's the one. How do you like that, John?" Boylan nodded appreciatively. Frayne continued, "I could just cut the first part of that track over, right?"

"Right," said Boylan, "but there's really no sense in it. You've got it down on the next two cuts, and I think they work better. There's a little mixup on the tempo of this one." The tape continued to roll through nine, and Boylan cut it off at the end. "Ten is coming, but there's really nothing wrong with that one at all."

Hagar, following the convention of self-criticism, interrupted briefly. "The steel was wrong at one point."

"Yeah," said Boylan, "you got a little bit behind on the change to Andy's solo, but that's all right. The basic rhythm track is OK, and I can overdub solos any time."

Kirchen chimed in, a little shamefacedly: "John, I played a bump note at the wrong place once."

The other rhythm instruments had fortunately been strong enough so that the gratuitous bump note had not accelerated the pace, and Grupp pointed out that with a little effort they could simply lift the offending note out with a razor blade. "Lord, Grupp," Kirchen groaned theatrically, "where have you been when I've really needed you?" With a grin, Boylan signaled Anderson to roll take ten.

As it played, the Airmen leaned forward intently. It was hard to tell whether their eagerness came from the craftsman's pride of perfection or simply the realization that if this track was as good as they hoped, they wouldn't have to play the song again for a while. Regardless of the cause, their excitement increased as they listened, and at one point—after a particularly complex piano-and-drum fill—Dickerson and Frayne slapped hands in the playground gesture of congratulations. Then they heard Stein's string break.

"Jesus, what was *that?*" Frayne exclaimed. His cues had been adjusted so that his own instrument and the rhythm section dominated, and he hadn't known until the playback that Stein's solo had been disfigured. One note was bent awkwardly out of shape, and then, after a brief arrhythmic hesitation, the rest of the solo was awkward, lower-register improvisation. The band began spontaneously to talk, but Boylan cut them off sharply: "Will you guys just shut up for a minute? We can do that solo over any time—unless you stopped playing the way you just stopped listening."

He directed Anderson to roll the tape back and cut the fiddle from the replay. This time, they listened only to the instruments behind the aborted solo, hoping that the broken string had not caused them to lose their concentration and divert from the rhythmic groove they'd spent the night finding. It hadn't. Not a note was out of place. Tichy was already leafing through his magazine to find his place when Boylan called a break.

14

By THEN, it was nearing midnight, and the break, like everything Boylan did in the studio, was carefully calculated. Knowing whether a band is still on the upswing or whether it is poised on the edge of a psychologically disastrous downturn is part of the producer's art. "I'm still not really happy with 'Keep on Lovin' Her,' " he said the next day, "and I think that by the time they really get to see what they can do in the studio, they'll want to go back and do it over. But it really is one of the best things they've done, and I don't think it would have gotten that much better last night, although they were still up for it. If they hadn't had an acceptable take, I certainly would have sent them out again—or maybe just kept them in the studio for another reel—but it was good enough. And after that, they sort of deserved a break as a reward. I didn't have any coke to give 'em."

Because of the great cocaine famine (which would shortly be ended), Boylan drew on his own energy resources to rejuvenate the band. The night before, despite the lateness of the hour, he and Frayne had gone out for "just one drink." That had turned out to be a misnomer, but it led, during the break, to a fifteen-minute stand-up comic routine, beginning with Boylan's elaborate imitation of Frayne's performance on a roadside sobriety test the police had ordered him to take ("Shit," said Frayne modestly, "I *always* pass those"), and concluding with his very own martial art, a Boylan invention called Kung Shoe. Given its practitioner's somewhat erratic aim, this demonstration was at least as alarming as it was amusing, since it involved Boylan's kicking his heavy wooden clog as hard as he could in the general direction of a door knob.

Just as Boylan was finishing, Rick Higginbotham arrived from the city with news from the contract front, beginning with the jubilant report that ABC had "backed off totally" and was now ready to pay for Boylan.

"That means," asked Boylan, "they're buying the record?"

Higginbotham offered a palms-up shrug and continued, "Hodge laid out the stuff on the option, and then Lenny" (one of the ABC attorneys) "got so out of line that even his own staff lawyers were kind of saying, 'No . . . no.' There's just no question at all that they're not going to get four. As they put it, 'We realize there's a, er, problem with the, er, option,' but if we weren't going to give them anything at all, they'd litigate. So we may compromise on two, and now the only question is how much money we get for them." Exhilarated by the news and refreshed by their break, the Airmen returned to the studio. Two hours later, after a score of false starts and a half-dozen near-misses on "Don't Let Go," they called it quits for the evening. Nothing had gone right.

Some of the problems were technical—it took two or three takes for Grupp to get the saxophone sound gravelly enough to fit Boylan's conception (Stein had switched from fiddle to sax on this one). Others were musical—the picking style that Kirchen had started out with produced a series of pops on every attack, and he had to find a less percussive approach. But most of the trouble came from fatigue. Dickerson especially grew more tired and less able to maintain his concentration as the evening wore on.

Dickerson was, after all, bearing the brunt of Boylan's attempt to change the Airmen's usual style. On the two songs the Airmen were trying to record that night, Dickerson was the typical rockabilly drummer. In traditional fifties style he avoided his toms almost altogether, and supplemented his kick primarily with snare and cymbals. The resulting fills, featuring a barrage of rolls and rim shots, were utterly foreign to Boylan's LA style. Dickerson didn't question any of Boylan's attempts to move him to the more contemporary sound, but the struggle to change his style took its toll. He had been playing this song in one style for almost a year, and the effort to adapt to the new one made him lose concentration on the basics.

An early sign had come during the very first playback of "Don't Let Go," when Stein mentioned that he needed more drums in his cues because he had missed a pickup beat leading into a chorus, and Dickerson grimly indicated that the problem was not in the cues but in the drumming. He had missed the absolutely routine beat.

From there on it got steadily worse. Six times in a row he rushed the drum fill that ended an a capella verse, sending them into the final chorus totally disorganized. And when Boylan attempted to calm the frustrated soloists by reminding them that he could change almost any of what they'd

played, Dickerson interrupted with, "Yeah, anything but the rhythm section," and banged his drums in anguish.

But Boylan, figuring among other things that Dickerson simply needed
to play the song several times to get comfortable with the new style, kept
them working. After the ninth take, he called for a slightly slower tempo:
"OK, that was good. But there are still some discombobulations where
things aren't together. And that is just a result of not concentrating. So let's
lay the tempo back a little—it's hard to stay together at that pace—and
everybody really concentrate on staying together, right."

It was actually beginning to sound a little better, and on the next take
everything worked except the transition out of the a capella bridge. Boylan ran through it a few times with the band, and then, with Farlow saying,
"Let's go now, maybe just a frog's hair slower on this one," they launched
into take eleven. It was by far the best of the evening, and Boylan was
enthusiastic: "All right! That was hotter than grunt. I'll mark it for
posterior and let's try one more for insurance. A dozen, a dozen." But it
didn't work even from the beginning, and he cut it after a few seconds and
started them off again at a slower tempo. At the end of the twelfth complete take, he called them in for a playback.

Nobody had anything bad to say about eleven—they were so worn out
by then that no one had much to say about anything at all—but there was
a general feeling that they could do it better. There was, however, no
great enthusiasm about rushing back into the studio, and after Boylan
surveyed the bodies slumped around the booth, he agreed to a ten-minute
break. They clearly needed one, for only two of the Airmen seemed
relatively unaffected by the night's labors. Tichy was indomitably working
his way through his second crossword puzzle of the night, and Farlow was
rolling yet another joint and singing "Got to have his rotgut, morning noon
and night" in a gleeful self-parody. Besides, Boylan himself, whose intensity had never wavered, finally needed a break. After the respite, when
the Airmen had gone back to the studio, he walked to the back of the
booth and collapsed in one of the reclining airline chairs, exhaustion in
his eyes and, more particularly, in his ears. "Let's reduce the overall
volume," he said to Grupp. "I'm *tired* from this."

While the Airmen were setting up, he and Grupp talked about the number of times during the evening that the sound level in the booth had
exceeded 100 decibels (well over the industrial safety limit for long- and
short-term hearing damage), and agreed to cut the volume by about 10
percent. Hearing loss, especially the loss of sensitivity at higher frequencies, is a major problem for rock musicians. Hagar's persistent feeling that
his steel guitar sound wasn't bright enough was probably caused more
by his twenty years on the road than by any actual problems in the sound,

and producers working at high volumes in the booth can have the same reaction.

But the lower volumes seemed somehow to symbolize the overall lowering of energy levels. The theory behind the break didn't work; the band never got back to the groove they'd begun to find on the eleventh take. As Boylan later admitted, the break was an error. It shattered whatever concentration they might have been able to muster.

"You can't tell," he mused. "Sometimes a band can go out there totally punchy and just do it all on instinct; other times they really can get energized from just a short break. I still sort of think they needed one—Ernie almost fell off his chair during the last take—but maybe they're tougher than I give 'em credit for."

The indomitable Boylan still didn't want to give up, but after five or six more tries, he asked Higginbotham how much longer the band could go without getting "a little squirrelly." Higginbotham, drawing on his experience with them, said they'd probably passed the point already. After one more try, during which they isolated on Dickerson's kick and heard its tempo wandering erratically, Boylan finally agreed and called it a night. "Listen, everybody, I've got eleven in the can, and that's a good one. It's time to knock it off for the evening now, and I'll see everybody here at seven o'clock tomorrow."

By then it was two-thirty in the morning, and the Airmen climbed groggily into their cars with hardly a word. They'd managed to come up with marginally acceptable versions of two songs. But only marginally acceptable. And they would spend twenty of the next twenty-one days repeating that night's exhausting routine.

15

THOSE NEXT THREE WEEKS in the studio were indeed exhausting for the Airmen, but they were exhilarating as well, because they could feel themselves playing better every day. Of course there were still problems. Kirchen, especially, thought they were wasting a lot of time with unnecessary engineering. "When you finally get something down so that it really feels right," he said, "and then you discover that Grupp was using that take to fiddle around with the sound some more, it just takes all the energy out of you for the next couple of takes. Without the energy going for you, it takes twice as long to get another good one." But there was also a sense of real progress. As Dickerson put it, "The difference isn't so much that we're playing better at the peaks, because I think we probably played every song at least as well once before as we did on the keeper take. It's that we're so much more consistent now. Even the bad takes are really close to being perfect. And the good ones are just *so* solid. . . . I can really feel the drums and Bruce being right there on every beat."

The beat, Frayne agreed, was the difference. "Sometimes when we're playing live, we get all excited, you know, and things get a little sloppy. Buff is always cool on the bass, and he never gets flustered, but the rest of us may let things run away. This time, Boylan's got Lance just crunching on those drums, and everybody's a little more on their toes. The trick is keeping the excitement going without letting the tempo get crazy. And we're doing it, right?" He paused. "I just wish someone would get on the stick and buy the fucking record."

That, of course, was Kerr's responsibility, and as the band continued its nightly grind in the studio, he and Hessenius began to implement the good cop/bad cop strategy that they'd decided to use on ABC. Kerr was to be as amicable and pliable as possible—partly because it suited his personality, and partly because if the band did stay with ABC, he would have to be their continuing contact with the company—and Hessenius would play the heavy. This too was in part a matter of type casting.

The general position was as Higginbotham had reported it to the Airmen. ABC was indeed stuck with a contract that Famous' failure to renew in timely fashion might well have rendered unenforceable. The company knew that it could very likely lose in court if it tried to enforce the contract, but it also knew that a protracted legal struggle would put the Airmen out of business. The stage was obviously set for a negotiated settlement. And, as Higginbotham had said, the only question to be negotiated seemed to be one of how much beyond the contract amount the Airmen would receive for giving ABC two records to which the company had probably forfeited its legal right.

Partly because they didn't know that the Blue Thumb dispute gave ABC an extra reason to litigate, such a settlement was certainly the direction in which Kerr and Hessenius aimed their efforts during the Airmen's early days in the studio. The first and most important thing to establish, from the point of view of negotiating a new advance figure with ABC, was the Airmen's value on the open market, so Kerr and Hessenius began to talk seriously with other record companies. Their aim was not so much to secure a firm contract as it was to give them another negotiating lever with ABC. Though they talked with a half-dozen companies, they focused on Warner Brothers, a company from which they'd already received strong indications of interest. They had even begun to discuss money, and both Kerr and Hessenius felt that all they needed to do was establish the figures solidly enough so that they could carry them back to ABC.

That, at any rate, was what they started out feeling, but when they made their initial visit to Warner Brothers headquarters in Burbank, the story of Famous' failure to pick up the Airmen's option in a timely fashion piqued the interest of Warner's legal department. Suddenly, the possibilities open to the Airmen changed dramatically. If Warner's was willing to take the position that their contract with ABC was no longer in force—and willing to uphold that position in the court action that would surely ensue —the Airmen could sign a contract with Warner's on the spot.

After returning to San Rafael from his Burbank trip, Kerr called the Airmen's staff upstairs to his small office. "Listen," he told them, "everything is changed now. The one thing that ABC has going for them is that they can sue us to death. We just can't afford to fight them, and they know it. But if Warner's is willing to come in on our side, then we can match them dollar for dollar. It gives us another great big chip when we sit down and talk to them. Even if they *think* we've got backing from Warner's, they're going to be a lot easier to deal with. And if we actually could get out of this contract—"

"Yeah," said Higginbotham, "there's no way ABC's gonna do anything for this record anyway. We'd be a lot better off on Warner's." _

Everyone agreed, and Hessenius was assigned to follow up the possibilities with Warner's legal department, but Kerr pointed out some further problems that muted their enthusiasm. "What I said was *if* we could get out of the contract. Realistically, I don't think we can. Even if we get the Warner's legal office coming in, ABC's gonna fight us. I mean, why not, right? They're paying all those lawyers all the time anyway; they gotta give 'em work to do. And if we tell 'em they're not gonna get anything from us, that the money they paid Famous for us didn't buy shit, then they've got no choice but to fight."

"But we'll win," Hessenius interrupted. "If we have the money to stay in court with 'em, there's no way we're not gonna get out of that contract." He had launched into yet another repetition of the legal merits of their case when Kerr broke in: "So we win. And it takes three years. What do we do for product?"

"Product," in the form of new records that are played on the radio, is the lifeblood of a touring band. Though the Airmen had earned almost no royalties from their last three albums, the records had nonetheless kept them alive as a concert attraction. Except for the special "oldies" presentations that appeal primarily to nostalgia or curiosity, concert-goers buy tickets because they've previously heard and liked the performers. Even a band that tours as regularly as the Airmen can reach exponentially greater numbers of people over the radio than they can on the concert circuit. Radio play creates audiences, and promoters therefore try to coordinate their bookings with the release date of a band's albums. More and more frequently, in fact, local promoters won't try to headline with bands on the Airmen's level unless there is new product on the market. In addition to the possibility of the record company's buying print and radio ads tying the new album in to the concert appearance, the promoters get the equivalent of free advertising every time a disc jockey plays one of the album's cuts. A period of no new product therefore means fewer bookings and smaller halls. It means, in short, less money.

"Look at the problems Rainey's having with the eastern trip over Thanksgiving," Kerr continued. "And that's with everybody planning on our having product by then. You gotta understand, man, this country's going into a fucking depression, and there's not gonna be anyone—no one at all—making a living unless they've got product that's selling. It doesn't make any difference if ABC has a case or not. All they have to do is bring it and we're dead. Look what those fuckers did to the James Gang."

The James Gang, a Detroit-based hard-rock band, had been one of the most commercially successful new bands in the country during their first year of recording, but they had not been happy with their company, ABC. Claiming a number of breaches of contract, they signed a new contract with one of ABC's competitors, and ABC responded with a suit to enjoin them from recording for any company except ABC. The resulting trials and appeals dragged on for some two years, during which the James Gang released no records whatsoever. By the time the case was finally decided, and the James Gang was declared free of ABC, their early fans had nearly forgotten them, and their new albums did not do nearly as well as would have been predicted on the basis of their early success.

They had subsequently filed a multimillion-dollar damage suit against ABC, and that suit was still in court as the Airmen's dispute with ABC developed. Hessenius had checked with the James Gang's lawyers and thought the band had a strong chance of collecting damages from the company, but the money involved could by itself do little to patch up its shattered career.

"Those guys are *vicious,* man," said Kerr. "If they did it once, they'll do it again. And all they lose is money. If we can't get bookings, we lose everything. If there's no money coming in, there's no more Cody. Period. I mean, sure it's worth talking with Warner's—and maybe they'll go for some kind of buy-out—but I think we have to plan that we put out two more albums for ABC. I just have to keep working with those chumps down there to convince them that we're not gonna give 'em the garbage and save the good stuff for whoever's next. Besides, I don't really think Warner's is gonna get into it. David Berson is the important guy for Warner's on this, and you didn't hear him talking about it. It was only the lawyers looking for something to do."

The Warner Brothers' lawyers, as it happened, had plenty to do quite soon. In a situation that had gone one step further than their contemplated relationship with the Airmen, they had signed a contract with British vocalist Rod Stewart only to find another company, Mercury, claiming a valid contract with Stewart that required him to deliver another album to them before he could record with anyone else. Mercury contended that neither a greatest-hits nor a live album that Stewart had given them, both of which they released, counted toward fulfilling his obligation to them, and that his contract had therefore been automatically extended. Though his new album had been completed early in the summer, a complicated series of injunctions left him unable to deliver it to either company until a court resolved the ambiguity. A hearing was scheduled to take place in November, and because Stewart's recordings could confidently be counted on to gross more than a million dollars for his label, the Warner's litigators were focused on that case.

Eventually, as Kerr had predicted, Warner's declined to get involved in the Airmen's dispute with ABC. By that time, however, Kerr had anticipated its decision and made arrangements for Berson to come to San Rafael to negotiate a contract that would take effect after the Airmen had delivered the two required—or perhaps unrequired, but unlitigable—albums to ABC.

Kerr was interested in the new contract as a negotiating tool with ABC, but it would nevertheless bind his band for the next several years of their professional lives, so he and Hessenius put in long hours preparing for Berson's visit. Sheets of yellow legal paper lined with Hessenius's precise notes contained a list of the provisions they would seek, but again because of ABC, they focused primarily on the advance. The current contract called for an advance of $55,000 per album, and they had decided to ask for double that amount from Warner Brothers. "They oughta go for that," said Kerr. "We're selling about 150,000 now for Paramount, and Warner's can do a lot better than that without trying. They should go to one-ten without any trouble at all." He sounded like a man trying to convince himself.

He was also, apparently, a man able to convince others, for after a three-hour session spent closeted with Berson and Hessenius, he emerged with a large smile and a handshake guaranteeing exactly what they'd wanted. The formalities remained to be arranged with Warner's home office, but the deal was theirs. At very worst, the Airmen would have to do two more albums for ABC at the old rate before picking up the biggest check in their careers. And armed with the Warner's offer, they might be able to jack ABC up to $75,000 or so for those final two albums.

"That's really all we need to make it perfect now," Kerr said happily. "With the Warner's thing coming, we don't really need the money, but those chumps ought to pay for all the crap they're putting us through They can afford it. Besides, it's probably the only way we can get them to work the albums once they're sure we're leaving them. The more they spend *on* you, the more they'll spend *for* you. It's a rule." By the time he'd begun his round of phone calls to tell the band what had happened, a couple of bottles of champagne had appeared, and his office was crowded with Airmen and Riders staff members. Smiling through the thick marijuana haze, he reminded Hessenius to call ABC.

"Tomorrow, Joe," said Hessenius from a cushion in a corner of the office. "There's plenty of time tomorrow."

During the next couple of days, while Kerr did his best to chat pleasantly on the phone with the ABC people he'd have to work with for the next few months, Hessenius played out his assigned role as the bad guy. Badgering ABC with phone calls, he tried to get the company to renegotiate the advance for the remaining two albums. It was all, however, to no avail. "It's not that they say they won't deal," he complained, "it's just that they won't say anything."

ABC, in fact, seemed to be pretending that the Airmen didn't exist. Its routine press releases carried no mention of them (though the band had been prominently featured in the trade-paper advertisements announcing ABC's purchase of Famous), and the publicity department would not cooperate with reporters seeking to do stories on them. To Kerr and Hessenius, the company seemed to be invoking its most potent threat. It could punish the Airmen by refusing to promote their album.

There was a certain plausibility in this argument—indeed, the James Gang had alleged similar mistreatment in their suit against the company— but Corb Donahue denied it. "What would we want to do a thing like that for?" he asked. "This company is in business to make money. Even if Cody is going to leave us when their option is up, we still want to make money while they're here. Besides, the more records they sell of their new albums, the better the 'best of' package will do after they're gone. How could they even *think* we'd do that?"

Nevertheless, the James Gang's lawyers had built a strong case that the company had done just that to them, and Boylan reported that when he tried to insert himself in the Airmen dispute as a figure with friends in each camp, Dennis Laventhal, ABC's vice president for promotion, had bluntly said that the Airmen were "not one of our high-priority projects." Kerr and Hessenius translated this as "no promotion."

It's a matter of debate within the record industry whether an album that sells badly is actually worse than no album at all, but it is sure that a sudden drop in sales will cripple a band's career. Radio station program directors regularly receive sales figures from their neighboring record retailers, and if a band's album stops selling, they quickly reduce its radio play. Such limitation in play further limits sales, for there is an indisputable relationship between how often a record is played on the radio and how many copies it sells. Under even the best of circumstances, the sheer volume of new releases virtually guarantees that some records will simply not get played on the radio at all. An album's chances of falling into that unhappy category are greatly enhanced if its label's promotion force puts its emphasis on other products. The threat of no promotion which Kerr and Hessenius had inferred got to them, though perhaps not in the way that ABC wanted. They decided to bring in Dick Hodge.

Hodge, according to Marvin Finnell of ABC's legal staff, promptly raised the stakes in a meeting he had with Finnell and Lee Young, the company's legal vice president. In careful legalese, Finnell said that Hodge had issued an ultimatum: unless ABC "agreed to pay additional money over and above that provided in the current contract, his clients would immediately arrange for the distribution of the album through another record company. He further stated that on behalf of his clients he repudiated any obligation by them under the existing contract." To some extent, of course, that was pretty much what Kerr and Hessenius had been implying all along, and Hodge himself said that he "was merely trying to get those gentlemen to pay some attention to the fact that they had a real problem on their hands." Nevertheless, ABC took his threat very seriously.

"I don't really know why," said an ABC attorney. "It was just the same old song, but there was something more credible about it this time. Mostly it was Hodge. Hessenius had been down here saying the same thing, but he's such a fucking lightweight that you don't have to pay any attention to what he says. He's all bluster and bullshit. But Hodge is a different matter. He's a very shrewd cookie, and he doesn't make threats unless he's prepared to carry them out. We were goddamn worried about that option thing—it's just so *automatic* to pick those things up; those guys at Famous couldn't pick their noses without putting their fingers in their eyes—and they really stood a good shot of having a court throw the contract out. They couldn't beat us on their own; they couldn't afford Hodge for the amount of work we'd make him do; but if they ever actually did hook up with another company . . . what could we do? We just had to stop that from happening, and an injunction looked like the best way."

On September 25, two firms of ABC lawyers, one from Los Angeles and one from San Francisco, applied to the California State Court in San Francisco for an injunction prohibiting the Airmen or any of their agents from making or agreeing to make records for any company other than ABC.

The logic that seemed inescapable to ABC seemed simply incomprehensible to Hessenius. "I don't know what they're doing this for," he told Kerr. "Hell, we're talking with them all the time about how much money we want for giving them these two records. We haven't talked seriously at all about going anywhere else with them. Now they're up here with their own lawyers and San Francisco counsel as well. I don't know why they came here. They could just as well have filed in LA and made us do the traveling. They're gonna end up spending more money trying to get this injunction than they'd have to spend to settle with us. It's really crazy. And I'll tell you something else," he concluded. "They ain't gonna get it anyway."

It is clear in hindsight that Kerr had no real intention of trying to break away from ABC; clear too that Hodge's reiteration of the threat was intended as another way of emphasizing the weakness of the company's legal position and encouraging them to negotiate. What seems likely, though unprovable, is that ABC so undervalued Hessenius that they almost necessarily had to overvalue Hodge, and ended up by giving his threat more weight than he'd intended it to have. But regardless of the motives or misunderstandings behind the company's decision to take the Airmen to court, the action still had to be defended. If ABC won its case, the all-important negotiations with Warner's would have to be postponed, and the band's financial future would remain an unsettling question mark. Kerr and Hessenius decided to do the only thing they could, which was to countersue for a declaration that the contract had in fact been rendered null and void by Famous' failure to exercise the option properly. As an added wrinkle, they also moved to transfer the case from state to federal court.

"Partly," said Hessenius, "that's just a way of buying time. We really aren't ready for a full-scale fight right now, and the argument over who has jurisdiction will let us spend time working on the case itself. But it also shortens up the appeal process, if there ever is one, and that's important to us. And finally, we want to throw a little scare in 'em about antitrust violations. Because their parent company is New York based, we can probably get it into federal court without too much trouble."

When ABC arrived in court to seek the injunction, Hodge and Hessenius were ready with the jurisdictional argument. ABC correctly sensed the move as a delaying tactic and petitioned for a temporary restraining order that would prevent the Airmen from offering the record to any other company while the jurisdictional arguments were being settled. But injunctive relief of the kind that would prevent the legitimate earning of a living is usually granted only as a last resort, and Hodge and Hessenius argued that the hardships even a temporary restraining order would cause the Airmen were so severe that it should not be granted without a full trial.

"To some extent," Hessenius recalled, "the scope of the injunction they were seeking was our biggest argument. They had it drawn in such a broad way that we had a shot at making it look punitive. We thought we could convince the judge that he shouldn't put us out of business without a hearing just because they alleged a whole bunch of stuff."

Though the judge gave no reason for his action, he did indeed turn down the company's request for a temporary restraining order. "Now," said Kerr, "maybe they'll be willing to talk business." But they weren't.

"How could we?" asked an ABC lawyer. "Sure we could settle with Kerr for his band, but who knows how many other options Famous had fucked up? If we have to renegotiate with every other act we bought, or even a quarter of them, we're going to be spending the rest of our lives making deals instead of records. We also, to be fair, would have ended up having to spend a *lot* more money. I was sorry to see Kerr caught up in the middle of this, because he seems like a fundamentally decent guy, but he's got to understand that one fucking little band just doesn't matter in the whole scheme of things. I mean, they're a good band and all that, but what the hell? There are lots of good bands."

And so Kerr's repeated phone calls to ABC went unreturned, and the court case and the album proceeded simultaneously. More important to Kerr, however, was another series of unreturned calls. Something seemed to have gone wrong with the "routine" approvals at Warner Brothers, for David Berson, who had been scheduled to call Kerr within a couple of days after he returned to Burbank, hadn't done so. Nor had he returned the phone calls that a harried Kerr had squeezed in between meetings with the Airmen's lawyers.

Finally, late one evening, Hessenius got through to him. "I don't know how to tell you this, Barry," he began, "but the deal's off. I've changed my mind."

Hessenius, stunned, insisted that Berson talk directly to Kerr. Berson tried to refuse, even using the argument that he was not legally supposed to talk about deals with anyone other than a lawyer, though he had of course been talking to Kerr all along, but he finally agreed to give Kerr the bad news himself. "But that's all it's going to be," he added. "I'm not changing my mind."

"Why the hell not?" Hessenius muttered as he walked down the hall to ask Kerr to pick up the phone. "You've changed it before."

Berson later described his conversation with Kerr as "one of the worst moments of my life. I mean, it was really terrible. I felt awful enough to begin with. I mean, I'd made a deal and then reneged on it, right? How could I be feeling? And then he just began pleading with me. He made every argument in the book, but, Jesus, I'd already been through them all before I made up my mind to back off the deal.

"Besides, when I went up there, I really thought Mo had committed himself to the band and that all I was doing was tightening up the details. When I got back down, I found out that Mo's commitment hadn't been that strong. And everybody felt that there were just too many uncertainties with the ABC thing—you know, suppose they did two albums that sold 30,000 copies? In two years, or however long it took them to get out, they might not be worth anything.

"You never can tell, of course. They might have had a couple of hits and been worth a lot more than $110,000, but no one down here really thought so. Anyway, there's no way you could plan on that; bands lose more than they win. Nobody ordered me to renege or anything like that, but I finally made up my mind that I had to do it. And so I did."

And talking to Kerr didn't make any difference.

16

THE NEWS that the Warner's deal had fallen through would have plunged the Airmen deep into despair had their time in the studio not already put them there. They knew that they were playing well, but were increasingly frustrated by what they regarded as Grupp's fussiness. "We waste three hours a night waiting for him," complained Kirchen. And of course Boylan refused to let up. They had simply not expected the work to be as intense, nor the concomitant waiting so boring, as it was turning out to be. By the end of September, the time they'd planned to be finished and take a vacation before their fall tour, they knew they were barely halfway through.

ABC, however, knew no such thing, for it dared not rely on Kerr's assurances that the album was coming along slowly. The Airmen's recording history indicated the strong possibility that the album was already finished and being played for interested executives at other companies. That, at least, is what Lee Young swore in an affidavit filed on September 29:

> I am informed and believe that plaintiffs scheduled the recording facility for fifteen days or less [from September 9]. Based on my familiarity with the procedures of recording, I know that plaintiffs under certain circumstances could produce a master recording which would be used for the manufacture of a complete long playing record album within a period of fifteen days or less. Further, I know that a record company like ABC Records could thereafter produce a finished long playing record album derived from such a master recording and arrange for commercial distri-

bution thereof within a minimum period of three days after receipt of
such master recording.

The Airmen were being sued to prevent their selling something that was
still painfully unsalable.

Part of the problem was Boylan's approach to recording. According to
the film journals, some directors work primarily on adjustments of camera
angles, lighting, and the intercutting of various takes, while others work
primarily with the actors. Similarly, there are record producers whose
backgrounds and personalities make the console their natural instrument,
while others "play" the band. Boylan fell into the latter category. He paid
attention to the console—just as directors of the second type obviously
do not ignore the technological niceties—but he used it as an instrument
for capturing a sound rather than creating one. The dials and switches
were Grupp's domain; Boylan worked with the musicians. Endlessly and
exhaustingly. It was, he said, the only way to do it.

"If you're working with really good studio musicians, it's possible to
build a record piece by piece. You get the drummer and the bass in together to get the rhythm track, then the rest come in one at a time and
just lay their parts down. I did a record that way once. It was with the
Association, toward the end of their career, when they really couldn't
play anymore, and I did damn near the whole thing with studio musicians.
But you can't do it with just anyone; you've got to start with guys who
have perfect time, and these guys just don't.

"Besides, they're a *band*. They really feed off each other's energy. The
more takes we can get with them all playing together, the better the
record is going to be." Also, by definition, the longer it was going to take,
and the more frustrating it was going to be.

For a musician who practices steadily and gets his parts down pat, repeating them endlessly as the others take turns botching things up is
sooner or later infuriating. Though Hagar was not invariably perfect in
his own playing (Barlow and Stein were the steadiest of the Airmen), he
was certainly the angriest. Unlike the other band members, Hagar didn't
live in the San Francisco/Marin area. When he was recruited to fill the
vacancy caused when the previous steel player left, he had been living in
Santa Cruz, a hundred and twenty miles to the south. And because his
wife, alone among the women associated with the Airmen, had her own
career established there, he continued to live in Santa Cruz after joining
the band.

Most of the time his distance from the other Airmen made little difference. He didn't get to spend social time with them, it's true, but as a
whiskey-drinking veteran of country music surrounded by dope-smoking

hippies, it was doubtful that he would have done much off-duty socializing with them anyway. When they were on the road, they were all on the road, but in the studio, when all the others returned to their homes and normal domestic lives during their off hours, Hagar lived in a camper parked behind the Record Plant. The distance was just too long for daily commuting, and Hagar's inability to get home grated on him. Even the weekend breaks didn't help all that much, because his wife's days off came on Tuesdays and Wednesdays, when the Airmen were invariably in the studio. After three weeks in the camper, Hagar was becoming increasingly irritable. Though he was occasionally sharp with other members of the band, his familiarity with them muted his anger; they were his traveling family for much of the year. But Boylan was an interloper. Besides, Hagar had been making records when Boylan was still in college, and as far as he could see there was no need for him to be at the Record Plant every day. He could come in and add his steel tracks any time. His anger gradually concentrated on Boylan, and at first took the form of a steady stream of complaints about the steel sound.

"John, the steel's not bright enough."

Ten minutes of adjustments—while the other Airmen stood around helplessly—then another take or two.

"It's still not bright enough," followed by a repetition of the adjustment process. The other Airmen had started out being instinctively sympathetic to Hagar—not only was he one of the band, they would have felt the same sympathy for any musician's attempt to get the sound he wanted—but the endless repetitions began to irritate them as well. Boylan could see it developing but did nothing, rationalizing his inaction by assigning physical rather than psychological causes to Hagar's distress. "He's been playing for too long," he said. "The noise has finally started to get to him, and he just doesn't hear the upper register as well as he used to. So when he says it doesn't sound bright enough, he's right. It doesn't sound bright enough to *him*. But he doesn't know me well enough, so I can't convince him of that. I've just got to wait until the other guys get so tired of things that they'll make him believe it sounds all right. I'm beginning to wish they'd hurry up, though, because this is getting to be one almighty pain in the ass." It is difficult to tell whether Boylan's reasoning was correct, but it is clear that his choice not to confront Hagar contributed to the very delays that had upset Hagar and Kirchen to begin with.

There were other problems as well. Frayne's lack of practice, which was not a problem during performances, was glaringly apparent in the studio. Three full nights went by in a futile attempt to record a boogie-woogie version of an old rock'n'roll tune called "House of Blue Lights." Not only was Frayne's timing inconsistent, but his hand tended to cramp

up after only a few tries, and the ensuing delays both infuriated the waiting Airmen and made it that much harder to establish the proper rhythmic
groove.

There were successes as well, of course. On the good nights, the post-
recording drink that Frayne, Boylan, and Grupp usually shared at a local
bar called Patterson's attracted a large crowd. Exhausted but satisfied,
the Airmen, sometimes accompanied by late-arriving wives or lovers,
enthusiastically poured beer down their throats and, when it was available, coke up their noses, occasionally making the conversation disappear
in a confused medley of a capella oldies.

And there was Kirchen's wedding. Like all social events more formal
than a post-studio beer, it was organized by "old ladies": the wives and
lovers of the Airmen and roadies. "Old ladies" is sanitized by quotation
marks because it seems an anomalous term in the seventies, but it was nonetheless the Airmen's usual way of referring to the women associated with
them. Though there is a certain degree of gently self-mocking campiness
in the term, and in the women's equally regular use of "old man," it also
carries a certain matter-of-fact recognition of reality.

Despite the widely accepted stereotype of the wild, drug-laden freak-
ishness of the rock world, the at-home lives of the Airmen seemed almost
to parody the domestic virtues of the fifties. The men worked, and the
women cooked and cleaned. The women who had been working before
their marriages found themselves under pressure from their husbands to
move full-time into domesticity. For many of them, it was at least
initially a pleasant move. The men had careers, but the women, with the
exception of Hagar's wife Yopi, had had jobs.

It is possible to see the logic behind the women's choices, though it is
hard not to feel as though they—and the Airmen themselves—existed in
a sort of time capsule. Certainly the Airmen did. Wherever they were on
the road, they were likely to be strangers, and to have only each other
for company. There was thus a sort of enforced physical intimacy to their
lives, but the necessity to stay together as a band made them keep their
emotional distance, and their conversations tended to dwell on the relatively neutral grounds of music, sports, and sex, the conversational topics
—if one substitutes "business" for music—of locker-room or hunting-
lodge masculinity.

To some extent, given their radically different backgrounds, traditional
machismo was all they had in common, and though the world was changing around them, the logic of their touring lives continually led them back
to old, safe assumptions. Their touring lives, of course, also left them
rootless.

"That's why we live the way we do," said Rick Higginbotham. "Unless
you've actually done it, you can't understand how sick you can get of

motels. When we finally get home, what we want to have is home, comfort . . . all that kind of stuff." The generalization was less true for the more flamboyant Airmen—Frayne, Stein, and Farlow, who came from the very ends of the class spectrum—but for the wives of the conventionally middle-class members of the band, life was bounded by cooking, cleaning, and kids. And if they did not eagerly embrace the strictures, they willingly accepted them.

"I'm not an automatic believer in nuclear families, or anything like that," said Ditka Dickerson. "I mean, I met Lance when I was into rock'n'roll and kind of hanging around bands, but that was a while ago. I'm not a crazy kid anymore, and I—we, actually—really wanted to have a baby. Now I don't buy the thing that a kid has to have two parents hanging around all the time, but I think they're entitled to one. And maybe there are people who can work out their lives so that they can really share that role equally, but there's no way that's going to happen if one of them is traveling all over the country. So I've got to be the responsible parent most of the time. But," she added, "not all the time. It's not true when Lance is in the studio, the way he is now, but most of the time, when he's home, he's *home*. And that may not be a bad way for people to live."

Kirchen's wedding, on a September Sunday, was to some extent a public validation of that life. It was also genuinely touching. With the exception of the bride's and groom's families, the guests were almost all members of the extended Airmen family: the band, the roadies and office staff, the New Riders' old ladies (the Riders themselves were on the road), Boylan and Grupp, and, on a California tour from their Texas base, Asleep at the Wheel, a band that Kerr had once managed. The guests assembled near the house, high in the Sonoma County hills, where Kirchen and Louise had lived for the past couple of years, and waited for the couple to appear. Soon a horse approached at a walk, and they came into view. Kirchen, his normally unkempt hair pulled back into a pony tail, led a large gray horse on which Louise rode side-saddle. The guests began to sing. As "Amazing Grace" filtered through the afternoon sunlight, Kirchen helped her dismount, a young relative led the horse away, and the minister stepped forward.

In his carefully pressed white cowboy shirt and black string tie, Kirchen looked somehow terribly young—as perhaps all bridegrooms do—to undertake the solemn vows presented by the minister. Louise seemed— as one remembers all brides seeming—composed and certain of what she was doing as she stood by him, her long, pale dress moving gently in the breeze. The vows, the horse, the ancient hymn, the cowboy's Sunday best, all denied the freeways surrounding the mountains and the troubles surrounding the Airmen—and it affirmed something in which they wanted desperately to maintain belief. As the ceremony ended and the guests walked back down the hill to begin the party, there were more than a few cynics surreptitiously wiping their eyes.

In an hour or so things were back to normal, and the cynics were instead wiping their running noses. In deference to parental presence, the coke snorting began behind the parked cars, but as the champagne began to flow, it became somewhat more public. With that mild exception, however, the scene remained something out of another time. The women in their long dresses tended to the children and to the food they'd contributed, while the men sat by themselves, smoking and swapping shoptalk. Dickerson discussed his new drumming technique with the Wheel's drummer—"I've learned something new every day"—and they all traded stories of the insect-infested motels, malfunctioning sound systems, and drunken audiences that marked much of their lives on the road. Even the arrival of the iconoclastic Frayne (who had deliberately missed the ceremony, he said, "because I was afraid I'd start laughing or something and fuck it up") didn't break the mood, and as it grew cooler during the afternoon, fiddles and guitars were dragged out of their cases and the musicians took turns playing jigs and reels while children and adults bounced happily around.

When it grew dark, reality intruded, for the Wheel had to go to work. Many of the wedding party, including the newlyweds, followed them down the mountain to the small bar in Cotadi where they were playing. Others drifted off in various directions, but all carried with them the inescapable sense of the Airmen's entourage as a real, if occasionally unruly, family.

17

THE FAMILIAL FEELINGS engendered by the wedding soon dissipated, not so much because of external forces like the ABC lawsuit, but because of Boylan himself. As a producer, he was just beginning to hit the period in his career when the supply of himself was no longer large enough to meet the demand for it. He had recently responded to the situation by upping his prices, but he was still burdened by overscheduling from his bargain days. After three weeks full time with the Airmen, he began to steal days from their project. A quick trip to Seattle to finish mixing the Danny O'Keefe album, a day in Los Angeles to remix a single from another album, an announcement that he was going to have to take a week off to do overdubbing on a Brewer and Shipley album for which the basic tracks had already been recorded . . . he seemed, to the Airmen, to be losing interest in them.

Kerr protected Boylan during his absences, pointing out that he was essentially working this project for free until the record company situation was settled, but the Airmen did begin to lose patience, and the exact moment when it began to show involved Hagar. Boylan's sense that they would begin to get on Hagar for his repeated delays had been correct, but he switched them back to Hagar's side early in the week after the wedding.

Monday had been a day off, a chance for the band to rest and for Boylan to go back to Los Angeles to clean up some business with Capitol Records, and Boylan had scheduled them into the studio at five o'clock Tuesday. Early that afternoon he called Kerr's office to say that he wouldn't be able to get there on time and asked Kerr to notify the Airmen to show up at nine rather than five. By the time Mary Hunt was able to call Hagar, he was already on the road. The other Airmen were reached in time, since none of them lived more than an hour from the studio. When Hagar finished his lengthy drive and pulled his camper into the Record Plant parking lot, there was no one there to meet him. Once inside, he discovered from the Record Plant staff that the session had been postponed for four hours. He got on the phone to Kerr.

"When he began talking, he was really pretty quiet," said Cathy Callon of the Record Plant. "But pretty soon he started really screaming. I mean, I hear some weird things going on over the phones here, right? But I never heard *anything* like this before. He was *hot*." Kerr quickly called Neil Fink and sent him over to the studio to try to calm Hagar, but by the time Fink was able to make his way over the mountains, it was a little late for rational conversation. Hagar had decided to cool himself down at the Record Plant bar. In an hour of steady drinking, one can get pretty drunk, and Hagar had clearly wasted no time. Fink did what he could, which was mostly just sit and watch tequila disappearing and listen to increasing threats of violence. At one point Fink managed to call Rick Higginbotham and suggest that he get to the studio as soon as possible.

By the time Higginbotham arrived, about an hour before the session was to start, any danger of violence had clearly passed, for Hagar was barely capable of standing, much less of throwing any punches. After a while, with the help of the largest and gentlest of the roadies, Higginbotham managed to ease Hagar into the Jacuzzi. Though he was annoyed at Hagar, especially because it was unlikely that they could get him sober enough to play, he was understanding; sobering-up duties were part of his road manager's job. He was, however, coldly furious at Boylan, and as the Airmen gradually arrived, he shared his fury with them.

"What the hell does he think he's doing?" he raged. "I don't give a fuck what Joe says about him not getting paid. He took this job on knowing he wasn't going to see any money for a while. If he didn't want to do it under those circumstances, he could've just said no. No hard feelings, everybody understands he's a businessman. But if he fucking said yes, then he can't just walk away whenever he feels like it. I'm gonna tell that to Joe tomorrow. Man, he's got to get on this guy and straighten things out." They continued talking for a while, Higginbotham and Kirchen coming down hardest on Boylan for his apparent irresponsibility, Barlow and Dickerson the most forgiving, when Cathy Callon came in the door: "Boylan just called. His flight was delayed and he missed the helicopter. Can someone come to the airport and pick him up?"

"Let me talk to him," said Higginbotham, and brushed by her to get to the phone. He was back in a few minutes.

"Well?" asked Kirchen. "What new and clever way to slow things down do we have now?"

"Well, what? Well, will somebody go pick him up at the airport so that he can get here at eleven instead of five? Well, will somebody go tell him to go fuck himself? Well, when he heard about Ernie did he decide he was just going to get a rent-a-car and go straight to the motel? And you guys can just go home? How about that one?"

"You're kidding," said Kirchen.

"The hell I am. Mr. Hot-Shot LA Producer is too tired to really get anything done tonight, he says. So you should all go home and be ready to start early tomorrow night."

This time, everyone was angry. Even Barlow, who rarely let anything disturb his equanimity, said something about "shitty behavior." But there was little they could do, and they gradually drifted out to their cars to begin a long drive home at the end of a wasted night. Cathy said that she would make sure Ernie got out of the Jacuzzi and into his camper before she closed up.

As Frayne was leaving, he broke the detachment he'd carefully maintained through the evening and called Kirchen—still the most upset of the Airmen—over to him. "Don't worry, Willy, I'll talk to him myself tomorrow."

He didn't, of course. For Frayne, the choice between an afternoon of surfing and an afternoon of sitting in the hot San Rafael office fighting with Boylan was easy. He did, however, give Kerr some explicit directions about what he wanted said. Kerr, bolstered by the icy presence of Higginbotham, said it when Boylan stopped by the office. Though he started out sternly in command, Kerr didn't stand a chance. Boylan's combination of apologies, implied assertions of his own importance, delicate reminders that he was not only working on the project on credit but had been covering all his own travel and living expenses, and music-business gossip about ABC and the Airmen soon disarmed Kerr completely. The conversation ended, as Boylan left to go around the corner to a secondhand bookstore he hadn't yet visited, with Kerr promising to see if he could find some way to reimburse Boylan and Grupp for their out-of-pocket expenses. After Boylan had gone, the seething Higginbotham stood up and stalked out of the office.

It had been a virtuoso performance, a reminder that Boylan's original career had been in theater, and a reminder as well that manipulativeness is a necessary tool in the producer's kit. But it is not a tool that can be applied without cost. Boylan's earlier decision to avoid a confrontation with Hagar by simply waiting for the band to lose patience with him had worked, insofar as he had protected his own image as just one of the boys. It had, however, led to Hagar's increasing isolation from the rest of the band—an isolation to which he was especially vulnerable because he was its newest member—and it had totally failed to clear the air between

Boylan and Hagar. It is at least arguable that a happier Hagar would have reacted differently to the scheduling mishap.

Boylan defended his style with a result-oriented argument: "I'm not a slave-driver type anyway," he said, "but even if I were, I wouldn't work that way with this band. They've been around too long to have someone come in and start giving them orders. I could probably do that with really experienced studio musicians or, at the other extreme, with someone who really didn't know his way around the studio at all. But not with these guys. Besides, I don't believe you can function in the long run with adversary relationships in the studio. The performer really has to feel that you're on his side, or nothing is going to work. I always have a pretty clear idea of where I want an album to go when I come into the studio, but unless I can get the band to want to go in that direction, it's not gonna happen. And even if it works on a note-for-note basis, it's not gonna sound like a band."

The creation of in-studio solidarity required the existence of an outside scapegoat to keep people unified. Boylan had led Kerr to focus on the "us against ABC" struggle; the night before, however, when he had changed his mind about going straight to his motel and had instead stopped at the Record Plant to talk with Hagar, he had left Hagar somehow blaming Kerr and the Airmen's office staff for not notifying him of the schedule change on time. It had apparently been fairly easy to do, perhaps because Hagar was also convinced at bottom that unity was the key to a successful album.

In dealing with the rest of the band as well, Boylan made it a point to work with them individually, and went to the studio early enough so that he could greet each of them as they arrived. Hagar, with whom he had made his peace the night before, was already there, and his calmed presence went a long way toward defusing any potential conflict. Boylan had called Frayne that afternoon, and had provided enough of an explanation to give Frayne—whose success as a leader was based partly on waiting until he was sure everybody wanted to be led—an excuse to avoid taking on a fight. Farlow had not been scheduled to be there the night before, so had missed out on the furor, and Stein, in his sleepy way, was likely to accept almost anything.

Fortunately for Boylan, the doves in this situation—Barlow and Dickerson—were the first to arrive. He simply apologized to them directly, and they were almost eager to accept the apology. They cared only to be sure that the Airmen were his prime concern, and the very directness of his approach was the perfect convincer. By the time Kirchen arrived, any opportunity for confrontation had passed.

"I wasn't looking for a fight or anything like that," said Kirchen. "I'm not all that sure that fighting gets you anywhere, and I sure don't think we would have lasted as long as we have if we were fighting all the time. But I thought we needed to talk things out. There was a lot of stuff that had gone down that I was unhappy with, maybe just because I didn't understand it, but I really thought we needed to straighten things out. I know that's the way Tichy felt too, because we talked about it in the truck on the way down." Tichy's feelings, if any, were not visible, and he may simply have been going along with Kirchen. At any rate, he did not seem eager to fight when he arrived at the studio.

"When I got there," Kirchen continued, "everything was all smooth, and I wasn't going to be the heavy. But I think things might have been better in the long run if Joe or George had really stepped in."

That evening itself went well, and the basic tracks were finished by the end of the week. But there was still some question whether the Boylan charm would work in his absence, and he was scheduled to work with Brewer and Shipley in Los Angeles all the next week.

Boylan said that Kerr had approved his taking that week—and specifically that week, for it was the only break in the Brewer and Shipley touring schedule—at the very beginning of their deal, but in the absence of any air-clearing confrontation, it left the Airmen unhappy again. The Airmen themselves had planned their own touring on the basis of their previous experience with studio work and were scheduled to leave the week after that for a five-day tour through Vancouver and British Columbia. The resultant two-week delay meant that even if ABC and Kerr reached an agreement, the album could not possibly be released in time for their major Thanksgiving swing through Texas and the Northeast.

The delay in the release date concerned Kerr more than any of the band's problems with Boylan in the studio, for the lack of new product meant a lack of record-company support that would hurt the Airmen at the box office. But he was too preoccupied with ABC to insert himself in the recording process as he had done when the Riders' album was similarly behind schedule, and, perhaps for the same reason, he didn't talk with the Airmen about Higginbotham's reports of their unhappiness with Boylan.

18

ADMITTEDLY, Kerr had more than enough reasons to be preoccupied, but the Airmen occasionally felt themselves abandoned by him as well as by Boylan. Their feelings were particularly acute now, because they were soon to begin what they considered the most crucial part of their album, the vocal overdubs. Boylan himself was not sure that the vocals would make or break the album; he tended to rely instead on achieving perfect basic tracks. At one point he dredged up an old experiment that revealed that baby monkeys preferred to hug a terrycloth dummy that pulsed with an absolutely regular beat rather than their real mothers, whose erratic pit-a-pat heartbeats disturbed them. "That's the way a record should be," he said. "If it's got that, it's three-quarters home." But the Airmen were not so sure; they felt that their singing had been the weakest part on each of the previous albums. They had raised their fears one afternoon at the rehearsal hall, and Boylan had told them not to worry, he had a few tricks that would help them through it. But they were still nervous when they returned from Vancouver to begin.

The first task was to cull the best versions of each of the songs they had recorded and assemble them on a collection of "A" reels. The process of relistening gave Boylan a chance to make his final decisions in an atmosphere uncontaminated by the excitement of the actual recording process. It also provided him with a couple of unpleasant surprises. At least one, and perhaps two, of the takes he'd felt were finished required more work. Some of the problems were surgically remediable, and Grupp promptly went to work correcting tempos by careful excisions and additions of tape, but others might require rerecording. In the interim, however, they had enough to begin with. On the first night back, Boylan scheduled Farlow at six o'clock and Tichy at ten.

Unlike bands that feature a single lead vocalist and use the other musicians simply to chip in with background harmonies, the Airmen had three leads (not counting Frayne's occasional novelty numbers), each one with his own strengths and weaknesses. Farlow was by far the most interesting stylist, but tended to wander off pitch at almost any opportunity; Tichy had perfect pitch and rhythmic control, but was by comparison so lacking in intensity that Neil Fink, who ran the mixing board during the Airmen's concerts, once claimed laughingly to have fallen asleep during a Tichy ballad; and Kirchen had a share of each problem. Of the three, Farlow had always been the hardest to record.

He was also the most nervous. For the first time during the sessions he arrived a little early, and he spent the first half-hour pacing around the booth while Grupp and Anderson worked at eliminating a mysterious microphone hum. He had also, for the first time during the sessions, brought Karen Toffler, his "old lady," with him, presumably for moral support. During the waiting period, her support was limited to reading a nineteenth-century children's novel. Finally, Farlow was allowed to burst from the booth into the studio.

"Let's try moving from one mike to another on this one," said Boylan. "We want to see which one is best for the famous Billy C. style."

"Which has never," said Farlow, only half joking, "been captured on tape."

"Well," Boylan responded in macho-gangster style, "Ah'm agonna gitchew, C." With that, the tape rolled on "Don't Let Go," and Farlow began the first take of what promised to be another long night.

The process they were working with was in its technical maturity, because the self-synching mechanism necessary to the night's labors had been invented in 1962. Using the equipment available at the Record Plant, Boylan could, on a track-by-track basis, convert the tape machine's recording head to playback. While the entire tape, except for one track, was playing back into the booth and into Farlow's headphones, the remaining track was actually recording. That track was reserved for Farlow's vocal.

The ability to switch the recording head to playback is crucial, because the studio tape recorder, like home models, has two separate electromagnetic connections around which it winds its way from reel to reel, one for recording and one for playing back. In a studio machine they are about two inches apart. At the speed at which Boylan chose to record, thirty inches per second, it took the tape about one-fifteenth of a second to travel from one head to another. Before the mechanism that allows the record head to be temporarily converted to playback had been invented, the sort of routine overdubbing that Farlow was doing was so difficult and expensive that it was out of the question for artists constrained by a budget. In the old technique two machines ran simultaneously, one playing the basic tracks, the other recording them as well as whatever additional tracks were being newly recorded. In addition to the expense of running two tapes (and hiring two engineers) simultaneously, the difficulty was that when the music on one tape was transferred to another, it also carried with it some portion of the inescapable mechanical noises picked up during the recording process. Even in the best of studios, where recording machines ran with the absolute minimum of extraneous noise, a transfer that included as few as three or four overdubs built up a backlog of tape hiss that ultimately rendered the original tracks useless. The invention of self-synch wiped out those problems with a stroke, not only allowing a string quartet to multiply itself into a symphony, or a single musician to become an entire rock band, but opening the way to the "perfect" record that has since become the minimum standard of the industry. Still, after his first take, Farlow complained: "Jesus, John, that sounds awful."

"Don't worry about it, C.," said Boylan. "It's just because it's playing back to you over the record head. When you come in for a playback and we get you both going over the right part of the machine, it'll sound fine."

Farlow seemed a little doubtful, but he continued singing alternately into the two mikes that still remained until they finally decided which one to use. They then began, but without much success, for Farlow's voice faded in and out arbitrarily during the first take. Grupp frantically adjusted dials to hold it within the proper recording levels, but to no avail. Finally he looked over at Boylan questioningly. Boylan pointed through the glass at Farlow, who was bouncing up and down and dancing as he sang. "Cut," called Grupp. "Listen, Billy, I don't want you to stand like a soldier or anything like that, but could you stay within four to six inches of the mike?"

Farlow shrugged an assent. "I sure could. But I'd 'preciate a little something to keep me concentrated on that distance."

"Oh, Christ," said Grupp, but by then Fink was already on his feet and chopping coke to the left of the console. After a moment's hesitation, Grupp reached into his pocket and tossed a small vial to Fink: "Might as well do some for all of us, Neil," he sighed rather theatrically.

With the coke in the offing, Farlow began his first serious take of the night. After a minute or so, Grupp cut him off: "What are you doing four feet away from the mike?"

"It's too loud," replied Farlow. "I was blowing my ears out."

"Well, just tell us, and we'll fix it. We need you four to six inches from the mike and no more."

"OK, turn it way down then." He paused, then grinned at Fink through the window. "I'm just not used to hearing myself on stage at all." Fink obligingly responded to the comment on his sound work with an obscene gesture, and Farlow giggled happily as his previously recorded voice counted down rhythmically on the tape. Another minute and Boylan interrupted: "You're doing great out there, C., but I'm not doing so good in here." He continued, talking to the booth at large, "We're playing a five-way game here: monitor level, the record level, cue level, the level he sings in and the limiter level. They're all factors." Farlow's voice boomed over the monitors, adding yet another—and perhaps more practical—consideration: "I'm gonna take a piss. Maybe then I won't hop around so much."

On the way back to the studio, he stopped for a quick snort. Toffler put down her book to join him, and there was a general pause. As he returned to the studio, he stopped for a minute. "You know, it's either drugs and no money, or money and no drugs. We're the brokest we've ever been, but we've got the most coke"—he paused a little self-consciously before deciding to plunge on—"and the best producer." He vanished out the door before Boylan could respond.

Twenty minutes later, he said his first words other than "uh-one, uh-two, three, four." They were, "Ooops, I swallowed." There had been other mistakes, but Boylan had let him get used to the cues and the playbacks before he began to point them out. As soon as Farlow had gotten enough into the studio frame of mind to notice his own mistakes, Boylan began chiming in. He began with an obvious one: "Billy, you dropped a word on the first verse."

When they rewound and played it back, Farlow was chagrined: "You know, I never even noticed that. You do that kind of thing live, and it's gone before anyone hears it."

"Right," said Boylan, "but we're doing this one for posterior. No mistakes allowed."

"Right," echoed Farlow, a bit glumly. Boylan assured him that it was all right, but signaled Anderson to rewind the tape. One of the major differences between his recording style during the initial stages of the project and during overdubbing was that he was no longer doing complete retakes. By this stage, he had the basics down, and was now concerned with recording individual tracks that matched the laboriously achieved perfection of the band's basic efforts. And so they rewound to give Farlow a chance to excise his extraneous swallow. The technique they used is called "punching in."

In the earlier stages of constructing the album, when Boylan had been working ensemble as much as possible, punching in and out would have made no sense, but in overdubbing he used the technique extensively.

When one of the singers or instrumentalists made an error, he simply stopped the tape, explained what the problem was, and played the critical passage again. As it played, the soloist sang or played along with it, duplicating the part earlier recorded. At the last moment before the mistake occurred, Boylan signaled Grupp to hit the recording switch, and the tape machine simultaneously stopped playing the key track and started recording on it.

When the soloist was simply picking up a phrase and continuing, the technique was elementary. It began to get difficult when singers or instrumentalists were correcting one note at a time, for then "punching in" had to be supplemented with "punching out," and the two-inch gap between the tape machine's heads became critical. "You can punch in as close as you can think," said Grupp, "but to punch out, you really need as much as a tenth of a second. You've got to get out when there's a 'hole' about that size *between* the heads."

What this all means is that, in addition to the technical skills required to operate the console, a good recording engineer must have the reflexes of a Walt Frazier. Grupp demonstrated his by repeated victories in a game which Frayne dubbed "Sausalito Five-O." It started out simply enough, with Grupp killing time in the booth by alternately starting and stopping the digital recording timer and seeing how many times in a row he could stop it at exactly 5.0 seconds. Very occasionally he would miss and hit 4.9 or 5.1, but he was never off by more than a tenth of a second. Frayne, who had been in the studio when Grupp first started playing, promptly took a chair before the start and stop buttons at the producer's end of the console. "Go ahead, Grupp, I'll match you." After a few false starts, during which he was getting used to the equipment, Frayne began to be able to hit four or five in a row. Grupp, however, was always able to keep pace with him. Frayne, a fierce competitor, finally quit in disgust, but spent the next several nights honing his skills for a rematch. When he was fully ready, he issued a challenge. It appeared, for a while, as though the game would never end, for each of them kept hitting 5.0's without a miss. Then Grupp said, "This is too easy, George, let's do it with our eyes closed so we can't see the clock." "All right," said Frayne, and immediately hit a 4.6. Grupp responded with a 5.0. Still keeping his eyes closed, he had hit three more in a row when Frayne pushed his chair away and stomped out of the booth to get a drink.

Working with the erratic Farlow, Grupp needed all his skills. Though his onstage persona was full of the ebullient self-confidence required to carry off a star's role, Farlow's insecurity showed through offstage. It derived partly, perhaps, from his position as house redneck in a modestly bookish band, but more from his striving toward his own definition of perfection. Other members of the band certainly wanted popular success, but Farlow was the only one who consciously embraced the idea of stardom. His models were not the hip, distant superstars of the seventies but the swaggering studs of rock'n'roll's early days, yet he was analytical enough to see the difficulty of combining the raw energy of the early rockers with the technical perfection required for radio play in the post-Beatles era. He knew that he could perform wonders with a live audience, bringing them shouting and stomping to their feet, but he was also painfully aware that the studio audience he had to please consisted of Boylan and Grupp, detached professionals who would not be carried away by any basically unrecordable displays of energy.

Farlow spent the next several takes forgetting the words of songs he'd sung hundreds of times. With each mistake he grew more nervous, and soon the occasionally forgotten lyric had escalated into a stream of "da-da-dum-de-das" followed by muttered apologies. "Shit," he finally said, "I sure would like a joint."

Boylan had cautioned the singers not to smoke dope while they were recording because it temporarily constricted their voices. Now he thought a moment and relented: "Well, come on in and have one then."

Farlow's face lit up like a child's at Christmas. "I can?" he asked wonderingly. Without waiting for an answer, he hustled into the booth, where Toffler was already removing their stash from her handbag. "It's not as though C.'s vocal quality is the secret of his success," said Boylan as Farlow made his way in. He paused, then turned to one of the roadies. "But, Kenny, you better call Tichy and tell him not to bother coming in tonight." After a few calming puffs, Farlow returned to the studio, and the real work of the night began.

It took about an hour and a half to get even a marginally acceptable version of "Don't Let Go" recorded, for Farlow was rarely able to sing more than a phrase or two before Boylan interrupted: "A little pitch thing, there . . . Pitch again, you're a little too relaxed . . . You're scooping to that high note, starting low and then sneaking up to it . . ." There were other problems besides pitch, but Boylan was working toward a minimally acceptable take. As their efforts proceeded, Farlow began to gain confidence in himself and in what they were capable of doing for him in the booth, and the final chorus went all the way through without a single correction. When it was completed, Boylan called him in for a playback.

"We got it, huh?" asked Farlow as he sat.

"Well, let's listen and see what you think. It's certainly OK, but I suspect that you can do better." They listened, and Boylan continued: "That's a perfectly acceptable take; there's nothing *wrong* with it. The timing and the pitch are fine all the way through. But I'm not sure about the dynamics. I think that maybe all the punching in and out caused you to lose the feel of the song a little bit, and if you're up for it, I'd like to try another one."

"You mean," said Farlow, "you're just gonna *erase* this one?"

"No, we've got plenty of tracks left, so what I'll do is just record the new take on another track. We won't throw this one away until we've for sure got something better."

Farlow visibly relaxed. "OK, let's get to it while I'm still thinkin' about all the stuff you said." He stood up, stretched, and walked out toward the studio.

"And then," Boylan continued in his absence, "when we get one better than we have, we'll keep it and go back to record even a better one on the track we just used. He doesn't know it yet, but we're a long way from through."

Regardless of what he didn't know, the dope, coke, and whiskey combined with the knowledge that an acceptable version was already locked onto the tape to leave Farlow free to explore the dynamics of the song. The second version, much stronger than the first, took only about twenty minutes to record from beginning to end. "That's real good, Billy," called Boylan. "It's really much more interesting than the first one was. We've got about a half-dozen little pitch problems that we should punch in, and then you can come in and give it a listen." Shutting off the talkback, he turned to Grupp. "I'm starting to flounder a little bit. Can you work through the punches with him?" Grupp nodded assent, and Boylan stumbled from the console back to one of the chairs in the rear of the studio, where he slumped, eyes closed, while Grupp and Farlow laboriously corrected the errors. Another twenty minutes passed before they were finished, and Farlow returned to the booth for a playback.

After the playback, Boylan revived and talked with Farlow about the theory of the song. "Don't Let Go" is an old rocker originally recorded by Roy Hamilton in 1958, and doesn't have the sophisticated development associated with later songs. "It's just the same thing over and over again three times," said Farlow, "so what I try to do is make up for that on the volume."

"Well, volume is one way to do it. It *feels* easy, too, but I think it's actually harder. Instead of trying to do it all by volume, why don't you try it this way? Do the first verse straight, putting on as much volume as you want. Then don't worry about volume at all on the second verse, but try and get variety in the delivery. Do it in a kind of half-talking way. We're going to have the hand claps behind you there, and it will work just fine. Then on the third verse, really *embellish*." Farlow went on out into the studio again.

As a way to both ease his throat and spur his concentration, before he stepped toward the mike he got one of the roadies to blow a fine mist of coke deep into his throat. He followed it with a little "sippin' whiskey," but Boylan, to whom both were offered, turned them down. "No, it'll just keep me awake all night, and I'm wasted enough as it is." The rest of the evening would end up belonging to Grupp. The tasks left to him and Farlow were largely matters of execution rather than creativity, but both seemed annoyed by—and tried to break through to—the exhausted Boylan.

Grupp's style involved occasional sharp questions aimed toward the back of the booth, to some of which Boylan managed a mumbled response, but Farlow, physically and emotionally distant from the dozing producer, had a more difficult time of it. Earlier he had been talking to Toffler about what was going on, saying, "Boy, I feel like this was the first time I've ever been in the studio . . . the level of perfection. Usually when I do the vocals, it's Andy and Cody in the studio, and they do three or four takes and then say, 'That's the one.' Mostly 'cause I jumped around a lot on that one or something."

"Yeah," Boylan had said, "but I won't look at you."

"I know, but I'm learnin' a lot of shit about singing."

But by the end of the night, as his best efforts were earning no more than an occasional cut and rewind from Grupp, Farlow finally came to within one inch of the mike and tried to attract Boylan's attention by shouting, "Of all the juke joints I ever played, I swear this is the worst. Not only do I get no pussy, but my goddamn audience is fallin' to sleep." Boylan didn't respond. He probably couldn't. For the first and only time in the studio, his face, sagging with the exertions of his LA week and the nearly impossible demands he had been placing on himself, looked as old as his gray hair. They finally ended up with a vocal which probably met his standards, but there was no way of telling that night. When Farlow headed home, he could muster no more than a surly good night to Boylan.

There is an argument to be made that Boylan was doing his job perfectly well, for the next day's listening revealed that "Don't Let Go" was everything he and Farlow had hoped it would be. Boylan's setting the broad patterns and then turning the details over to Grupp for execution probably worked almost as well, in terms of the final outcome, as his own constant attention would have. Yet that argument, whatever its general validity, just didn't apply with the Airmen. Even after six weeks in the studio, they were not quite at ease working with an outsider. More than that, the singers were nervous about their vocals; in addition to guidance, they required a certain amount of hand-holding, which Boylan was unable to provide that week. He was exhausted, he said, and nursing himself back to health after a "totally crazed" week with Brewer and Shipley. Necessary though it may have been, his recuperative parlay of lots of health food and no cocaine had left him alternately cranky and dozing.

It lasted for only a few days, but it happened with Farlow, then with Tichy. When it happened with Kirchen it was even more noticeable, because he had not been called to the studio until Tichy had finished his work relatively late one evening, so that he received none of the attentiveness Boylan was able to draw from himself during the first few hours in the studio. Finally, and most important to the Airmen, Boylan channeled his remaining energies into the hard work of recording; driving himself to the limits of his physical endurance, he simply had nothing left to invest in the defusing processes he had used before. The only thing holding off an explosion was the Airmen's separate studio schedules; there was no way they could get together to confront Boylan. Finally, however, the opportunity arose.

A week earlier, as the first of the month slipped by with no payments made on even the most pressing bills, Kerr decided that the need for income outbalanced the need for rest and booked the Airmen for a four-night stand at a San Francisco club called the Boarding House. The booking was not in high favor with the band—both because it meant afternoon recording sessions in the midst of a two-show-a-night schedule and because half of them lived more than two hours away from the club—but they realized its financial necessity. What they hadn't realized, until they got together in the dressing room before the first night's show, was that it gave them a chance to talk about their unhappiness with Boylan. As they recited their grievances, Frayne listened quietly. It was clear that they had reached a consensus and needed merely to be catalyzed. He knew them well enough to know that they now wanted him to lead. Finally, after a period of silence as they turned to him, he spoke. "Let's get him in here on Saturday and tell him all the stuff we think is going wrong."

Perhaps because he'd sensed what was going on, but more likely because he'd finally worked through the effects of his backbreaking week in the Los Angeles studios, Boylan's intensity returned that Friday and Saturday. On those two afternoons he brought the Airmen into the studio one at a time to add or correct any required instrumental solos. But two afternoons of progress did not make up for the real and imagined slights accumulated over a six-week period, and the Saturday-night confrontation was still very much on.

There were two differences between this one and the abortive attempt after the Hagar incident. The first was in the band itself; they were meeting as a group, rather than allowing themselves to be picked off one by one. The second was that Frayne had responded to the challenge by exerting leadership.

There was no shouting behind the Airmen's closed dressing-room door; there didn't need to be. Boylan certainly knew that he'd overextended himself, and was freely prepared to admit it. He was also able to claim with a good deal of justice that he had recovered his energies. He was ready, he said, to drive them down to the wire and get the album finished.

The band, armed with the evidence of his performance the past couple of afternoons, was ready to believe him. They certainly didn't want to change horses in the middle of their complex financial stream. Moreover, the confrontation gave them a chance to rebuild their own confidence by reminding Boylan that he was—literally—working for them. The dust-clearing, though not melodramatic, freed them to follow his studio directions without the accumulated irritations getting in the way. They sealed their new pact onstage, when Boylan came out and played guitar with them during their final two numbers. Once again they were ready to go back to the studio and face what he'd said were the last two problems: a few overdubs, and a new basic track on "Southbound."

19

THE MEETING, though useful, did not entirely overcome Boylan's pench-
ant for avoiding confrontations; the problem he had scrupulously avoided
mentioning to the Airmen was Frayne's piano playing. After countless
listenings and relistenings to "House of Blue Lights," he had decided that
the piano was irremediable. There were twelve versions recorded straight
through, and on each of them the piano's tempo was radically different
from that of the rest of the instruments. He had talked with Higginbotham and Kirchen about what could be done, and they had both
agreed that there might be nothing left to do but scrap the track. But it
turned out that there was another alternative. After the Boarding House
stint, Frayne arranged to take three days off to fly to Philadelphia and
visit a woman friend. As soon as he was sure Frayne was indeed going
to be gone, Boylan checked with Kirchen and Stein. With their reluctant
but understanding approval, he called Roger Kellaway.

"About a third of the records in the country are recorded on the West
Coast," says an A&M executive. "On about half of those records, Roger
Kellaway plays piano." In other words, anyone buying a rock album
anywhere in the country has about a 15 percent chance of listening to
Roger Kellaway. But only the most devoted of fans have ever heard of
him, for unlike performers who make their livings by traveling and recording, Kellaway has chosen anonymity. He is a studio musician, a hired
gun who comes into a recording session prepared to play whatever the
producer wants him to.

Studio musicians in general are an odd breed; in the midst of an industry where success is measured by sales, they hear a very different drummer.

Success for them involves the fine tuning of their craft; the resulting sales of whatever songs they've worked on are irrelevant. Even those who have broken through to the point where their names have become public property maintain the studio ethic; Eric Weissberg, who had a number-one hit with a song called "Dueling Banjos" that he recorded for the film *Deliverance,* once responded to an interviewer's question about his best recording with "I guess it's the double-tracked fiddle I did for a Doctor Pepper commercial."

Weissberg's attitude is in many ways typical. The measure of his craft is keyed to the moment of recording rather than its commercial outcome. The studio musicians exist at the peak of their trade, capable of producing whatever is asked of them in the studio. At worst, they are paid the union-scale minimum per session, and the best of them can command more than that. Some of them eventually tire of their anonymity and go public—as when the ubiquitous New Orleans pianist Mac Rebennack surfaced as the glittering Doctor John—but many of them are content with their anonymous $50,000 a year.

They are not anonymous in the trade, however, and the Airmen, who had spent many studio hours talking about session musicians with Boylan, were excited by the chance to play with Kellaway. "It's a whole new standard," said Kirchen. "If we can play with him, we can play with anybody." Frayne was their leader, and they knew he was a good piano player. "The only reason George doesn't practice," said one, "is so that he can knock everybody out about how good he is without practice." But playing with Kellaway would be something special. So special that it muted any pangs of disloyalty they might have been feeling.

When Kellaway stepped off the Marin helicopter a half-hour before the band was to begin recording, he looked every inch the hired gun. At least, with his fringed buckskin jacket and carefully creased cowboy hat, he looked that way until one got close enough to see his developing potbelly and his standard show-biz T-shirt. On the drive to the studio, during which he and Boylan discussed commercial possibilities for a film score he was working on, the impact of his swaggering helicopter entrance dissipated. But when he arrived at the studio, the hired gun image rapidly returned.

After listening to a playback of the best existing version of "House of Blue Lights" Kellaway asked for some blank scores. Owing to its location, the Sausalito Record Plant is not usually home to studio musicians, and records self-contained bands almost exclusively; Cathy Callon, the Record Plant receptionist, was momentarily stunned by his request. "You mean," she asked, "the kind of paper with the lines on it?"

"Right," he said, as laconically as Gary Cooper.

After a certain amount of rousting about, during which the first few Airmen arrived, she found some and delivered them to him. "Thank you," he said politely, then lapsed into Bogart mode: "Play it again, John." The tape ran again, and as the Airmen watched dumfounded, he took down Frayne's part by dictation. Andy Stein, the most musically sophisticated member of the band, started out looking over Kellaway's shoulder, but was soon reduced to helpless giggles and escaped from the booth. Lurching around the pong machine, Stein said when he could speak, "He's kidding. I know the problems with that part. He can't play that without practicing for a month.

"I mean"—he paused—"I'm really impressed by what he's done already, but he can't play it. In fact I'll bet he can't even write it down without . . ." Stein stopped again. "What do I mean can't *even* write it down. If that's all he can do, he's already amazing. But he can't play it. It's *very* hard."

Stein's prediction notwithstanding, Kellaway took only one more replay to doublecheck what he'd taken down, and then he was ready. Buckskin fringe flapping, he strode toward the piano to exercise his fingers. After a few minutes, while the other Airmen were arranging their instruments, he called Boylan into the corridor. "I don't know if I can play this," said the hired gun. "It's not the way I play boogie-woogie, but even if it was, it's an impossible key."

"Don't worry," said Boylan, "you'll get close enough, and what I'm really looking for is time."

"Well I can do *that,* but it's not going to be easy."

It was difficult primarily because the Airmen were indeed a band rather than a collection of Kellaways. The arrangement they had chosen had not actually been chosen at all. It had grown from the idea that it would be fun to do a rock'n'roll song in Dixieland style, featuring a chorus with Kirchen on trombone and Stein on sax.

Kirchen was not a very good trombonist, and he could play only in the most basic key, which for a trombonist is B♭. "It's like my C," Frayne had explained, "and if he's gonna play trombone at all, that's gotta be the key. The only thing is that it means I have to go from C, which is where the song was written and is really easy, into B♭, which is really hard." Kellaway, the prototypical studio musician, had wandered into the middle of the constraints imposed by a live band. The temporary awe which his dictating skills had instilled in the Airmen was about to disappear. "All right," he said, "let's try it. But I don't know if it's gonna work."

It didn't. After a few takes in which Kellaway was excused because everything was new to him, the Airmen suddenly faced the problem that Frayne's part was unplayable. In addition to the tempo difficulties, Kellaway couldn't keep his left and right hand together.

Kellaway, instead of being the solution, had rapidly become part of the problem. His left-hand lead, which set the pace for the rest of the instruments, was stuttering. His right hand, though all the notes were correlated exactly to what Frayne had earlier played, was awkwardly out of phase with his left. "John," said Kellaway as he raced into the booth, "I just can't do it." Compromise was clearly in order.

One would think it might be hard to work out a compromise with a hired gun, but it was easy, at least partly because Kellaway *was* a hired gun. He had little ego invested in this project; it was, after all, only one of a half-dozen that he might have been doing. He and Boylan were quickly able to work out an alternative approach to the song. To begin with, they temporarily abandoned the right hand, and set about playing it through with Kellaway using only his left. Once he was freed from the complex rhythmic coordinations and could concentrate solely on establishing tempo, Kellaway played with a metronomic solidity that anchored the rest of the Airmen. After a couple of takes, everything except the transition from the opening piano bars to the Airmen's entrance was firmly established. Just before take eight, Stein stumbled on the solution.

He and Kirchen, killing time in the isolation booth to the right of the studio, began a trombone and saxophone duet on "Tin Roof Blues," the old Dixieland standard. The other players joined in and had begun an impromptu jam session when Boylan cut them off. "That's it," he said. "Just do that for twelve bars, until everybody is really comfortable in the tempo, *then* go right into the piano intro. OK? Twelve bars of Commander Dixie, and then right into it. Let's go now, rolling on eight."

It worked. Although they did a few more for safety, take eight was the one they kept. After the playback, Kellaway returned to the studio to add the right-hand piano part on another track. In two takes—the second one required only because of mechanical troubles during the first—he had it down, and was on his way back to the heliport. In less than two hours, Kellaway had earned two hundred dollars and the Airmen had made a perfect take of the song that had eluded them through the previous six weeks. "You know," said Stein after Kellaway had gone, "he's *very* good."

But as good and as necessary as Kellaway had been, Frayne was hurt and angry when he returned and discovered that Boylan had brought in an outsider to do his part. "You guys," he said accusingly to Boylan and Grupp, "didn't give me a chance. You didn't tell me what was going wrong, you just went out and got somebody else. You didn't treat me like a serious musician."

With that, he went out to the studio and played it perfectly. He returned somewhat calmer, and was further mollified to learn that even Kellaway had needed to play the part one hand at a time: "I kept on *telling* you guys it was hard." But even though he had just gone out into the studio and proved that he could play it, Frayne was still angry, and

Boylan suggested compromise: they would do a playback of the band and Kellaway's left hand, and Frayne could add a right-hand part that would be used in the final recording. Frayne brightened immediately and went back out to overdub the right-hand part.

Even normally there is something a little eerie about the overdubbing process. Only one musician is visible in the studio, but the music of an entire band pours from the studio monitors. There was something even stranger about this effort, which resulted in a record with a piano part recorded in Sausalito by two different people: the left hand by a man who was in Los Angeles when the right hand was recorded by a man who'd been in Philadelphia when the left hand was recorded. From the sound that was finally put down on the tape, however, there was no way a listener could guess. "I guess it was a good thing," said Boylan to Grupp as the highly pleased Frayne added his part, "that Roger didn't do it all on one track." When Frayne had finished—and it took him only one try—they went back to work on their nemesis, "Southbound."

Of all the songs the Airmen had chosen to record, "Southbound" was the one they were counting on as their single release. It had been given to them by Hoyt Axton, a prolific writer of hit songs (and a follower of family tradition: his mother had written "Heartbreak Hotel" for Elvis Presley a generation earlier) who'd opened several shows for the Airmen as a performer during recent tours. They had heard him sing the song several times, and had liked it enough to include it in their own concerts. Beyond their merely liking it, however, they felt that it was a potential hit. "Southbound" was in fact so unabashedly commercial that they had been a little embarrassed when they first played it for Boylan at the rehearsal hall. "I like it," he'd said.

"Right," Kirchen had responded. "Commercial Cody and His Lost Planet Airmen." The open recognition that this song represented something unusual for the Airmen had both eased their nervousness and given Boylan the clue that this one was one of their songs that they were really eager to have him shape. And shape it he did.

Some of the changes were rhythmic, but the basic shift came when Boylan substituted acoustic for electric guitars as the song's basic propellant. The resulting arrangement was certainly more polished than anything the Airmen had recorded before. It was also less true to their past and considerably more true to the LA present. Nevertheless, despite some misgivings from Kirchen, who spoke fondly of Hoyt Axton's "more rock-'n'rolly" version of the song, "Commercial Cody" welcomed the new arrangement, and after twenty-three takes, they'd finally gotten a version they considered good enough to keep.

Unfortunately, when the time came for Frayne to add his piano overdubs, it turned out that they'd been wrong. At the end of each chorus they had mysteriously slowed down, and it had taken them twelve or fifteen bars of almost imperceptible acceleration to get back into their original rhythm. "I think it must have been all the coke that night," said Frayne. Whatever the cause, the out-of-rhythm passages had become glaringly apparent because they threw Frayne off during the overdubbing. Grupp had argued for fixing them with a razor, slicing gradually decreasing slivers of tape from each bar following the choruses and thus establishing a steady rhythm, but Boylan had vetoed the suggestion: "It would be an enormous amount of work, and even then I'm not sure you could do it. And let's face it, the track's not that hot. I think it makes more sense if we just do another."

They had begun doing another one the night before Kellaway arrived. After thirty-six takes, they had nothing. They had tried another ten after Kellaway departed. Still nothing. Hagar had even given up his usual restless pacing to sit off in a corner by himself, grimly flipping the pages of a paperback. Dickerson, equally frustrated but sensing Hagar's anger, went over and sat by him. "What are you reading, Ernie?" he asked.

"A book," was Hagar's only response.

"Oh, I, er, see." After another minute of sitting in the chill of Hagar's surly silence, Dickerson gave up and walked away, right into the middle of a fight between Grupp and Boylan. They were arguing, not with the theatrical bravado of the Airmen, but with the hushed and venomous intensity of longtime lovers. "Do you think," said Boylan, "I need you to tell me it's not working? Do you really think that's some form of hot news you're giving me? If that's your idea of being helpful, I might as well just run the fucking board myself." Grupp walked out of the booth without a word. Ten minutes later, when he'd come back from a furious walk around the parking lot, Boylan had already decided to call it quits for the night. There was no post-studio beer.

The next day, though the session was supposed to start at four in the afternoon, Grupp didn't arrive at the studio until nearly six. And when he did arrive, he was pale and shaking. An adverse reaction to an antibiotic he'd taken to stave off a cold had sent him to the emergency room of the local hospital. He explained away his petulance of the night before as the first stages of the reaction, and he and Boylan had certainly managed to make peace during their long wait at the hospital. Boylan had not wanted Grupp to get out of bed at all, and was preparing the board himself when Grupp walked in. "Dummy," Boylan said affectionately, "I thought I told you to stay in bed."

"Yeah, but I don't trust you not to fuck up the board. Let me just set it up, then I'll go back."

The effort of setting up the board was really about all Grupp could manage, and as soon as Frayne finished adding the right hand to "House of Blue Lights" Grupp adjusted the dials for "Southbound" and left.

With Grupp safely on his way, the Airmen dispersed into the studio. Boylan himself was playing acoustic guitar in the isolation booth. Frayne, Dickerson, Kirchen, and Barlow took up their instruments in the main studio. The other Airmen had been given the night off, and with Grupp out sick, the control booth seemed strangely empty. It did, however, provide a certain advantage for Tom Anderson, the Record Plant assistant engineer, who didn't have to climb over bodies in his race to handle all the mechanical duties by himself.

"OK, T.A.," Boylan called over his microphone. "Let it roll on one. Here we go now."

This time it began to sound a little better. Boylan had earlier said that the absence of a piano had hurt them the previous two nights, and it seemed he might have been right. Boylan and Dickerson had decided to try a slightly choppier rhythm this time, and the fills that Frayne floated above it kept them tied together. After six takes, they came in to see how the new arrangement sounded. "Playback number five, T.A.," said Boylan. "I think that was the best one, but I couldn't really tell." When it was finished, he continued, "What do you think? The tempo's just fine, and there's no mistakes that I can hear."

"I think it sucks," Kirchen responded. "It's ugly this way. It doesn't flow at all." Frayne, who liked the new arrangement, disagreed, but Barlow and Dickerson sided with Kirchen. When Frayne tried to argue his case, Kirchen cut him off: "George, you may think you know something about 'Southbound,' but let me tell you, until you've played it four fucking hundred times and have it still sound like shit, you aren't even qualified to talk." He paused. "Goddamn, you know something, John, I bet we're never gonna get this sucker. We might as well just forget about it. We've got enough other stuff for an album anyway."

Boylan, for once, was without snappy response, and could only urge Kirchen not to get discouraged.

"I'm not discouraged, I'm just stymied."

"This," said Frayne, "sounds to me like a case for Doctor Cuervo," and he wandered out to the bar to pick up a bottle of tequila. When he returned, they passed it around and took long pulls from it while they tried to figure out some new approach. Finally Boylan spoke. "Maybe you're right about the flow, Bill. Let's see if we can play it with the same energy, but with a little more . . . finesse."

It was not particularly concrete advice, and Kirchen responded by ostentatiously picking his nose. "Duh, what's finesse, John?"

Unable, through his own haze of discouragement, to find any useful words, Boylan said only, "Come on out into the studio and I'll show you." They did, but "finesse" didn't seem to help; on take seven Boylan actually started off in a totally wrong key. There was a great deal of good-natured razzing, which served so splendidly to break the tension that one wondered whether Boylan's "mistake" had been accidental after all. Then he began to hit his guitar again.

"Hit" is very close to the exact word. Instead of letting the chords ring, as he had in previous takes, he was coming down hard across the strings with his fingers, then damping them instantly with the heel of his hand. The resulting sound was almost drumlike, though with each of the beats prefaced by a melodic hint. After a minute or two Barlow joined in with a high, sliding bass run. "That's it," called Boylan. "Do it again now." Right behind the second bass riff, Kirchen came in with a series of rapid guitar arpeggios. By then Dickerson was moving in and out of the rhythmic flow, using his tom-toms almost as much for pitch as for percussion. When Frayne once again added the high piano fills he had used in the preceding takes, it was complete. "You know," said Boylan, "I think we just might have something going here. Let's go on take eight. First the acoustic, then Buff's two runs, *then* everybody else. OK now, rolling on eight." As they played, delighted grins began to break through the intense concentration on their faces. It certainly wasn't the Airmen's characteristic sound, but it felt and sounded good. "One more," said Boylan as soon as they'd finished, "while we've still got it." That one finished, they returned to the booth to hear what they'd done.

"Play 'em both, T.A.," said Boylan. "And if they're both as good as I think—"

"We'll make you an honorary Airman," Frayne cut in.

The tapes were indeed as good as they'd hoped. Half-afraid to believe it, they finally began to respond. Kirchen, who had been perhaps the most depressed, led off the recovery by rising and laughingly beginning an exaggerated series of jumps. "I'm excited again, John. Excited! I didn't think I'd ever feel this way again."

Boylan grinned. "You fucking well better be. Let me just call Grupp, and we'll go have a beer."

20

GETTING "SOUTHBOUND" out of the way seemed to mark a turn for the better in the Airmen's fortunes. The remaining overdubs went so smoothly that the album was ready for mixing by the time the band left on its late-October tour, and there was finally some movement in the situation with ABC. Hodge and Hessenius had worked out a two-pronged legal strategy, hoping that one of the two avenues they proposed to follow would eventually lead somewhere. The first developed from their attempt to transfer the action from state to federal court.

"One thing that these guys are getting away with," said Hessenius, "is that they're pushing us around without anyone really knowing it. If we can use the court action to make the big guys in New York understand what Lasker is up to, the real craziness of it all, they may just call him off. So what we've got to do fairly early on is make it clear that we're developing a restraint-of-trade argument, and to make sure that they know in New York that the guy who runs their two-bit recording division is pushing a lawsuit that may end up costing them millions of dollars. And while that's going on, Hodge can get to Marty Pompadour." Martin Pompadour was the head of the ABC parent corporation in New York and likely to be sensitive to the threat of an antitrust action. "And when he does," said Hessenius, "he's gonna warn Pompadour that Lasker is putting ABC's head into a buzz saw. At that point he's gonna have to check with his own lawyers to find out what's going on. And I'll tell you this: he's not gonna like what he hears."

When Pompadour checked with his lawyers, he would find that the parent corporation was indeed well on its way to being dragged into a lawsuit, a suit that it might have no great interest in entering. The first clue to what was going on came in a letter that the Airmen's attorneys wrote in response to a request from ABC's attorneys for "a written list of questions concerning the substance of jurisdictional questions." The three-page, single-spaced letter contained seventeen questions, ranging from the basic question of the state in which ABC Records had been incorporated through increasingly detailed queries concerning the exact nature of its relationship to the parent corporation. Although most of the questions were straightforwardly related to the jurisdictional question, others indicated that tangential approaches might be taken. One of these was a question about the amount and geographical distribution—determinable by state and local tax payments—of the company's annual earnings. It was clearly not a question the company would wish to answer publicly.

In fact though the request for written questions had stated that "we will let you know what ABC Records' answers will be prior to the hearing referred to," the company's response to the list was a sharp refusal to provide any information before the hearing and a statement that they did "not consider relevant, for example, 'the gross and taxable income given on such tax return' filed by ABC Records in all states in 1973."

"We didn't really expect any answers to those questions, anyway," said Hessenius. "That was just a little something to let them know what they were walking into. The sort of thing that maybe makes 'em think twice." Hessenius's main interest was in the other portion of the case, for he had arranged to review the court papers from the James Gang's suit and had been intrigued by what he found. "You know," he said, "those bastards did the exact same thing to the James Gang that they're doing to us. If the court down there finds that ABC violated their rights, our case suddenly looks a whole lot better. We can really show a pattern of malicious and destructive acts that will cost them a pile of bucks. If I were them, I'd be starting to get a little nervous along about now."

As further pressure on the company, Hodge and Hessenius announced their intention to file additional suits for personal damages. Unlike the action which they'd filed in federal court to have the contract declared void, these suits would be not only against ABC but against its president, vice president, and chief counsel as individuals. "Listen," said a grimly smiling Kerr, "Lasker's not gonna be president of that company forever. They're gonna get rid of him at one point or another, because the only way you get to stay president of a record company is to buy it. He's just another employee. And someday he'll screw up, or somebody's nephew will need a job, and he'll be out in the street.

"Now Lasker is a prick, but he ain't no dummy. He knows what's gonna happen to him someday. And what *I* want him to know is that when he's gone—and when ABC isn't gonna take care of his damages or his lawyers—he's gonna have a personal liability for a few hundred thousand bucks hanging over his head. I'm kind of sorry to do that to Lee Young, because he's just doing what Lasker and Stark tell him to do, but maybe when he sees his own name on some legal papers, he'll start telling them to shape up.

"Hodge is still working with them to try and set up some sort of buyout, and maybe they'll begin to listen to that. So far, though, they've treated it like a joke. Lasker said he wanted $200,000 to release us from a contract—which we say they don't have any longer—and he wants to keep all the rights to our back catalog. Which means if some other company buys us and really pushes this album, he can then slap together a greatest-hits package out of the albums we've already done for Famous and cash in on the work the new company does. Shit, with that kind of deal, nobody's gonna be interested in buying us, and he knows it."

So while Hodge and Hessenius continued their legal maneuverings, Kerr had to assume that the album would be coming out on ABC and make his preparations accordingly.

Though Lee Young's affidavit had sworn that a record company could arrange for distribution of an album three days after receiving the master, ABC's practice was to allow six weeks, primarily to prepare cover art and packaging. The Airmen's contract, standard for the industry, called for them to submit their own cover art for the company's approval (which approval "shall not be unreasonably withheld"). For this album, Kerr had commissioned Chris Frayne, the Commander's brother, to do a "classy" cover.

Frayne had done all the art work for the group's previous albums, as well as logos for their stationery, designs for their T-shirts, the sign on the side of their bus, and all the other graphics associated with a rock group. The style was an amalgam of cowboy, spaceman, and truckdriver images. This time, to go with the smoother sound the band was reaching for, Kerr wanted a smoother visual image.

When Frayne's painting was first uncrated, it looked as though he had designed it for one of the German "space-rock" groups that were beginning to appear on the best-seller charts. Designed for a double-fold album, the rectangular painting, twice as wide as it was high, featured a flock of terrifying fire-breathing pterodactyls chasing a group of spacemen across an arid extraterrestrial landscape. The spacemen, wearing what looked rather like deep-sea diving suits, were racing toward the rear door of a rocket, while from the front door a man in a metallic-blue wetsuit was firing his own flame-producing gun at the nearest of the menacing animals. His other hand rested on the thigh of an extremely pneumatic space woman whom he was urging into the rocketship. When someone suggested that it was really a little too futuristic for a group that specialized in reviving old country and rock chestnuts, George Frayne was quick to defend it. "Look at it again, man," he said. "It's a goof. Didn't you ever read sci-fi pulp when you were a kid?"

A second glance revealed that Frayne was right. The lurid purples and oranges, the lettering of "Commander Cody and His Lost Planet Airmen" were loving parodies of an illustrator's style that flourished during the period from which the Airmen drew many of their songs. Some observers were skeptical, feeling that it might be too subtle an evocation of the period, but the Airmen themselves were enchanted by it. Because their contract allowed them to choose their album covers, it was their approval that was critical.

"Artists' approval" clauses are relatively new in the record industry. They began to be used when some of the San Francisco groups allied with the psychedelic illustrators who created the poster art of the mid-sixties sought the right to have those artists design their album covers. Though the record companies retained the right to veto any design for reasonable cause, they really seemed not to mind giving up that element of product control, partly because packaging represents a relatively small segment of product costs, but mostly because there is no evidence that a record's cover influences its sales figures. Before they gave up control. Columbia Records commissioned a survey, quoted in *Communication Arts'* definitive survey of album art, which revealed that only an insignificant number of buyers purchased an album without already knowing what was in it. They'd heard some of it on the radio, or they'd read a review or been told about it by a friend, or they were familiar with the performer's earlier work. When that survey leaked out, it confirmed a variety of unhappy experiences in which first-rate packaging had done little to help sales of second-rate artists. Thus the record industry truism: "If it's in the grooves, you can sell it out of a paper bag. If it's not, wrapping it in mink won't help."

Like all clichés, that sentiment achieved status because it contained enough truth for people to repeat it. But it also admits the exceptions stated by John Berg, the energetic vice president and creative director of Columbia Records, who is generally regarded as the best in the business. "Artists' control," he says, "is 20 percent good, 80 percent bad. The main problem is that some of these groups are on gigantic ego trips. They come in with some picture that a girl friend or a cousin took and they say 'This is our cover.' And when you try to explain a few things to them, like the fact that there's no room to get their names on the top of the package, they just say, 'That's all right, man, our fans know us.'

"Well, nine times out of ten they're wrong. Probably their hard-core fans *do* know them, but it's only the biggest groups that have enough of those kinds of fans to make consistently good sales. The rest depend on

people who go into a store thinking about buying an album—not a particular album, but some album—and they've got maybe four or five in their
heads. They'll go for the one they find first.

"Now a lot of that depends on in-store display, which is one of the
things our sales department works on—and we help them out with special
display materials whenever they want it—but a lot also depends on the
packaging of the album itself. If it doesn't have the performer's name in
big letters across the top, it's simply going to be lost. When someone is
scanning a display rack or shuffling through a stack of records on a
counter, they're going to go right past it. And that customer is going to
buy another album by some other artist, maybe even his second-choice
album. And I really don't care what some of these guys think about
'artistic control,' we're in the business of selling as many records of as
high a quality as we can. And we should have the right to use whatever
tools make sense to us in doing that job. They're supposed to make the
records; we're supposed to sell them."

To as large an extent as possible, though he complains that he doesn't
get the kind of backing he should in disputes with artists, Berg practices
what he preaches, and the Columbia art department is the largest in the
business. Columbia accepts or commissions a fair amount of outside design, but the bulk of the work is done by the in-house staff of forty-seven
that Berg supervises in New York, Los Angeles, and Nashville. Berg even
does a fair amount of the design and photography work himself, and has
a framed Polaroid photo of Bob Dylan hung on his wall. "See that," he
said, "I took that myself one morning. Then we used a standard type face
to say who it was and used it on the cover of *John Wesley Harding*. The
whole thing cost about 87 cents, and the album was one of Dylan's best
sellers. Now that's a real star, a guy you can sell with a Polaroid photo.
But these lunatics who come in with 'I've got a brother who's into design' "
—he gestured despairingly—"most of the time, they're just hurting themselves."

Chris Frayne, though undeniably George's brother, was more than
"into design." In addition to his work for the Airmen, which was almost a
hobby, he was a highly successful commercial artist. All in all, acceptance
of his design by ABC should have been a routine step in the series of
events that precede the release of an album. But as with so much else
connected with the Airmen's project, the routine broke down again. ABC
refused to pay for Frayne's design until they had "more information"
about it. Kerr, angry because he felt their refusal was simply petty harass-
ment, arranged to fly to Los Angeles with a photograph of the painting.
"Well, what the hell," he said, "at least I can get to see a few of the other
people in the company while I'm there." But he returned the next day

angrier than when he left: "I don't know what kind of games they're playing down there, but everybody I wanted to see was 'in a meeting right now, Mister Kerr.' I mean, if they're gonna treat us like that, why don't they just let us go?"

"What did they think about the cover?" asked Higginbotham.

"I didn't show it to 'em. If they're not even gonna see me to talk about the album, what are they gonna say about a cover? Now, I don't even want to give 'em this cover. It's too good for 'em. We just ought to go out, have someone take a straight photo, and let them turn out their cheapo package. There's no reason to think they're gonna do anything for this record, and we might as well just save the painting and use it for Warner's or whoever we end up with when we get through with these chumps."

Higginbotham and Hessenius shared Kerr's discouragement, but Mary Hunt had a somewhat different view. Talking to one of the other women in the office, she said, "I don't understand what's going on in Joe's head. I wanted to call up and make some appointments for him down there, but he wouldn't let me. His idea is that people are just going to stop whatever they're doing and say 'Hiya, Joe. Glad to see you. Come on in.' Well, that's not the way it works. Not everyone in the world is a Marin County doper. Those guys are running a business, and they aren't about to stop all their work so they can chat it up with Kerr for a couple of hours. Particularly when he's about to sue them for a million bucks. They may be a little crazy, but so's Joe. And Barry's just up there egging him on and getting him even crazier. We're broke, and while they're getting their rocks off and running their big important trips, the band is getting fucked."

The band, as a matter of fact, hardly knew what was going on. Kerr was very careful about making his daily round of phone calls both to keep his allies in the music industry informed of what was going on and to solicit their advice, but he hadn't so much as seen one of the Airmen since they had performed at the Boarding House. The recording was nearly finished by now, and the uncertainty about distribution was getting to them. Dickerson and his wife talked about it one night during dinner at a small Sausalito restaurant. "It's funny, here we are in the middle—really at the end, I guess—of making the best album we've ever made, and we don't have any idea what will happen to it. The only thing we do know, I guess, is that we'll be off ABC after we do this one and another one. But we don't know where we'll be then.

"That kind of stuff was OK when we were all hanging out together in one house in Berkeley and living on fifty dollars a week, but that was five years ago. I've got—we've all got—the kind of responsibilities now that we didn't have then. Ditka's baby is due this winter, and we had planned to use the money from the Warner's signing to move in a little closer to the city. So when that fell through, we both felt really awful for a week. I know that Joe is doing his best for us and all that, but I just wish I knew what was going on."

"Right," said Ditka, "and when you put that together with how hard Boylan is working them, we're all fighting a lot. The other night, Lance was grumpy again, and I finally told him, "Unless you can act like a decent human being, you should just move on out of this house until you finish at the studio.' I was really mad, and I went out to get in the car and drive over to Debbie and Bruce's to talk to her, but just as I was getting into our car, she pulled into the driveway. She'd come over because she and Bruce had just had the *very same fight*."

"Yeah," Dickerson laughed. "That was when we figured it wasn't us. It was just . . . everything."

Kerr probably could have managed to find a way to tell them more about what was going on, but there really wasn't much happening. The hearing on ABC's request for a temporary injunction had been set for October 25, and until it was over, Kerr and the lawyers could do little but plan for it.

Ten days before the hearing—and a few days before the Dickersons' conversation—Kerr went into San Francisco to meet with Hodge, Hessenius, and John Keker, another attorney who'd been brought in to help handle the heavy work load imposed by the tight deadlines they were working against. At that meeting they tried to figure out what to do with the record once it was finished. Their first decision was to hold onto the record, not giving it to anyone until after the hearing. Kerr agreed only reluctantly, because the delay would make it nearly impossible for the album to be released in time for the big Christmas buying season, but he was persuaded that the long-term impact of the lawsuit was worth the costs of delay. As Hessenius pointed out, there was no guarantee that ABC would release the album in time for Christmas in any case. The Airmen's contract called for the company to accept or reject the record within fourteen days of receiving it, but it did not require them to release it within any specific period of time.

That settled, the lawyers began to plan what to do after the hearing. Hessenius summed up their final strategy: "If their motion for an injunction is denied, we'll give them the record anyway. But a letter saying that we've been coerced into giving it to them will go along with it. The letter will just state the truth: that no other company will make a deal with us because of the litigation, and that if it weren't for the litigation, we'd be able to sell it to CBS or Warner's for a lot more than ABC is willing to pay for it. We also point out that their case has no merit, and that their bringing it is an unwarranted interference with our very real business opportunities. Finally, we announce that tendering the record in no way waives our rights in present or future litigation—in which future litigation we will seek damages for business coercion.

"If they win, of course, it's a different story. The first thing we do is try to have the court make them post a high bond against possible damages if it turns out that the permanent injunction is denied after a trial. We try to get it as high as we can by telling the court the same things we'll put in the letter if ABC loses their argument, and maybe toss in a letter from some record company saying they'd buy it if ABC weren't suing us. Then we try to get the court to agree that if ABC doesn't accept it within fourteen days, the injunction is automatically dissolved and we're free to sell it anywhere we want.

"Actually, we're almost better off if we lose than if we win. That way, if they turn the album down, we're free. If they take it and don't promote it, which is the kind of thing we can always find out from their initial pressings and stuff like that, then we've got a great suit for damages."

But neither of their plans came to pass, for ABC suddenly capitulated. The decision in the James Gang case was announced; the band was awarded more than $600,000 in damages and given the right to bring a subsequent action for even higher damages. It may have been merely coincidental, but shortly after that ABC called Hessenius with the first serious counteroffer. For $100,000, ABC would terminate its contract with the Airmen, agree not to bring out a "greatest hits" Airmen package, and let the band rerecord its older material for a similar collection on its new label.

It was a very generous offer, particularly in ABC's waiving of its absolute contractual right to prevent the band from recording anything that had been issued on the Paramount label, and Hessenius immediately began preparing the band's formal acceptance. "I still think," said an ABC lawyer, "that we would have won that case, and none of us here were very pleased when the company decided to drop it, but I guess they finally figured it wasn't worth the risk. This way, at least we get some money out of them. The other way, they might have gotten a lot of money from us. Besides, one of our guys heard that their record was really not so hot."

21

IT'S HARD TO TELL what, if anything, the ABC people had heard to steer them off the record. Certainly Boylan and the band were becoming increasingly enthusiastic about it as they wound into the project's final days. More to the point, all the Airmen's Los Angeles friends and allies, fired by the band's enthusiasm, had been bombarding ABC with messages about how this was going to be the best of all the Airmen's albums. The hint that the company had heard negative reports on the album seems more a self-protective explanation for its failure of nerve during the game of legal chicken than a factual one. No one, not even Boylan and the Airmen, really knew how the album was going to sound. Before any of them could tell, it had to be mixed.

Mixing is a rather new phenomenon in the recording industry. As recently as the first days of rock'n'roll, recording was a relatively simple process in which a band lined up in front of microphones, each one controlled for volume from the control booth, and played their music. Generally it went right from the microphones to the final tape; only the most sophisticated of recordings allowed even some overdubbing. No matter which method was used, when the recording session was over, the record was finished. A producer might, of course, have had second thoughts and wished that he'd used more volume on the violin, but thoughts were all he could have. The only way to correct the problem would have been to bring the entire band back and record the tune again with different levels on the fiddle.

What this meant, among other things, was that studio life was in some ways easier for the Airmen at the Record Plant than it had been for bands

136

in the days when there was no punching in and out, no opportunity for one musician to correct his mistake without involving the entire band. Though Boylan had tried to record as much as possible with the band working together, the final two weeks of production consisted to a great extent of correcting individual flubs and adding background vocals and even completely different instruments (on "Southbound," Dickerson had added a raft of percussion instruments and Kirchen an instrumental bridge using a special speaker that produced its own phasing by means of a rapidly rotating horn). But all the modern techniques that made recording marginally easier ultimately produced their own problems. The separate tracks that had been recorded at various times had to be combined into a mix which would have, not sixteen channels, but only the two which the listener would eventually hear over his stereo set (and in the case of any single chosen for release, a mono mix suitable for radio station use). The work the Airmen had done in the studio was necessary but not sufficient for their album. The mix was equally crucial.

Because of its importance, mixing has come to be regarded as something of a mystical art. It does partake of alchemy (one of the machines Ed Freeman had used in mixing the Riders' album bore a sign reading "Your basic sow's ear to silk purse converter"), but it can't do everything. As one exasperated producer finally screamed to a performer who was complaining about the quality of the mix: "Listen, you can't polish a turd."

But you can, of course, try, and many a studio-weary producer has made trouble for himself by saying something like "Don't worry. We'll get it in the mix," a promise which, as Boylan dryly observed, is about as reliable as "The check is in the mail."

Compared to the recording process, mixing is a very private art. At least during the preliminary stages, no one is in the booth but the producer and as many engineers as the sheer physical demands of a mix-down require. The process begins simply enough, with an assistant putting on an A reel while the chief engineer sets the equalization, limiters, and panning as they were during the recording process. This is not simply a matter of memory or aural recreation, for a careful engineer will, as Grupp faithfully had, copy down the various settings every time the band finishes working on a song. But neither is it exact, for the take finally selected for the A reel may have been recorded relatively early in the night, and various adjustments made subsequently. Still, that is generally a problem solvable by trial and error, and at the point when each instrument both sounds the way it should and is positioned where the producer wants it, the producer and the engineer will be ready to achieve a rough mix by playing the tape through and raising and lowering the volume on each track as they go along. Meanwhile their work is being recorded on a separate tape. Then, after they listen to it, the fun begins.

If, as in the earlier example, the producer decides he wants a little more volume on the fiddle solo, he can no longer use the techniques he employed in the studio and hold the other tracks constant while replaying the fiddle track with a different adjustment. The final master tape, if the records made from it are to be listenable, must have an absolute minimum of tape noise, and repeated overdubbing is simply unfeasible. So they start all over again, with the engineer's hands flying across the board, moving the volume sliders up and down *exactly as he did the first time*—except for the fiddle. Then they listen to that. And then the producer decides that maybe the steel guitar should be echoed a little bit behind the final vocal chorus. And then they start again. Clearly, even under the simplest of professional recording situations—sixteen tracks mixed to stereo—the work load is enormous. The engineer and the producer must combine disciplined physical dexterity with the aural equivalent of a photographic memory—not to mention good taste.

That is the most basic of situations, and since Boylan and Grupp between them made an impressively competent team, they were generally able to establish an acceptable mix. But even they, and however many other hands would be required to assist theirs, faced nearly insuperable difficulties when the mix required something more complicated, like the conversion of twenty-four channels into quad. In the end, the producer's ability to achieve a mix satisfactory to himself, his band, and the record company (plus the people who will eventually decide whether or not to buy the record) is constrained by the physical and psychomotor limitations of his engineering crew. Just as the basic recording is a compromise between the producer's ideal and the performers' musicianly capabilities, the mix is a compromise between his ideal and the physical capacities of his engineering crew. Every album is twice compromised by the time it reaches the consumer.

The extent of the demands and the likely compromises is indicated in a situation in which a producer wants to do more than just bring up a fiddle solo or echo a steel fill. Suppose, to quote from an admittedly self-serving advertisement for a new mixing device, his instructions sound something like "OK. Look. Take out the strings on the second eight of the first verse, raise the horns on the 'do-dum-dums,' bring up the vocal group on the 'la-las' but keep them down on the 'lu-lus.' The lead voice is flat on the first eight of the second verse, so take him out and bring up the Flugelhorn. The bridge is weak, so let's restructure the whole mix at the second eighth note of bar two. You know, bass guitar and drums up, and start panning everything else in circles, but watch the 'la-las' and 'lu-lus.' "

Faced with that series of demands, and the need to get each of them absolutely perfect without somehow messing up a minor adjustment or two in the basic mix, the average engineer will opt for compromise over suicide.

Yet such demands are not unusual. The Airmen's record tracks involved ten or twelve instruments, some grouped together and two—the piano tracks on "Southbound"—with only half an instrument; a track or two for the lead vocal; and at least one for background vocals. Punching in and out, leapfrogging from track to track, adding echo and adjusting volume, Grupp and Boylan would have their hands and minds full, and they would have to make compromises. At least they would have to unless they could manage to obtain an invention that two companies (one on the West Coast, and the other based in Nashville) had developed a few years earlier: an automated mixing system.

For the first couple of years the system had met a certain amount of resistance, apparently because many producers feared that anything having to do with computerization would produce a "cold" sound, but it had begun to win acceptance in 1974, when as important an artist as Stevie Wonder used a computerized system to mix his *Fulfillingness' First Finale*. Boylan himself had used a computer system in mixing the Brewer and Shipley album, and very much wanted to do the same thing with the Airmen's record. "It's not so much that you save time," he said, "though I think you probably do, but that the final product is so much better. You really achieve a kind of precision that fallible humans just can't match."

Though fully automated consoles are now available at prices in the range of $150,000, the basic unit most often used is a fourteen-thousand-dollar product called—evocatively, if ungrammatically—Memories Little Helper. It is more or less exactly what its name implies, and is properly an automating rather than a computerizing device, for it does not so much combine inputs as remember them. Perfectly. The automated mixing process begins when the Memories Little Helper is linked to an existing console by cutting the wires of the fader levers which the mixer uses to adjust volume and rerouting them through a connector plugged into the automated unit. The mixing engineer will then use these levers exactly as he would to control volume in doing a nonautomated mix. The difference is that before he begins, the Memories Little Helper unit is patched to two nonadjacent tracks of the master tape. Once that is accomplished, the engineer establishes a basic mix, riding the volume levels only as much as he comfortably can. When he and the producer are satisfied with that rough mix, they hit the input button on the automated programmer and go through it once again. When they are finished, the programmer will have recorded all the mixers' movements on the master tape's data channel. At that point, the rough mix is "locked in."

From then on, the mixer need not worry about repeating his basic movements, and can instead concentrate on refinements—doing nothing, for instance, but subtly adjusting the levels of the background vocals. Because the process can be broken up into manageable tasks, the fatigue problem is virtually eliminated and a previously unimaginable level of precision is attainable. Producer Phil Shier cited one instance to an interviewer from *Recording Engineer/Producer:* "Suppose for example that you come into the studio with one of your tapes and you hear that the drummer was playing something wrong. Instead of the bass drum going dum-DUM-da-dum, you wanted it to go dum-dum-da-DUM. With automation, you can ride your level so precisely that you can really re-accent the beat."

Boylan had good reasons for wanting to use automated mixing on the Airmen's album. Unfortunately, however, the Sausalito Record Plant had not yet installed a programming unit, and the tapes would have to be mixed elsewhere. Even more unfortunately, since the tapes had not been paid for, Chris Stone refused to allow Boylan to take them from the studio.

"It's the only way you ever get paid," said Michelle Zarin. "Once the tapes are out of your hands, there's no incentive for anyone to pay you. I trust Joe Kerr, but I also know his money problems. If he had only enough money to pay one bill, he'd pay the one that got the most for him. That's just good sense. The band pays him to make those kinds of decisions. We just want to make sure that he has a real good reason to pay our bill as soon as he can."

Zarin's explanation made sense. Wally Heider had once released some tapes to Kerr before being paid for them, and the Airmen still owed almost $15,000 to the Heider Studios for the taping of the Armadillo concerts used in the band's live album. That album had been released, and though Kerr had been allocating sporadic payments to Heider, he had no incentive to divert money from salaries or other necessary expenses. He had, in fact, once sent Heider a check for several thousand dollars, but the studio had mistakenly put it in the wrong envelope and mailed it back to the Airmen. By the time it returned to Kerr's office, other debts had become more pressing, and the money was promptly used to pay them. "I figure it's their mistake," said Kerr. "We tried to pay them and they fucked it up. They'll get it eventually, but they know they're gonna have to wait." Though Kerr had since made several small, erratic payments on the debt, it was clearly going to be a long time before the Heider studios saw their money.

The Record Plant was not about to make Heider's mistake, but they were not about to offend Boylan either, if there was any way to avoid it. Kerr, with his two bands, was good for an absolute maximum of four bookings a year; Boylan represented potentially twice as many. Besides, as Zarin put it, "Boylan is in the same position as we are. He hasn't been paid either, so he's not going to let them get away with anything." Finally they agreed that the tapes could go to Los Angeles—not to Westlake studios, where Boylan had mixed the Brewer and Shipley album, but to the LA Record Plant. "That way," said Zarin, "we both get what we want.

We have the tapes secure, and he gets to computer-mix." And, assuming that some record company eventually bought the tapes, the Record Plant would get the income from the mixing as well as from the recording proper. Thus the tapes went down to Los Angeles, where Boylan and Grupp were able to use an automated mixer. Within a week, they were ready for the band to hear the rough mix, and Boylan—accompanied, "just in case," by a Record Plant employee—brought the tapes back to Sausalito early in November.

Late in the afternoon that Boylan returned with the tapes, the Airmen, Kerr, their roadies and the office staff all gathered at the Record Plant for a playback. Coming into the studio, they all felt good, and when they'd actually heard the tape, they felt even better. There were suggestions, of course, but with the exception of universal agreement that Kirchen should once again redo the vocal on "House of Blue Lights" (during which he'd been suffering from an extremely sore throat), most of the changes were minor. Though Higginbotham was visibly angry that Boylan was going to be vacationing in Mexico during the rerecording and would have to leave things to Grupp, even he grudgingly admitted that an outside producer had made a difference. Now that the recording was substantially finished, the only question was which company would finally release it.

22

THE INITIAL NIBBLES came from Atlantic, CBS, Arista (the company headed by Clive Davis, who had signed the New Riders to their CBS contract before being forced out in the payola scandal), and—surprisingly—Warner Brothers. "Once we heard that there was the possibility of a buyout at a reasonable price," said David Berson, "it was a whole new ball game. I have to admit that I was a little surprised to hear from them after the way they'd been treated, but Hessenius just called me up, told me what was going on, and asked me to get back to him within a couple of days. They obviously knew we wanted them—Mary Martin, our A&R person on the East Coast, had been particularly strong on Cody—but it still must have been a little humiliating."

"What's humiliating?" said Kerr. "We're in the business of making records; they're in the business of selling them. I mean, Berson is pretty clearly a flaming asshole, but we like Warner's okay. They're obviously one of the companies we'd very much like to be with. I'd like to knock the chump off his platform shoes, but if I let my feelings get in the way of the best deal I can make for the band, then I'm as big a chump as he is. Besides, if we do go with Warner's, one of the elements in the deal will be that Berson has nothing to do with us."

Kerr's instincts proved sound. The nibbles from Arista and Atlantic were no more than that; both were scared off by the size of Warner's initial $110,000 offer. CBS, however, remained in the picture, and its first offer very nearly matched the Warner's figure. More important, CBS indicated a strong willingness to better that figure if Kerr would allow them to hear the new album.

"Look," said a West Coast CBS official, "at $100,000, that band is a pretty fair investment. They've got a solid track record; they tour hard; they've got strong management. But they may turn out to be more than that. They're also a band capable of turning out a hit or two and really taking off. We know—everybody knows—their troubles with Paramount and we also know their history in the studio. But you put them together with a Boylan, and you can never tell what will happen. Blind, they're worth $100,000, but if we hear that they've really got something to sell us, well then, we're willing to pay more."

Kerr was not sure. "If I have a sure $110,000 in my pockets, why do I want to risk having someone hear the album and say 'This is shit'? I'm happy with Warner's; it's a good offer. Besides, if we play it for CBS, Warner's is gonna hear about it and want to listen to the album too. It's too big a risk." But Kerr hadn't been in the studio with the Airmen. They *knew* this was the best album they'd ever done, and Frayne was their leader. A born gambler, he gave simple instructions: "Play it."

There was, however, a knotty problem about what they were going to play. The Record Plant management, picking up the vibrations that the Airmen were about to make a major contract deal, became even more cautious about letting the tapes out of their hands. Finally, after Kerr had done some fancy talking on the telephone, they agreed to let Grupp cut two acetates (records made from so soft a plastic that they cannot be used for anything other than a handful of demonstration playings) and one cassette (recorded at a speed too slow to be useful for rerecording, but adequate for playbacks). "They were really paranoid," Grupp remembers. "When I was doing the acetates, they sent someone right into the booth with me."

When the records were made, Kerr went to Los Angeles with Hessenius to pick them up and play them for CBS. The records they picked up, two thick, unidentified disks that felt like old-fashioned 78s, contained eleven of the twelve songs they'd recorded. Eleven was one more than Boylan had wanted to include in the album. "I hate to go over sixteen minutes a side," he had said, "because you begin to lose fidelity then. You used to be able to put more on, but the sound standards were a lot lower then, and besides, the vinyl was thicker." But he had relented and added "The Devil and Me" as filler on the second side. Tichy had written it, and would receive songwriter royalties for every album sold.

"I tried to bury it as best I could," said Boylan. "It's right smack in the middle of side two, and everyone knows that's where you put your weakest stuff. Most of the radio stations won't even listen to those tracks. I hope." He hoped so primarily because "Devil and Me" was a pretty weak song, a lachrymose, repetitive country ballad that almost everyone in the band except Tichy, whose economic interest overwhelmed his taste, referred to as "The Turkey and Me."

"It was a pound-off," Frayne said. "This real sad slow song about a guy who got busted in his motel room with a sheep. We wrote it after we saw the Woody Allen movie where Gene Wilder is in love with one. Only Tichy somewhere along the line stopped singing the last verse. Anyway, it's a couple of thousand bucks for him, so it's certainly not worth fighting to keep it off the record. Besides, there's so much good stuff there that we can afford a turkey or two. It's not like we took off a good one to put it on. We think of it," he said, grinning, "as a bonus for our many loyal fans."

Except for that song, however, the Airmen were proud of the album. "I had my troubles with Boy Johnlan," said Kirchen, "but this is the hottest album we've ever done. I guess I kind of like side two better—it's really more my kind of music—but the guys at CBS are gonna fall over when they hear side one."

Side one, which began with the album's two strongest cuts, "South-bound" and "Don't Let Go," moved through two soft acoustic songs before concluding with a boogie-woogie tune featuring the hard-driving horn section that the Tower of Power had overdubbed one afternoon at the Record Plant. It was clearly influenced by Boylan in a way that side two, with its assortment of Airmen standards, was not. "It's actually a double album," Stein said. "Side one is entitled *Commander Cody Sells Out,* and side two is *Good Ol' Cody.*"

Whatever lingering ambivalence they may have felt about "going commercial," Frayne's and Kirchen's business judgment was good. By the time Kerr had finished playing side one for an assortment of CBS executives, the company was already set to up its offer. The listener from their country division was especially enthusiastic about "California Okie," a despairing ballad of contemporary unemployment that featured Kirchen's vocal and Farlow's twenty-mule-team harmonica. "Give me *this,*" he bubbled. "Give me this kind of stuff. This is the kind of music we can really *sell.*" Though they found songs to like on side two as well, they listened to it almost as a courtesy before telling Kerr that they would check with the East Coast and be back to him within forty-eight hours. It didn't take that long; the next day Kerr learned that CBS was willing to better Warner's advance by $10,000 and to throw in some other goodies as well. Armed with the CBS offer, and with new confidence in the album, Kerr was ready to go back to Warner's and seek a better deal from them. Warner's heard the album and promptly came up with one.

"I can't believe it," said Mary Hunt. "This is crazy. We're really the brokest we've been in years. Not only do we owe the Record Plant all those bucks for this album, but our travel agent has cut us off until we pay our bill. We may even have to send the band cross-country on the bus unless we can find someone dumb enough to sell us airline tickets on credit. In another week or two we're all going to be living on nuts and berries, and at the same time, Joe and Barry are talking options and deals like we've never heard before. This whole business is crazy."

While their staff desperately juggled creditors back and forth from one charge card to another, Kerr and Hessenius were trying to juggle the corporate giants. CBS, which was a little hesitant about matching Warner's latest offer, allowed as how they'd like some of their East Coast people to hear the album before coming up with any new figures. Since both the Riders and the Airmen were due to play in New York during the Thanksgiving holiday, Kerr and Hessenius clutched their precious acetates under their arms and came east as well.

"You have to understand our position on this," said a CBS publicity woman. "We're really talking about two bands instead of just one. We've got the Riders already, and we're very happy with them. Their album is selling really well, but their option is coming up, and we want to keep them. We can't actually tie the two together, because it would be unethical for their management to do that, but we think that if Kerr is pleased with what we can do for Cody, he'll certainly be receptive to any deal we offer the Riders.

"More than that, I think we'd be just as happy if he didn't go out and have a positive experience with any other company. We know that right now we look very good to him—how could it be different after Paramount and ABC?—and we'd like to keep it that way. If he takes Cody somewhere else and they do a great job for the band, then he's got to think about moving the Riders too." She looked pointedly around the room. "That's really one reason for this party."

"This party" was a reception and dinner for the New Riders in one of the private rooms at Lüchow's, a century-old landmark in Lower Manhattan. In addition to the Riders, their "old ladies" and their management, it was attended by key CBS personnel, each of whom made it a point to chat with Kerr and Hessenius. Though the party was also sprinkled with a few of the New York area's more important rock writers, it was less geared to publicity than to impressing Kerr and Hessenius. And it worked. Everything—except the food, which was one of the gross Germanic overfeeds typical of Lüchow's—was understated. "You gotta admit it," whispered Hessenius as a waiter once again refilled his wine glass, "this is a class operation." Only after the band had gotten into their CBS-supplied limousines and been driven back to their hotel was there any mention of the Cody contract. And even then it was tasteful. Over a final cognac, CBS Vice President Bruce Lundvald told Hessenius that his company would at least match the Warner's offer. They could work out the details at the office later in the week. There was certainly no need to spoil a lovely party by discussing business.

Hessenius was delighted and returned to the hotel in triumph, yet two nights later, when the Airmen gave a sold-out Thanksgiving-night concert at the Academy of Music, the only record company personnel in their backstage dressing room were from Warner Brothers' New York office. "They are going to sign with us next week," Mary Martin said emphatically. Nothing was actually decided, however, until the Airmen finished their holiday tour and returned to the West Coast for a band meeting.

They met on December 5, in the San Rafael office. There were six items on the agenda, but the key one—a comparison of record-company deals—was first. Hessenius had put the comparison together, laying out the Warner Brothers and CBS packages side by side. He went through them in order, beginning with the term and album commitment offered by each. CBS offered a two-year deal with two eighteen-month options and Warner's a fifteen-month term with the same options. CBS expected three albums plus a "best of" during the two years; the Warner's offer called for only two new albums plus a "best of" during the fifteen months. Each company, after Kerr's spirited encouragement of their bidding war, was willing to advance $150,000 for the new albums and to pay ABC the $100,000 it demanded. Though neither would pay advances for the "best of" album, each would contribute to the recording budget for any songs from the Airmen's Paramount days that needed to be rerecorded. CBS would pay up to $25,000, Warner's up to $20,000. Each of them also demanded that a certain percentage of the advances be paid back by assigning the mechanical royalties that would normally come to the band's publishing company to the record company if the albums didn't sell enough to pay back the advances. CBS's cross-collateralization clause would come into force only on the third album (if the first two didn't reach a still-to-be-agreed-upon sales total), but would be against the full $150,000 advance for that album. Warner's would take effect immediately, but was for only $45,000.

"CBS is also," Hessenius explained, "willing to work out some sort of a deal where the advance will be retroactively increased at certain sales plateaus. What we're talking about now is an additional $100,000 at 300,000 units, but the exact figures are still up in the air. Whatever they are, they'll be close to that. Warner's has already refused to include any provisions of that sort."

As far as the options went, each company offered and required the same thing: two albums during each eighteen-month option period, the first two at $225,000 each, the second two at $300,000. Royalties, though calculated differently, were also substantially the same. CBS offered 22 percent of wholesale-less-packaging for a total of $.5818 per unit; Warner's offered 11 percent of retail, less packaging and 15 percent free goods, for a total of $.5797 per unit (CBS's failure to mention free goods did not mean that it didn't make deals with retailers, but only that it had included such arrangements in the basic royalty rate). Each offered automatic increases in royalty percentages at 250,000 and 500,000 units, and each offered proportional increases in royalties during the successive option periods. Under either offer, the album the band had just completed would have to sell about 250,000 copies for the band to see any royalties beyond the advance. At that sales figure, royalties from CBS would total $161,400; those from Warner's would total $158,100. "All of which comes down to saying," Hessenius summed up, "that with the exception of the basic time commitment, which guarantees us another album at $150,000 but delays our moving into the higher advance figure by nine months—and the possible added advance at a specific sales plateau—the dollar deals are pretty much the same."

There were some minor differences. Though each company would substantially subsidize a European tour and would give the band the right both to supply their own album covers and to approve any company art work on their behalf, CBS would not pay for an outside public relations firm and Warner's would. More important, CBS would pay all costs for the band's participation in the annual country-and-western DJs convention in Nashville, but Warner's country division was so weak that it didn't even participate in country music's major sales and social event.

Yet these differences were marginal. What the final choice came down to was a CBS guarantee of two years at a total advance to the band of $475,000 versus a Warner Brothers guarantee of fifteen months at a total advance of $320,000. If the band made it, and the options were picked up, the Warner's offer was clearly preferable. But that was a gamble, and because of its longer initial guarantee, the CBS offer was safer. Hessenius argued for the security and prestige of CBS, while Kerr pointed out the practical difficulties of doing business with an East Coast company.

Frayne expressed some preliminary uneasiness at the near nonexistence of Warner's country division. Not only had Famous achieved substantial country sales for the Airmen on its Dot label, but the band gloried in their ability to cross the hippie-hillbilly boundary and had been genuinely thrilled when the country music DJs voted them the "best new band" of 1972. Finally, though, Frayne came out for Warner's. His argument, cold logic leavened with his gambler's kamikaze instincts, was simply that at the end of the initial period of the Warner's contract, the Airmen would have made seven albums and traveled together for almost ten years. If they hadn't made it by then, they were never going to.

After a pause during which Kerr reminded everyone how nice it would be to have everyone at Warner's know that Berson had cost the company $100,000 by backing out on the first deal, the band voted unanimously to go with Warner's. Then they got on with the rest of the meeting.

The next item was a review of the album project just finished. It was, they agreed, to be titled simply *Commander Cody and His Lost Planet Airmen,* and Chris Frayne's painting was to be sent immediately to Warner Brothers for processing. They then reviewed the costs of the album, which totaled $58,155.85, over $3,000 more than ABC had been willing to pay them for it. The major item was more than $39,000 in studio time at the two Record Plant facilities and at the Capitol Studios in Los Angeles, where Grupp had done some final editing and mixing work. Producer's costs, the next largest item, amounted to some $14,000 ($6,000 to Capitol Records as the fee for Grupp's services, $5,000 to Boylan as an advance against royalties, and $3,000 for the two's accommodations and expenses). The remaining $5,000 included slightly more than $1,000 for studio musicians (Kellaway and the Tower of Power horn section); $1,000 to Chris Frayne for the cover art; a similar amount for publicity photographs and album layout; another $1,000 in miscellaneous expenses; and, to the Airmen's mild chagrin, $820 for "entertainment" that had vanished up their noses during the recording sessions.

Once those bills were paid, they would have almost $100,000 left to divide. Most of it was already committed to back debts and legal fees, but even after settling those debts—and making a down payment on a desperately needed new bus—they could anticipate bonuses of $4,000 each. It would be the first time in their history they'd been able to indulge in such largess.

The year 1974 had, in fact, been the Airmen's most successful ever. With concert earnings of more than $285,000, the record company advance, and their publishing royalties, they had grossed over $471,000. Even after all their expenses had been deducted ($81,000 in salaries, $79,000 in travel expenses, $60,000 for recording the album, $33,000 in legal fees, $32,000 for office and promotional expenses, including a $6,000 telephone bill, and a host of miscellaneous smaller bills, their net income was $149,000, and each Airman had earned more than $15,000. They were solidly in the black for the first time in their history. And with a new album and a new record company, 1975 looked even better.

23

ONE REASON for the Airmen's optimism was Warner Brothers. To some
extent, any new record company would have felt good to them (in rather
the same way that a mid-season change in managers will temporarily
improve the morale of a baseball team), but Warner Brothers was special.
In the record industry the two companies that performers and managers
consistently spoke of most highly were Atlantic and Warner Brothers.
Atlantic, which was regarded as somewhat grudging in its contracts, was
on the performers' list of favorites primarily because of its management.
Jerry Wexler and Ahmet Ertegun are old-time record men, with roots
deep into rhythm and blues and early rock'n'roll. Warner Brothers,
though it is a parvenu by Atlantic's standards, gets high points partly for
its generosity, but also because it too is headed by veterans of the music
business, Joe Smith and Mo Ostin. "Joe and Mo" (or "Mo and Joe,"
depending on whom one is talking to) are a disappearing breed in an
industry where company presidents are increasingly plucked from the
fields of law and business.

Warner's strength is also indicated by a running argument within the
industry over whether Vice President Stan Cornyn or Vice President Bob
Regehr is the most intellectual man in the business. But it is Smith and
Ostin who really make the difference. As Arlo Guthrie once said, "I like
Warner's because I can go to the top and walk up to Mo Ostin and say,
'How you doin', Mo? What's happening?' And I don't figure I can do
that anywhere else." Warner's had a particularly strong reputation in
the Airmen's San Francisco circles. It had been the first record company
to move into that area during the flower-power era and sign up large
numbers of burgeoning talents.

In his Burbank office Stan Cornyn talked about that moment in the company's history. "In sixty-seven I went up to San Francisco with Mo Ostin, who was at that time general manager of Reprise, because someone had told him that something was happening up there. Now this was in the midst of the most extreme Berkeley and Haight-Ashbury scenes, and we walked through it much as we might have walked through the market place in Tangier. But Mo just listened to *everything,* and when he'd heard what was going on, he started signing people. Between him and Joe—it was really *all* Joe who got the Dead—Warner Brothers/Reprise signed Neil Young, Joni Mitchell, Arlo Guthrie, the Grateful Dead, and Jimi Hendrix. And that was only the beginning."

"The beginning" Cornyn spoke of, though certainly the beginning of an era, is the middle of the Warner Brothers story. The company was formed in 1958, when the Warner Brothers studio started a record company primarily to release its soundtracks as albums. Early in the sixties, when Frank Sinatra was running into some trouble with a company called Reprise that he had started a few years earlier, Warner's acquired Reprise in return for the rights to distribute three Sinatra films. When they acquired it, Reprise's largest sellers were Sinatra and Dean Martin. "It was not the most distinguished of labels," said Cornyn.

It was a label in trouble, locked by Sinatra's loyalties into an MOR roster, and totally unable to cope with the burgeoning of rock. Shortly after the acquisition, it almost went under and was saved only by the success of Peter, Paul and Mary, one of the first mildly adventurous acts signed by the merged company's new management. The success of the folk-protest trio led Warner/Reprise to begin signing other contemporary acts, a process that got a boost a few years later when Jack Warner sold his company to a firm called Seven Arts, the miniconglomerate that had already bought Atlantic Records. The purchase coincided with the San Francisco rock explosion, and the new company, Warner Brothers/Seven Arts, was sitting on top of a potential gold mine.

But overextension had taken a toll, and a bad year in the film industry left the new corporation unable to support further expansion of the records division. Facing reality, the directors of Warner Brothers/Seven Arts agreed to merge their company with Kinney International, a company that had begun as a chain of funeral parlors in the Bronx and had expanded into a thriving car-rental business. The company had gone on to buy up parking lots to store the rental cars and to allow other drivers to rent space in those lots for their own cars. Within a handful of years Kinney had grown into one of the nation's large corporations. Its search for profitable ways to invest its steadily multiplying capital eventually led it to the "leisure" fields, and it acquired the New York–based Elektra Records. A few years later, at the same time that Warner Brothers/Seven

Arts was reaching out to expand its artists' rosters on its two labels, the corporation was merged with Kinney. The resulting company was known as Warner Communications.

Two further changes had occurred since the merger. The first involved a group of artists managed by Geffen-Roberts, Inc., who had left their various labels (including Warner/Reprise) to record for Asylum Records, a company David Geffen had started that was distributed by Atlantic. That too was acquired by Warner Communications and was merged with Elektra; Jac Holzman of Elektra Records was then either promoted or kicked upstairs to become senior vice president of the parent corporation, and David Geffen was put in charge of the new Elektra-Asylum label.

Warner's acquisition of new companies coincided with both the expanding artists' rosters of the original firms and a general explosion in the rock record market. The upsurge in volume made it possible for the company to break away from independent distribution and establish its own nation-wide system. With the creation of that system, known as WEA (Warner-Elektra-Atlantic), the company officially entered the ranks of the "majors." It had also become, partly because CBS was slow to realize the potential of rock, the largest company in the rock industry. By coincidence, each of its constituent companies had tapped a separate major source of rock talent: Warner/Reprise had the major San Francisco acts; Elektra had a solid core of New York folkies, some of whom, like Carly Simon and Judy Collins, developed into major pop artists; and Atlantic's long history in the rhythm-and-blues field made it a natural home for newly developing soul acts. In 1974, even as they were faced with a recession that was crippling the singles market, the three constituent companies earned a total of fifty gold records (singles selling more than a million copies, or albums selling over a million dollars' worth at wholesale).

Yet the Airmen's new home was, paradoxically, a small company, for the five music-business constituents within Warner Communications were rigidly separate. The only mild exception was that the management of WEA reported to a committee made up of the heads of the three labels. As for the rest, "I think they figured they had a good thing going," said Joe Smith, "so why fuck it up? We haven't even talked about merging the kinds of things that no one would even know if we merged. You know, payroll, data processing, and stuff like that."

Warner's was organized a little differently from most record companies. In addition to the housekeeping departments, the legal and administrative areas, it had three coequal divisions involved in the company's artistic decisions: A&R (artists and repertoire), responsible for the quality of records made by Warner's artists; sales and promotion, which was far more involved in artistic decisions than its name implied; and Cornyn's own creative services division, which in his words "has to do with everything that sells records, except for radio play." The tripartite arrangement had several advantages. For example, the separation of sales from A&R insulated the sales team from pressures involving "their" artists; Cornyn's restless mind had led Warner's creative services division to be first with any number of promotional processes that had subsequently been adopted by the industry; and keeping promotion separate from publicity meant that Warner's promo men were free to do nothing but get airplay for Warner's product. But the system was not without disadvantages, and one was the potential for communications breakdowns among the divisions. Warner's is therefore one of the most meeting-oriented companies in the industry, or in any industry. Several times a week Cornyn's office is jammed with a collection of representatives from the company's various divisions who exchange information in a relentlessly ordered but nonetheless interminable fashion. Even these meetings are not enough, and the basic mode of communication seems to be shouting. When something is happening—or when someone would like to *think* something is happening—doors along the second floor's narrow corridor pop open and closed in a farceur's delight, and executives race from one to another, gesticulating wildly. When someone in Warner's is excited about a record, everybody knows it. And almost everyone in the two-story rabbit warren that served as the company's LA offices was excited about the Airmen.

Part of the excitement was spontaneously generated when the staff people first heard the acetate, and some of it resulted from the Airmen's having long been a favorite band of many key Warner's personnel (including Joe Smith). Much of it, however, was carefully orchestrated. "Getting people inside the company excited about a product is half the battle," said Ron Goldstein. Goldstein, a slim young man given to aviator glasses and layered-look clothing, was one of three "general managers" in the company. As general manager of the Cody project, Goldstein was assigned to shepherd the Airmen's album through its various prerelease phases. Each month he was given three or four new albums to work with; though he didn't actually *do* anything himself, he was responsible for monitoring everyone who did have something to do. As soon as he'd learned of his assignment, he sent out an enthusiastic memo announcing the Cody signing.

The memo followed a more businesslike one sent out a week earlier by Nena Nevard, whose job was to act as liaison between creative services and sales and promotion. Her spare, factual memo outlined the non-monetary aspects of the contract (including the commitment to a European tour and probable international distribution of the album), stated the release date and the fact that Kerr would be conferring on the promotional tour with Bob Regehr, head of artists' relations for Warner's, and contained a summary of the Airmen's recording history and sales figures. Reportorial rather than judgmental, her memo included such understated phrases as "Kerr says they are tongue in cheek characters" to describe the band, and concluded with a promotional note on the markets that the Airmen might be able to break into: "Kerr is looking to us to break the group in the pop market. His organization is familiar with what he terms 'progressive country' and will be working the album that way. He is anticipating tremendous sales development—to 400M."

Goldstein's more effusive memo began with a review of the Airmen's appearance the previous weekend at the Santa Monica Civic Auditorium: ". . . fell 350 seats short of selling out, including no record company affiliation for a year, no album out in the market place, Forum show starring Loggins and Messina with Poco on same night (same type of audience). The show was overwhelmingly successful. Lots of encores and tremendous enthusiasm. This band has it live."

Goldstein then moved on to hype the album ("Many of us have listened to the album and the consensus is that the product is there. Group does not write, but they know how to select material. . . . It's all good and there are possible singles") and to give their touring history. He wrote that the sales department was ready to send prerelease copies of the album to Chicago stores when the band was appearing there, talked about merchandising possibilities, and ended, "If you will allow me a little hype, I have to say that this looks like an excellent signing. The product is good, the group works, the management seems experienced and together, and the atmosphere out there seems right." The two memos, taken together, both prompted and reported on activities in the record company's various divisions.

The legal department, for instance, was monitoring the details of the buyout agreement between the Airmen and ABC. Since the original contract had been between the Airmen and Famous (now ABC), Warner's had no direct standing in drawing up the agreement, but their lawyers worked closely with Hessenius to make sure that no vestige of the previous contract would mar the Airmen's arrangements with Warner's. When the lawyers were satisfied with the wording, the Airmen individually signed the agreement with ABC. It was a full and complete termination of the contract with Famous, and as soon as Warner's forwarded the $100,000 buyout fee to ABC, the band was legally free to sign the Warner's contract. With that, the legal department's involvement with the album came to an end, but work was just beginning in the areas of product management, creative services, and sales and promotion.

24

As soon as she heard that the Airmen had been signed to Warner's, Lorrie Janson, in product management, began filling out a page for them in the series of thick black looseleaf folders that lined her bookshelves. Though sound equipment dominates nearly every other office in the building, hers was only a small portable stereo. Janson, a former character actress who bears a more than passing resemblance to Dorothy Malone, is in charge of scheduling the production of Warner's records. For other people in the building, the Airmen's album might be The Next Big Hit; for her, it was job #404,132. But for all of them, the Airmen's album was a commodity.

On the form for this particular commodity, she checked off the receipt of art work, liner copy, label copy, and copyright clearances. According to her records, the final tapes had been received on December 27, and the master recording had been made at Capitol Studios on the next day. The following day she had received the metal parts that the factories would use for stamping out albums and had forwarded them to the three plants that manufactured Warner's albums. On January 9 the first test pressings came back ("We don't get tests from all three plants," she said, "just from Santa Monica, because it's the closest"), and she distributed them to the company's various divisions. She also sent one up to San Rafael for final approval. "This was a very novel situation," she said. "I always get a certain number of tests, you know, a standard number. But it seems that everybody wanted this one. New York wanted extra, and I think the whole second floor was down here asking for copies at one time or another. I actually had to reorder test pressings, and I don't think that's *ever* happened before."

Had she listened to the album? She smiled politely. "Well, no. I've been meaning to, you understand, but it's just always so busy down here . . . but I do know that everyone is very enthusiastic about it."

Goldstein continued his pump priming, an effort to whet the appetites of the people who would take over after the record was released. After his initial forays within the office building itself, he reached out to the salesmen and promotion staff. Since he could hardly fly all over the country to talk with them individually, he did the next best thing: "I wanted our promotion people to understand how this album came to-gether—we're a big company and ship a lot of product—so I went up to George's house and taped an interview with him and Joe. George is such an amazing character that I figured he could turn them on better than anyone else could. I edited it down to about fifteen minutes, then shipped it out on cassette to all the regional promo men. And it really worked. I started getting calls the very next week: 'What's the single?' 'When are they touring here?' All that kind of stuff."

Goldstein's job involved more than simply generating excitement. Un-like the linear and ordered processes of the studio, where things flow along one after another in a readily discernible order, everything happens at once when a record is released. Publicity, shipping, advertising, tour promotions, and a hundred other details come together in a synergistic process that is at once as complicated and as routine as an army's taking up a new position in the field. As general manager for this album, Gold-stein was sitting on top of everything, and one of his first jobs was to find out whether or not there was going to be a single.

Historically, Warner's had not been very much interested in singles. Many of its acts, including some of its biggest money-makers, had never had a hit single, and the company's general policy had been to build its artists gradually through album sales, bringing singles out only after a performer had become established. Because radio play was traditionally focused on singles rather than albums, Warner's had been forced to develop new ways to promote its artists.

"We've always been, and we still are," said Joe Smith, "a company that's known for its ability to break new artists. And because it's sometimes hard to get airplay for an unknown, we've developed—mostly Stan Cornyn developed—a whole series of non-airplay ways to sell records."

Under Cornyn, Warner's pioneered "FM Print" ads, a series of type-heavy, irreverent advertisements that ran both in national publications like the *Voice* and *Rolling Stone* and in hundreds of college papers and the alternative press. The ads, featuring bizarre events like the "Win a Fug Dream Date" and the famous "Pigpen Look Alike Contest," created an image of Warner's as *the* hip company. Cornyn also introduced the "loss leaders," double albums made up of cuts selected from a variety of

Warner's albums, about half by well-known acts and the other half by acts the company was trying to get someone to listen to. These albums were sold, by mail order only, for the nominal price of two dollars each. The company had been doing one a year since Cornyn came up with the first one seven years before, and each one had sold in the neighborhood of fifty thousand copies.

"All of that," Cornyn said, "was a response to the question of how you break an artist like Randy Newman: someone you really believe in—who's a goddamn genius, when you get down to it—but who is simply not going to get played on the radio. I think we still do that kind of non-airplay work better than anyone else, and we finally *did* break Randy Newman this year."

During the few months before the Airmen signed with the company, the recession's effect on the music industry had created a gradual change in Warner's policy. As Joe Smith put it, "The money out there is getting tighter all the time, and people are less willing to take a chance on a record unless they're really familiar with the performer. And a good solid hit single is still the best way to get the kind of airplay that will make people want to hear the rest of a performer's work."

That had certainly been the case with the Airmen's first album. It had entered the charts with a flourish, at 176, with a "bullet" indicating the chart-makers' judgment that it was a potential hit, but five weeks later had slipped back to 200. Subsequently, though it didn't fall off the charts completely, it drifted back and forth in their lower quadrant. When "Hot Rod Lincoln" first appeared on the singles chart, at 98, the album was at 158.

For the next six weeks, however, "Hot Rod Lincoln" was winging its bulleted way up the charts, and the album gradually followed it, eventually breaking into the top 100 before stalling at 82 and beginning a stately descent. The album would have sold well for a debut in any event, but the single got the airplay that sent the album to success.

"So now," Smith continued, "if we think we have a single, we're a lot more likely to release it ahead of or simultaneously with the album than we would have been a couple of years ago." The Airmen presented Warner's with an opportunity in that while they were not quite well enough known to be automatically assured of airplay for a single, the company considered them established enough so that station programmers would at least listen to any single that a Warner's promo man brought in and pushed. The question, then, was whether or not the album contained a potential single.

"Actually," said Goldstein, "that wasn't really the problem. We all knew that there were maybe a handful of possibilities on the album. The question was which one. There were a lot of people who liked 'Willin',' but there was also a feeling that it doesn't really sound typical of the group. Finally it came down to 'Southbound,' and I think our A&R people would have gone along either with that or with 'Willin'.' But there were a whole lot of people who liked 'Don't Let Go.' " Faced with a difficult choice, Warner's sought help outside its walls, and sales vice president Ed Rosenblatt sent the two cuts to Dr. Thomas Turicchi at the Psychographic Research Lab in Texas.

Turicchi, a former professor of music theory who was also trained in educational psychology, had backed into the popular-music business some three years earlier, when his research work came to the attention of a San Francisco program director. Turicchi's work was based on the irrefutable premise that listeners have physical responses to music. Those responses can be measured on a variety of instruments, and the results can be recorded in the same way that a subject's responses to a lie detector test can be recorded on a polygraph. What was special was the model that Turicchi built after conducting thousands of tests on panels of teenage listeners whom he had monitored for internal body responses while they listened to popular records. The model allowed him to move from measurement into prediction. Turicchi believes that by monitoring physical responses to unreleased records he can predict whether or not a given song will become a hit. He can do so, he told a *New Times* reporter, with 92 percent accuracy.

Word of Turicchi's dream machine had spread through the industry. Other predictors—the ubiquitous tip sheets among them—offered what appeared to be mere guesses compared with the hard evidence visible on Turicchi's graphs. Galvanic skin response, heartbeat, pulse, all are comfortingly concrete and apparently free of hype. By May of 1974 Turicchi had left his teaching position to work full time at his Psychographic Lab.

His first clients were radio stations testing the acceptability of the new releases they received, but soon record companies began sending him prerelease records as well. "It's all a little eerie," said a record company executive, "but who's going to argue with success? The guy is right a *lot* of the time."

"Of course he is," responded another, "but a lot of his 'magic' is the same kind of self-fulfilling prophecy that happens when Gavin or Rudman [two tipsheet authors whose judgments provide a security blanket for timid radio programmers] gives a big play to a record. The word gets out that Turicchi is hot on a record, so stations start playing it. Once they hear it on the radio, the kids buy it. Presto, it's a hit.

"I'm not denying that he has something going for him—as far as I understand it, he was predicting things pretty well even before he got to be a star himself—but now he's become just another promo man's tool. You send a record down to him so that if it gets a good response, you can tell everybody you've got a guaranteed hit and they better start play-ing it. If it doesn't get a response, you just don't talk about it. You have to realize, from the way he's got his panels organized, that the kids are gonna like *something* he plays, even if it's only because it follows a couple of turkeys. What it comes down to is that I'd never make a de-cision based on his work, but I'll sure use it to sell a record we've already decided to release."

At Warner's, the general attitude toward Turicchi seemed to be fairly skeptical, but they too used his services occasionally. "It's a way of test-ing our own ears, maybe," said one vice president, "but really not much more than that. By the time we've made a record, we've already absorbed most of our costs. Releasing a single to see if it'll fly costs practically nothing compared to what we've already put into making the album. If it hits, you're way ahead; if it doesn't, you haven't lost that much." Nonetheless, to help resolve the argument over the Airmen's single, Ed Rosenblatt decided to give "Southbound" and "Don't Let Go" the Turicchi treatment.

Turicchi's methodology leads to two separate reports, one a percentage indication of audience acceptability (compiled at least partly by observa-tion and discussion) that measures conscious response, and a second based on the unconscious emotional responses captured by Turicchi's electronic sensors. The second indicator is reported in integers from 1 to 50, with a reading of 20 or below totally negative, and one of over 30 signaling a potential top ten hit record. Turicchi's report was not en-couraging. "Southbound" scored 21; "Don't Let Go," 23. "Experience has shown us," Turicchi wrote, "that records which have an overall score of 28 or higher have excellent potential in terms of both sales and chart potential. Neither cut submitted scored in this range. However, 'Don't Let Go' was by all our measures the stronger record, although there was a significant level of irritation in the teen subjects." By the time his report arrived in Burbank, however, Warner's had already begun to press copies of "Don't Let Go."

"What's exciting about this album," said Goldstein a couple of days before its official February 15 release date, "is that we've had so much enthusiasm *prior* to release. There's lots of times when product comes in and we say, 'What the fuck? Where did this come from?' But on this one, Gary Davis—he's the head of promotion—said he thought 'Don't Let Go' was a single. And then the next record to come blasting out of Russ Thyret's office—as well as running sales, Russ is our office DJ—was that one. And then Ed Rosenblatt got on it.

"On a new act, for us to release a single early is very rare, but when Ed said, 'Let's *go* on this,' we did. If you've got Davis, Thyret, and Rosenblatt all going for the same record, then you've got the sales and promotion department. You don't have to worry about pushing the guys out in the field when their own bosses are telling them they've got a hit on their hands."

At the same time Rosenblatt's division was preparing a major push on "Don't Let Go," Cornyn's end of the company was organizing its own work for the Airmen. To begin with, the publicity department was putting together a thousand copies of a press kit to be mailed out to music writers along with complimentary copies of the album. "We can't really work on a single," said West Coast publicity director Gary George, "because we've got such a long lead time. Occasionally you can get something in one of the daily papers if you're really hot, but most of the stuff that we set up won't even be published until after the single has either made it or disappeared.

"We've been able to do a couple of special things on this one. We've set up stories on Cody and Emmylou Harris [another newly signed Warner's act] in *Rolling Stone* and *Country Music,* which we certainly can't always do. But most of the things we do at this stage are really routine. Check out the press kits, mail out the albums, set up a guest list for the showcase Troubadour gig in LA—all the standard stuff."

It is, of course, the feeling that record company publicists can do only the standard stuff that sends managers out to look for independent public relations firms. Under the Airmen's contract with Famous, the record company had provided a monthly retainer to one of the industry's best-known firms, Gibson and Stromberg, to publicize the Airmen. Though ABC had suddenly cut off payments to the firm, Kerr had kept up an informal relationship with them. He was thinking seriously of retaining them again for the new album, but first he wanted to see what Cornyn's various divisions could do for him. "Right now," he said, "it looks as though the company is going to push us. If they do—and we'll just have to wait and see what that means—I'm not sure that an outside PR firm is worth the bucks."

The basic question was whether, given the enormous amount of effort Warner's could put into its promotion, there was any use at all for the vast number of small publicity firms that dot the rock landscape. In 1974, as the recession began eroding the edges of the music industry, some people were answering in the negative. As money grew tighter, independent firms found their client lists shrinking, and many had to shut their doors. Even Gibson and Stromberg was finally overwhelmed by debts, and closed during the same week the Airmen's album was released.

Kerr, however, was at least initially unwilling to rely completely on the Warner's publicity arm, and sought out Patty Faralla during a mid-February LA trip. Faralla, who had toiled at Gibson and Stromberg for a couple of years before leaving to start her own firm, had grown close to Kerr and the Airmen during that time. She was also, though embarked on what was clearly a risky business, confident about the future of independent publicists.

"Bob Gibson and Gary Stromberg created rock'n'roll PR. Actually, Bobbi Cowan and Helen Noga had the first firm in town, but you can just imagine the chance that two girls had in 1966. It was really a whole new field. The big firms had all sort of started their 'contemporary' offices, but none of those people related to the *music* at all.

"Then Bob and Gary had the hot idea, and no one was ever able to touch them. They worked at putting the loonies in touch with the loonies, and they got all the best clients—the Stones, Yes, James Taylor . . .

"But then about two years ago they started to take it too much for granted and lost their instinct. If it isn't fun anymore, you lose it.

"The changes went beyond just the money thing, too. I mean, when they started out, there was almost no one who couldn't use what Gibson and Stromberg offered. Also, they really knew what they were doing. But now it's no longer automatic that a good publicist is going to know more than any manager that walks in the door. There just are no more dumb managers; the business is too sophisticated for them to survive. The managers"—she laughed—"are starting to catch up with the road crews."

When Hessenius and Kerr dropped in to talk to Faralla, she was in the same office building once occupied by Gibson and Stromberg, a green-stuccoed complex in a neighborhood peopled more or less equally by failed screenwriters and budding geniuses. Her office was plain, decorated only by publicity photographs of friends and clients and cluttered with heaps of trade magazines, but it had its advantages.

One of those was illustrated when, as Faralla sipped Italian wine and discussed the Airmen with Kerr and Hessenius, a door at the back of her office opened and Patrick Snyder-Scumpy walked in. Snyder-Scumpy is the unofficial name of Patrick Snyder, the West Coast editor of *Crawdaddy* magazine, one of the major rock publications. (He added the Scumpy in college because it sounded "seedy and decadent.") Scumpy had come in the back way just to say hello to Faralla, but his sudden materialization through the wall provided Kerr and Hessenius with a graphic illustration of the firm's connections with the music press.

Later that evening, sitting in the living room of her modest Studio City apartment, Faralla talked for a while about why firms like hers existed. "Personal relationships have a lot to do with it. I mean, there are a whole lot of groups that have a family sense about what they're doing, and they really want a whole lot of contact with whoever is doing their PR. The independents can do that. An individual human at a record company can never get really close to the performers. Because what happens if the company decides that they're going to put all their energies into someone else this month?

"A record company PR group can do the trade press and service a record, and that's about it. They can't take a group on tour and contact the key press and radio, including colleges, at all the stops on the tour. Unless they've really been around for a long time, most of them just don't have the skills or smarts to do that. There's too much internal bullshit going on for them to get out there.

"So they get the major stations all right, but anything else is too much for them to bother with. They just have too much to do, too many groups to handle. Warner's has maybe half a dozen people handling three hundred acts. We've got two for only six or seven clients. And because of Regehr's operation, Warner's is very much the best of the big companies."

Gary George, however, later defended the Warner's operation. "Look, I'll admit that when I was a writer, the independent publicists were my friends and maybe they did seem to have more time for me. But I've come to take a much more jaundiced view of them. They've got to prove to their clients that they're doing something right, so they're really in the business of sending out lots of carbon copies of every letter they write. They even send out memos of their phone calls. I do everything that they do, but we can't send out carbons to every manager."

Kerr eventually agreed with him, and chose not to engage an outside firm, but while he was making his decision, the first bit of outside feedback came in on "Don't Let Go." KHJ, the largest and most powerful AM rock station in Los Angeles, had decided during its very first week of release to add it to their playlist. It was a solid indication that "Don't Let Go" might actually be the hit that Warner's hoped it would be.

25

_____

WARNER'S RESPONSE to the KHJ action illustrated the extraordinary symbiosis that has developed between the American broadcasting and recording industries. Record companies provide inexpensive programming to broadcasters—the records themselves are free; the broadcaster pays only a token amount to the songwriter and publisher for each play—and broadcasters provide what amounts to free advertising to the record companies. In most other countries, where there is little discernible pop-format radio, record companies must market their products in a variety of ways. In America, the land of the dashboard radio, there is one prime way of selling records: airplay.

One can't, for instance, tell what effect a series of radio ads has on a record's sales, but one can—and Warner Brothers did, using an elaborate array of computerized record keeping—develop an exact correlation between the quality and quantity of radio play in a region and the number of records bought there. To some extent, Warner's salesmen are really delivery boys, and as soon as KHJ picked up the record, WEA automatically began placing reorders for all its accounts. "To be on the KHJ playlist," said Russ Thyret, "is 30,000 units. Good as gold." More important, KHJ's early play was a potent tool for the Warner's promo men to use when they went to radio stations in other parts of the country. If they did their job getting airplay, all the salesmen would have to do was deliver enough records to the stores.

KHJ's decision to play "Don't Let Go" was a surprise. KHJ is not as notoriously conservative as New York's WABC, but it usually adds records to its playlist only after they have started to move in some other section of the country. It had never played the Airmen's "Hot Rod Lincoln," even when the song broke into the top ten nationally. But this was different. "Late last week, I guess it was Thursday," Ed Rosenblatt said, "the local promotion man took the album up to KHJ and played it for Gerry Peterson, their program director. Next thing I hear is five o'clock Friday. They've added it right out of the box. They aren't waiting for any other stations. I really couldn't believe it.

"I guess it's just that we came along at the right time with something they needed. That Billy Swan thing is starting to fall off now, and he doesn't have a follow-up ready. So we come in with two minutes of 1955 good feelings, and we're on the list. It's all a crap-shoot anyway.

"You really can't figure it out ahead of time. We once had a group that I was really hot on, and I decided we'd do a car giveaway for radio station people. We had this big contest, you know, with the car parked in front of the Troubadour at night and everything like that. Well, I sold 20,000 albums and no singles. And it cost me $7,500 for a Firebird. And now we've got KHJ taking this one right out of the box and going on it . . ." He grinned. "You know, we haven't really done *anything* on this one yet, but Joe Kerr is going to be giving us all head onstage at the Troubadour next week."

Kerr, who had been in New York over the February 15 weekend when KHJ started playing the record, may not have been ready to entertain the Troubadour audience in that particular way, but he was so delighted that his long-distance phone bill for the weekend totaled well over a hundred dollars.

"He was calling *everyone*," said Ron Goldstein. "We were out when he called us, and my son says they talked for about half an hour anyway."

Kerr knew that KHJ meant sales, and so, of course, did everyone else in the music business. Though the record had sold only a handful of copies during its first week in the stores, it began to appear on the charts. *Billboard* carried it at 100, *Cashbox* at 107, and *Record World* at 81 with a bullet. The differences among them largely reflected their different methods of measuring a record's movement. *Billboard* relies primarily on sales to distributors, *Cashbox* on sales to one-stops (the subdistributors who service jukebox operators), and *Record World* is particularly sensitive to radio play. Taken together, the overwhelming import of their listings was that "Don't Let Go" was on its way. It was, everyone knew, only the second time since Gerry Peterson had come to KHJ that a nonsuperstar record had been added to the playlist directly on its release.

One day after the record began playing on KHJ, Russ Thyret demonstrated the power of radio and put out 5,625 singles into stores in the station's listening area. Orders for 2,000 each from two large chains were expected early on Monday morning, February 17, which would bring the total layout to nearly 10,000 copies in the Los Angeles area. An internal follow-up memo confirming KHJ's importance read "I have asked the singles order department at the LA branch to figure with Marc Mait-land's help how many singles are needed when all West Coast stations add a record [to their playlists] and then to order that many Cody singles. We know we have a smash and might as well order them now so as not to be in a back order position." On the same day WPLR, a rock FM station catering largely to the Yale University community, added the single to its playlist. It was the first East Coast add. "The thing that's so great about Cody," exulted Ron Goldstein, "is that they can go AM and FM."

Goldstein would not have needed to make his remark ten years earlier, when AM was the only radio. There were FM sets on the market, but not many were bought. A few large cities supported one or two struggling FM stations with classical or ethnic music, and a number of colleges used their FM stations to train budding journalists in radio techniques, but FM had no serious impact on the popular record market. Since then the growth of FM programming of popular music had outstripped the growth of the record industry itself. Though FM play was still not enough to break a single, it was regarded as the critical component in album sales.

Two imperatives created the FM mushroom, one technical and one aesthetic. The technical one was that FM could broadcast in stereo, the medium through which serious listeners were accustomed to hearing their music. The aesthetic one was related to the first: there is a community of serious rock listeners. No one would have accepted this in the early days of rock'n'roll, when it was considered exclusively teenage music, what the *New York Daily News* in 1956 called "a barrage of primitive, jungle-beat rhythms, which when set to lyrics at all, quite frequently sound off with double-meaning leer-ics few adults would care to hear." The stations which made their money from teenage audiences were exclusively on the AM band.

In the sixties those stations were severely shaken by the payola scandals and, according to the conventional explanation the "top-40" tight play-list format burgeoned as a result. Broadcasters hurried to protect them-selves from charges of payola by limiting their disc jockeys' freedom to play records of their own choosing. To police what was going on at their stations, owners and managers centralized control over what songs were to be played in the person of a program director. With one person re-sponsible for assembling the playlist, opportunities for corruption were minimized, at least in theory, and the radio stations that had discovered a gold mine when they tapped into rock'n'roll could continue their business without interference from the Federal Communications Commission.

Other explanations for the existence of the tight playlist involve the success of KHJ. In 1965 KHJ hired Bill Drake, a programmer who had achieved considerable success with smaller West Coast stations, to boost its ratings. Under his formula, there was less DJ chatter, shorter station promo jingles, fewer (and clustered) commercials, and, as his stations' promos endlessly.repeated, "Much More Music."

The claim of more music was true only in the grossest sense. Though KHJ did increase its minutes of music per hour, it radically cut down on the number of songs DJs were allowed to play. The old "top-40" format, with a handful of permissible album cuts and oldies thrown in as extras, went out the window. Instead of a sixty-song playlist, KHJ disc jockeys had a playlist of thirty-five, and those thirty-five were to be played in a strictly weighted order; the top ten, for instance, were to be played more often than the bottom ten, in a predetermined ratio. Remarkably, the station's listenership suddenly took off. Within two years after Drake's arrival KHJ was number one in Los Angeles, and Drake was on his way to a hefty consultant's business as the savior of struggling stations. Apart from the ramifications of the payola scandal, one thing was immediately apparent to radio station operators all across the country: tight playlists made money.

There have been a number of guesses, educated and otherwise, about the success of tight-playlist radio, but the clue probably comes from a survey Drake commissioned in Los Angeles. Its aim was to determine what made listeners do the worst thing that station owners could imagine —change the dial. There were any number of things that annoyed listeners, but by far the largest number—47 percent—said they changed stations when they heard a record they didn't like. Drake's response was simplicity itself: by cutting down on the number of records his stations were allowed to play, he minimized the chance that a listener would hear something he didn't like. As he told an interviewer, "It stands to reason: If you're play-ing the thirty-fifth worst record in town, and somebody else is playing the eighty-seventh worst record in town, you're better off than they are." Like many simple systems, Drake's was riddled with absurdities—e.g., his mea-sure of "goodness" was sales, which meant that the identical record grew objectively better or worse from week to week. But, again like many simple systems, it worked. Not only did his stations soar in the ratings, but those that followed his playlist as published in the weekly trade-paper listings also flourished. All over America listeners began to hear the same songs—with the same frequency—over their radios.

All of which was good enough as long as Drake's fundamental assump-tion about radio held true: that it was a medium to which one listened while doing something else. To some extent, of course, it held true because no one could possibly manage to give full attention to a Bill Drake station for any length of time. The sound was nearly perfect as a background for driving, doing homework, or ironing, but it was not meant to be *listened* to.

That assumption went by the boards with the arrival of the Beatles, the

Jefferson Airplane, the Grateful Dead, Bob Dylan, and the new pantheon of rock stars. Suddenly, perhaps even embarrassingly, rock was art, and a new generation of listeners was born. They felt (perhaps with long-range negative consequences for the music) an elitist contempt for top-40 radio. They listened to records.

At least they listened to records until late in 1966. That fall, the next stage of the radio revolution occurred. A displaced New York City disc jockey, Murray Kaufman (better known as Murray the K, from his AM days as "the fifth Beatle"), persuaded the management of WOR-FM to let him try a new programming concept. What he proposed was "quality" rock—album cuts, lengthy sets, no screaming DJs. Because WOR had already thrown away its potential FM audience by simply duplicating its AM programming (adding little to their advertising base), it was willing to give Kaufman's idea a try. Within a year, prompted by an FCC decision limiting duplicate programming for FM stations, progressive rock radio had moved to San Francisco and Los Angeles. By 1967, it had spread to nearly every major population center in the country, and had become a new medium for breaking records. Acts no longer had to have a three-minute melody to make it, and a whole host of performers moved to stardom through the new medium.

Warner Brothers was one of the first companies to anticipate the growth of the non-AM rock market, and its roster bulged with artists who never had a hit single, but whose albums managed to break even, and sometimes to take off. Arlo Guthrie, Randy Newman, the Mothers of Invention, Joni Mitchell, Black Sabbath, the Grateful Dead, Jimi Hendrix, and others were sustained for years by album sales fostered by FM play. FM had become so important to the success of an album that, as Stan Cornyn sadly told a music-industry convention in the spring of 1975, "Warner Brothers Records won't put out an album unless we think it'll get airplay."

The AM stations had not watched their older listeners switch to FM without coming up with counterstrategies of their own. A few attempted to duplicate the FM format, but they were generally unsuccessful. In addition to its superior sound quality, FM could afford long stretches of uninterrupted music because its initial licensing costs were significantly lower than AM. Until well into the FM boom, an FM station in a respectable-sized city cost only about a tenth as much to purchase as a comparable AM station. So the top-40 stations responded, not by enlarging their playlists, but by further narrowing them. First it was top thirty, with an ever-shrinking number of "chart-bound" specials, but even that narrowed, to the point where New York's WABC had a regular playlist of only eighteen singles. It had become harder and harder for new artists (and it was such a long time since the Airmen's last AM hit that they fell pretty well into that category) to get the kind of airplay that would move them to the top of the charts. Over the past two or three years, a pattern had developed of records breaking quickly in one geographical region, being picked up in enough others to start a good run up the charts, then getting stalled somewhere just below top-40 status. It was up to Rosenblatt's men to keep that from happening to "Don't Let Go," primarily by getting it played by key stations across the country.

"It's all done with mirrors," said a CBS promotion man. "We're all out there trying to convince program directors to play our product. And they say, 'Let me see your sales.' But we don't have any sales to show until they start playing the record. So you finagle a little. You bring in figures from other cities. You show 'em Gavin and Rudman." There is, as he indicated, a certain Catch-22 inherent in the job; promotion men are frequently in the position of a Washington hostess trying to get two political lions whom she knows only slightly to come to dinner. First she calls up A: "You may not remember me, but B is coming to dinner here on Tuesday and told me that he would like to have you come as well..." Then she quickly calls B with the news that A would like to meet him at dinner on Tuesday. The game is obviously not without its pitfalls, because the promo man needs the radio station a lot more than the station needs him. As Ed Rosenblatt put it: "Radio stations don't give a fuck about selling records. All they want to do is keep people's fingers off the buttons. As long as there's no one reaching out to change the station, they're happy."

But Rosenblatt agrees that the record industry is dependent—some say frighteningly dependent—on radio. It is a situation which, in most normal business situations, would simply lead to straightforward payments from the record companies to the radio stations. The amount of the payments would be negotiated between the station's estimate of how many listeners (and hence how many advertising dollars) it might be expected to lose by playing unknown records and the record company's estimates of what sales return will be generated by the desired airplay. But the broadcasting industry is in quite a different position from, say, fan magazines that cheerfully (if tacitly) sell their news columns for advertising dollars or free trips. According to the laws of the United States, radio stations are a public trust, and as such are heavily regulated by the FCC. Except under certain specific conditions, payments of the sort described are illegal. They are called payola.

Payola has been around almost since the beginning of the record industry. The forms it takes have included the assignment of publishing rights, stacks of free records, airline tickets, paid vacations, and good old-fashioned cash. Record company and radio executives are pious in their denials of the practice, but a number of federal grand juries have alleged that it still exists today. In its flashiest form, at least the form most beloved of headline writers, it is called "drugola." There is no question that the record industry—from studio through promotion—is rife with drug use. Such drug use is illegal, of course, but that is not the same thing as saying that it is dishonest.

One CBS promotion man put it this way: "Listen, particularly with the whole grand jury thing coming down now, I'm not about to lay an ounce of coke on anyone. No way. Not for top-three rotation for a month. It's just not worth it. There are people out there who want to put us in *jail*, man."

Lesser quantities, however, were a different matter: "If I've got some coke—and there's no way I'm going to travel to some of the places I go without some nose in my suitcase—then of course I'll turn a guy on. And if I've got enough, I may lay a half a gram on someone or sell him a little at cost. I can buy it better and cheaper than he can, so if I sell him some of my personal stash at no profit, or maybe even a slight loss, I'm doing us both a favor. As long as I'm not giving him enough to deal or anything like that, I don't see anything wrong with it. You've gotta understand that a lot of these guys are my *friends*."

Whether the various United States prosecutors now poking around the payola questions will see coke sharing in such a relaxed way is a matter of some concern to the record companies—so much so that one division of CBS was reported to have hidden a camera in the mail room of the corporation's London headquarters, to film another division's rumored smuggling of coke into the United States inside film cans. But it is of only marginal concern to most promo men. If they're having lunch with a program director who drinks, they'll buy the martinis. If he prefers to take his chemicals up his nose, they'll oblige that preference as well. As the CBS representative said, "It's no big thing."

The general sense of most promo men's work is that they are, by their lights, honest. They do try and curry favor with program directors in a variety of ways ranging from always having a supply of promotional T-shirts for radio station personnel (the Warner's briefing form for station visits includes a listing of proper sizes) to a stack of albums that the station can use for giveaway contests. Sometimes, of course, those records find their way to a local record store, where they are exchanged for cash that goes to the program director's personal welfare fund, and for which the performer receives no royalties. Even in those cases there is rarely a direct quid pro quo. Instead, there is a continuing relationship, a "contact."

"I've got maybe a half-dozen stations in my district," said the CBS man, "where I know that if I go in and really pitch on a record—and if I can show *something* that indicates it's moving in some other region—I can get that record played. I can't do it too often, of course, but when push comes to shove and my boss is really riding my ass, there are people I can depend on."

When such relationships don't exist, promo men have to adopt other, occasionally more bizarre strategies. Warner Brothers' Texas promo men delivered the Airmen's record to their stations wearing rented space suits, a bit of costuming that led to an embarrassing encounter in Houston, where a steely-eyed Secret Service man detained the Warner's representative until President Ford had safely made his way out of laser-beam range. But what the promotion men were really selling, and what they could sell after KHJ added the record, was that "Don't Let Go" was going to be a hit, and that the stations that played it early could remind their listeners that they were "hit makers."

Within a week, "Don't Let Go" was playing on KLIV in San Jose, KFRC and KSAN in San Francisco, KAKC in Tulsa, KKDJ in Los Angeles, KUPD and KRUX in Phoenix, and KGW in Portland. None of them were as important as KHJ, but they added up; by February 20, when the Airmen arrived in Los Angeles to begin a four-night showcase stand at the Troubadour, a survey of one-stop distributors reported that "Don't Let Go" was the largest-selling WEA single in the Los Angeles area. With *Billboard* reporting it as a regional breakout, Rosenblatt was ready to start working the record nationally.

Rosenblatt, a restless, bearded forty-year-old much given to anxious pacing and patently unfunny jokes, administers half of the Warner's annual advertising budget, but he does so with considerable skepticism. "I don't think advertising sells records. It creates an ambience for doing business with an account; when we pay for a store's retail ads, it helps keep them healthy enough to sell our product—but that's about it.

"Some people, primarily managers who either don't know what they're doing or are having trouble with their acts, come in and scream for things. You know, they want an ad in *Rolling Stone,* a billboard on the Strip. They think that's gonna give them a hit. And a while ago it probably looked that way—any record that had a billboard on the Strip was a hit. But that was because nobody was buying billboards unless they thought they had a hit to begin with. Now that everybody's putting up billboards, and not everybody is getting hits, people are beginning to understand that advertising isn't magic. You know, it's still the same game: if you want a hit record, get it played on the radio. There are other kinds of exposure that help—touring, TV, placement in stores, airplay in stores—but nothing, *nothing,* is as important as getting that song on the radio.

"That's why our promo men do nothing but radio. Cornyn and Regehr do a whole lot of stuff that's very helpful in the long run, but if people don't hear the product somewhere, they're never gonna buy it. And I'm not unreasonable with our people; I know that there are real geographic differences. I mean, just because WABC in New York isn't gonna play a record until it's 18 nationally with a bullet doesn't mean that the promo man there is an asshole. Same thing in Chicago, a place that doesn't have a decent FM station. Well, there are some of our records you're just not gonna move in Chicago. But wherever there's a station that *can* play a record we want played, I want them playing it.

"Now that makes for some problems, because the stations obviously can't play them all. So we have a strong regional marketing manager who can tell the promo men straight out, '*This* is the one to push.' And because they direct our salesmen too, things stay coordinated. But we're also big enough that even with the incredible flow of product, there's always gonna be one or two of our guys who really like any given record, and they'll go out and push that one on their own. And if it gets a little action, if the station's phones start to light up or the store reports look good, we've got the kind of communications setup that will let us give that word to every other promo man. That's why we have the conference calls."

Every Thursday morning at nine-thirty, Rosenblatt's office is the scene of a conference call between the nine regional marketing managers and the central sales and promotion staff. After the predictable amount of static and phone-company problems, the call for the week that the Airmen were playing in Los Angeles focused on an area-by-area review of the February releases. The February package included two sure hits, one by Robin Trower and one by Gordon Lightfoot, a half-dozen gambles, and two albums—the Airmen's and Emmylou Harris's—for which there were high hopes. But they were going to have to be worked if they were to make it. The first problem came up on a debut album by a little-known British singer-songwriter named Brian Protheroe that Warner's had released in January. Rosenblatt spoke to the Cleveland regional manager. "Look, we're getting the beginnings of a pattern on this one. It's sort of like the one we got on Leo Sayer, and we've just gotta keep it alive for long enough that someone hears it and really goes. What we need on this one, Al, desperately need, is WAXY up there in Buffalo."

A tinny voice responded through the speaker phone: "Right. I don't know what's going on there, but I think the problem is the salesman not getting his ass where he ought to be. They played it a few times, but we've got no store figures to show them."

"Well, then fire the motherfucker, man. We're gonna blow a record, and that's terrible. If you think you've gotta make an example of someone, go ahead and do it."

"OK."

The review continued with Rosenblatt's directing one final push on the Doobie Brothers' "Black Water." "That's gonna be three and two on the charts this week, and I really want to get it up to number one next week.

I know it's not gonna stick, because Olivia Newton-John is gonna go right by it, but I'd like to see if we can get it up there for a week." The mention of a woman singer prompted Dino Barbis, the West Coast promotion man, to report that KHJ had taken on Maria Muldaur's single, "Midnight at the Oasis." The brief murmur of appreciation was interrupted by the voice of Gary Davis, who was out on the road that week.

"I don't want anybody pushing that record; I think they're just going after demographics. Look at their playlist now." He pointed out that KHJ had found itself playing a lot of records by male groups and needed a woman or two—and "an FM sound"—for balance. "They went on that one for a whole different reason that doesn't have anything to do with where it's going. That record's on the end of its run. Phoebe Snow, Olivia Newton-John, they're gonna knock it out of the box."

"Yeah," Barbis responded, "but we don't want to leave him out on a limb like that. He adds it and it takes a nose dive. That's no good."

"I know that, but I still don't want anybody going into WFIL and taking a slot away from Cody or Leo Sayer just because KHJ went on it. I mean maintain on it, and work it in LA, but we've got to bring Leo and the Commander home. We've got a lot of people ready to go on them if we can deliver some good store reports."

"Right," said Rosenblatt. "The Cody particularly. If we don't get a good jump on that one, KHJ is gonna think they went on it too early."

"More than that," Thyret added, "you need a big jump on that one because it's gonna have a shorter life than Leo. We aren't gonna have time to develop sales in the secondaries when the major stations are starting to go on it already."

Rosenblatt again: "I think that because we got the heavies on it, you guys might have started out to lighten up on it, and we can't let that happen. That's a good record, but it's still only two minutes and nineteen seconds of 1955, and it's gonna have to be pushed.

"Listen, this is a very peculiar kind of time for us. Look at our radio play. We're getting four, five, six slots in the majors and the major secondaries, and it's very heady. It feels to me like its time to get back to the basics; we've got to keep the store reports coming in to those guys. It's like we've been in the cellar for years and we just signed Jabbar. If no one can bring the ball down court, he's not gonna score forty points."

After a brief interruption for the hoots and Bronx cheers his metaphor produced, the call went on with a report on the radio and newspaper ads for the succeeding week. Each touring act was supported in varying degrees, and though the regional managers made no suggestions about the overall commitment to any performer, they were quick to suggest the appropriate media for the advertisements. Russ Thyret then took the phone to announce that Tower of Power's "Urban Renewal" was going to be reserviced in conjunction with a single release and with some ad buys in black AM stations. "We've got a little problem with Tower, in that their management feels that we've dropped the ball on the R&B side. They came to us to move over to the pop side, and they're reasonably happy with that, but they feel they're not now being represented at the black one-stop and account level. What I want each of you guys to do during the week is to check out the heaviest black one-stop in your district and compare how many 'Urban Renewals' that account has sold versus the latest product from Rufus, Blue Magic, the Isleys, and Ohio Players. I want those figures first, and then I want you to find out that man's opinion on whether we're being adequately represented, on a sales level, in those black one-stops. I want that stuff ready for next week's call.

"I know," he said over a babble of protest that all the other groups he'd named had hits, "that they're all gonna have sold more than Tower has, but I want to see whether the spread is the same everywhere, or if we really have let them down. Finally, and this is the last thing from me before Ed takes over again, Brian Protheroe is in town here now, and is available for interviews, so you should talk with the artist relations guy in your neighborhood if you think there's something you'd like him to do. Dino has worked with him and says he's very cooperative. And now, he-e-e-ere's Eddie!"

"No applause? What's the matter with you guys? OK, let's go on with the February releases now. What's happening in Cleveland?"

"Right now Commander Cody looks very strong. I think we might be able to get some play on the single next week if we get a good jump in the charts. But even now, we're getting some progressive FM. Not much action yet on Emmylou, but there's good street talk, and we'll get some progressive on it. Everyone sort of likes Bonaroo, but it's gonna take action somewhere else, maybe San Francisco, before there's much movement here. For the rest, we've got so many star LPs this month that it sounds like I'm repeating myself—Robin Trower is so far the strongest. All the stations are working the shit out of it. Chris Christman is really the only negative."

"OK, Dino, what's LA–San Francisco look like?"

"Basically, I've got the same as Alan. The sleeper is Bonaroo, though. We're getting some airplay on it already. Good vibes from Emmylou, with a few first reorders. Obviously Cody, you've all got that. The two weakest are the Lenny Bruce reissue and Christman. I still have DJs in the stock-room on that one."

"Down here," said Murray Nagle from Dallas, "Emmylou Harris is gonna be the strongest. At Austin, in the live gig, she really stood out over Cody."

"I heard that," Barbis interrupted, "but wasn't that when Farlow couldn't sing at all? Out here, their album is looking very strong; it just has to be worked."

"Right," said Rosenblatt, "but the best way of working that album right now is to get the single played. It feels really good right now, so get those store displays out, and once the single starts happening, I think we're gonna bust the album wide open. OK, who's next? What's going on in Chicago?"

"Cody, Lightfoot, Wet Willie, and Trower all doing well, with Bonaroo and Emmylou starting to pick up. Dionne Warwick is getting some MOR play in Milwaukee and Minneapolis, so maybe we ought to try working that one on those stations. The Trower especially is getting real good airplay, and for the next week we're going to be concentrating on AM airplay for the Cody."

Alan came in from Cleveland again. "Yeah, we just got our first shot on WCUE yesterday and got the single added. And we've got a whole hour on the album in Buffalo coming up Sunday night. We've also got a few store displays set up, and I don't think we're gonna have any problems on this. And one other thing, a lot of FMs are going on the 'Willin'' cut from that album."

"OK. New York?"

"As far as the release is concerned, we're now in the second phase of layout, and I've got the same thing on Dionne Warwick that Cliff had in Chicago. NEW-AM was on it from the beginning. There's generally good reaction to Emmylou, and Bonaroo is wailing pretty good on the air. We came in kinda light on that one, because no one here knew anything about them, so we'll see what happens on next week's layout sheets and start looking around for reorders."

"Before you send us any more Bonaroo," cut in a voice from Philadelphia, "you should know that our salesmen feel as though they're short of Leo Sayer. They also feel that the Robin Trower reorder pattern looks very heavy, and that it's likely to be every bit as strong as the last album. We're also getting good reorders on the Lightfoot. Emmylou was a little slower starting, but we had one account take three hundred, then come back in less than a week with a reorder for a thousand. I really can't say much about Commander Cody yet. It's getting good airplay, but we haven't seen much reaction on the retail level. But the big word here is that Leo Sayer looks like it's busting out."

"All right, we'll make sure we get some fucking stock out on that one," said Rosenblatt, making a note to himself as he talked. "Boston?"

"The Bonaroo is getting some FM play up in Maine, but nothing at BCN yet. It's still pretty much of an educational process there. We don't have a lot of play on the Cody single yet, so the album is just out as an album. Out of the box, it's doing better than anything they've had in years.

We're doing an ad with U.S. Records, and they've taken three fifty each of Cody, Lightfoot, Wet Willie, Emmylou, and Trower to back it up, which is the best we've ever done with them."

"OK, it all sounds pretty good. Russ has some word on next week's singles now."

"Right, there'll be two new ones next week. We're pulling a second one, 'Willing to Learn,' off the Tower of Power album to see whether we can do something with it. And we've got a new Seals and Crofts." There was a chorus of moans at the last one, for many of the promotion men felt that Seals and Crofts were uncooperative and condescending. "Listen," said Thyret, "it's the title cut of their goddamn album, and they did just fine with 'Diamond Girl,' 'Unborn Child,' and 'Soft Summer Breeze.' Let's just go with it. And now the closing prayer from Doctor Rosenblatt."

"It all sounds very good out there, but I don't want any of you guys to get caught in the jackpot we got in with Leo Sayer, so these are the minimum reorders I want on the Emmylou album. We only shipped seventeen thousand of those to begin with, and if what I hear is right, it's gonna be a lot bigger than that, so let's get stock rolling on it." After listing a series of numbers, he continued, "Dionne Warwick is showing up lighter in your reports than I'd like to see. You ought all to push that MOR as well as black. Cody's coming in; Lightfoot and Trower look good. Right now we're so fucking hot—it's a pleasure to be in this situation. Especially after January. So let's just keep pushing, and we'll talk to you next week."

When the conference call ended, Rosenblatt stayed at his desk, rapidly flicking through the daily IBM sales report. After a few minutes he stopped and looked up: "You know, twenty years ago I was selling dresses in the garment district. And if I was a forty-year-old dress salesman now, I'd . . ." He shrugged. "This is just a great business, that's all. You can wear jeans and feel twenty." By the time of next week's conference call, he felt not only twenty, but better. "Don't Let Go" had climbed to number 90 on the *Billboard* chart, 92 in *Cashbox,* and 66 in *Record World,* and both *Billboard* and *Record World* had given it the all-important bullet, a clear indicator to program directors that the record was on the rise and worth adding to their playlists.

26

THE ENORMOUS AMOUNT of work being done on the Airmen's album and single by the promotion staff represented only part of Warner's effort. It had to be an illusion—there were, after all, dozens of other albums in the works—but it sometimes seemed as if the Airmen were the company's number-one priority. Sales, merchandising, editorial, publicity, and artist relations were all pushing the Airmen as well, and most of those activities fell under the aegis of Stan Cornyn.

Cornyn, Warner's senior vice president, was one of the few record executives to have achieved Dr. Hook's dream and seen his picture on the cover of *Rolling Stone*. To some extent, the magazine chose Cornyn because of Warner's close identification with San Francisco music, but he also belonged there because he was an artist in his own field. In addition to having charge of all the company's national advertising and publicity, he was responsible for knitting all the firm's divisions together, making sure that as little as possible fell through the cracks. With "Don't Let Go" apparently starting to move, Cornyn's role was critical.

Cornyn, who had been with Warner's since its earliest forays into the rock field, talked about what had made the company a success: "There were a whole series of things—FM, Monterey—that all conspired to make it the right time for a record company that wasn't intransigent. What we tried to do was make the company as flexible and as creative as our artists, even in little things. Like changing our art department from one that knew how to do record covers better than any performer to one that *suggests* alternatives. To say that the artist is automatically sensitive and accurate about the package of his project is absolutely false, but to say that the record company always knows best is equally silly.

"It's a little tricky trying to hold all that together in the midst of this economy. We're obviously concerned enough about what's going on in the business that we're taking a little bit more control of things, but basically I would a whole lot rather do what we're doing than get trapped in the rigid old attitudes that caused the semidownfall of so many record companies. Maybe it's just personal. I like the existential life, where one has to choose whether to take a next breath or not. And this"—he grinned —"is certainly the perfect business by those standards. Besides, every now and then, you get lucky. We certainly didn't sign Cody because we thought they'd do nice album covers, but look at it."

Though all Warner's signings are finally decided by Mo and Joe, Cornyn had been heavily involved in the decision to sign the Airmen. "The whole bidding war changed things only slightly. Any decent record company can figure out what an act will make, and will have the money in their pockets to pay for it. It turns out, I think, that finances aren't ever really the issue; it's what a band wants from a company. CBS can point to an excellent distribution system and a large, on the whole excellent, New York staff. Our strengths are in the success of our A&R staff, our creative and artist relations divisions—where we really work on *career* development, not just product development—and our own distribution system, which is as massive as CBS's. Plus, of course, we're a West Coast company.

"Those are reasons why they might want to choose us; there were also reasons that we looked toward them. Artistic considerations aside, we look at the financial and marketing side as well, because we're being asked to make a major commitment. The question finally is, 'Are we likely to be profitable in this situation?' The consensus on them was yes, though there is a policy that if one person feels strongly enough about signing an act, it can be signed regardless of negativism.

"With them, you start out knowing that there's a minimal downside risk, that there's not going to be a $200,000 developmental period. Also, the act has been known to break singles before, and the up side is quite exciting. Most important, they're not dependent on external factors, no reliance on one producer or one songwriter. To a company entering a long-term commitment, their being relatively self-contained and dependable is a big plus.

"Finally, and this relates to their upside potential, they don't sound quite like anyone else in the business. I mean it's not as bizarre as Tiny Tim, or anything like that, but they're certainly not at all like one of those identical bands that suddenly exploded behind the Kingston Trio. Besides, they ring bells in my head; they play the kind of music that got me involved in all this stuff to begin with. It's joyous, which is what I think music is all about.

"Now I clearly don't go around suggesting that we sign only acts I like—there'd be only about three if I did—and that's not my job. My job is to see that the art of the people we do sign meets the greatest possible public. There are patterns, certain things you do next in moving a band from 100,000 to 250,000, and we have all those down.

"Some of them are things that all record companies do—and that I find a disturbing pattern, actually—like depending on airplay. You can't sell anything else that way; you have to go out and *market* it. There was a time when we did that fairly well, at least partly because we had artists who couldn't get airplay. And we still, I think, do the non-airplay end of it better than anybody else, but we also put enormous effort into the relatively free exposure that comes from airplay. And when a KHJ goes on a record, we know what to do about it.

"What we do is fairly basic: get extra copies into the stores, so that people can buy it, and start telling other radio people that the great KHJ is on it. The first is just as important as the second—partly because a record could get played every ten minutes on the radio and we wouldn't get a dime from it unless it was in the stores, but also because if a program director puts it on, he's going to be examining how the record is doing in his market. If it's not in the stores, nothing can happen. So it's clearly our duty as a record company to be able to handle that.

"But mostly what we do is listen very hard to see if there's any kind of initial movement on an album. Every night, every promo man in the country calls a toll-free number and tells us what has gone on in his area that day. So do the regional managers, and so do the artist-relations people. In the morning, someone comes in and transcribes the tape-recorded messages, and by the time we get here, we've got a nationwide report on our desks. When we see something moving—when there's something in *this* piece of art that people are responding to—we then gear up to follow it."

For the Airmen's album, once the action began with "Don't Let Go," Cornyn's staff began designing a more intensive merchandising push. "It's not that there's a 'two-hundred-thousand-dollar treatment' or anything like that," he said, "just that you begin to get a sense that money spent promoting this particular item isn't going to be thrown away." As soon as "Don't Let Go" began to break, the merchandising department put out orders for two new items: an "ad-mini" featuring the single's title, and a "contains hit single" sticker to be applied to the album's shrink wrap.

Ad-minis, stickers, and the like are the province of Adam Somers, a bouncy, enthusiastic veteran of the Berkeley/San Francisco scene. "If it's a produced item—except for radio spots—it comes through this office," he said. Despite his deliberately funky appearance, Somers is a stickler for efficiency. Long before the Airmen's album had been released, he had prepared a series of merchandising aids, some of them routine, others less so.

The first batch of ad-minis were routine. "The basic problem, if you want to use a picture of an album in an ad, is that there's generally not enough tonal quality in it for the title to be visible. So we put together a package, in eighty-five- and sixty-five-line screens, of headlines, prices, captions, and a version of the album cover that has the title and a couple of tunes blown up big and spread across the top. That way it still looks like the album cover, so that people can recognize it when they go to the stores, but it's also readable for a guy who's going through the Sunday papers and stops to scan an ad from Licorice Pizza or Sam Goody's. When we did Cody's, we didn't know there was going to be a single—and certainly couldn't know that it was going to get this kind of amazing response—so the tunes we pulled out didn't include 'Don't Let Go.' Now, of course, we're doing a new bunch of minis with the single listed. When we do cooperative ads with record stores, we'll be able to make sure the single is plugged."

The in-store display, however, was special even to begin with. "Well, you start out with the idea that an in-store display isn't out of the question. These guys have sold records before, they have a track record. Anyway, that end of the job is really the creative and exciting part. I thought of taking the album art and stretching it out along the side of a big trailer truck. I mean, I was in Berkeley in sixty-eight, and the juxtaposition of that cosmic ozone stuff together with the most basic and functional piece of equipment you can imagine captures the whole gamut of their music. So we did that for a poster and for a hundred model trucks. They're almost a yard long—big enough to see, but small enough so our salesmen can handle them—and they make a great in-store item. From there, once we got the truck thing going, we came up with little glass trucks full of candy to send to the radio stations. It's not expensive, and it's the kind of thing that might sit on a program director's desk for three or four days until he takes it home to his kids. That's a part of building his consciousness of a band. But none of that is the kind of stuff you do for just any record, and I really wasn't going to do it until I met Kerr.

"When you hear him talk, it's like a record company dream come true. He really understands what's going on. When Kerr talks about their tour schedule, and you hear him listing their weak and strong markets, breaking it down into places where they can help us and places where we'll have to help them, you say, 'Shit, this is an organization I can spend money on and it's going to be maximized.' Let's face it, when somebody in my position is motivated to spend money on a group like Cody, it's because of the way the organization is presented.

"Like right now, for instance, we're really cutting back on T-shirts.

Everybody in the business has so many shirts already that it just doesn't seem worth the expense to us, except in special cases. Well, they really want some T-shirts for their own purposes, and when Rick Higginbotham came down and explained why, it sounded like a good idea to me. What I decided to do was to give them the color separations so that they could reproduce the album cover, which I think is a classier graphic than the one they were going to use, and agree to take sixteen dozen shirts for us to use. Put together with what they were going to get for themselves anyway, that makes a large enough order so that they can get a real good discount. I guess partly I said yes because everybody around here was so hot on the band, but also it's that they're reasonable people who know the difference between demanding and asking.

"I'll tell you this. There's other people I wouldn't go across the street for. I've got an eleven o'clock this morning with an organization that's the complete opposite of Cody. Seals and Crofts, man, and they suck tit. It's all cousins and wives and aunts and uncles who just show up with a list of 'gimmies.' And when you go out of your way for them, they never give the company credit for what it's doing."

Among the ways that Somers kept track of what Warner's was doing, whether for the Airmen or for Seals and Crofts, was a computerized mailing system through which his merchandising materials were delivered. "It used to be," he said, "that we just shipped everything to the branches, which is really what Stanley calls 'singing into a dead mike.' The only way we could ever tell whether stuff got used—or whether it ever even got out of the salesman's trunk so that stores could think about using it—was to go out and physically inspect the stores. Well, that's obviously pretty crazy, and Stanley came up with the idea for DMS."

Direct mail service begins with a computerized file listing every important record outlet in the country, the categories of records it carries, those that have windows, those that have walls, those that use rack dividers with performers' names on them, and other basic information. It also includes key radio-station personnel (and those T-shirt sizes), and may eventually be expanded to include the thousand or so rock reviewers on the publicity department's lists. Instead of bulk deliveries to the WEA branches, most of Somers's materials now go directly to the point at which they are to be used. "It took two years and a lot of money to develop," said Cornyn, but both he and Somers thought the system was worth it.

"I think in the long run," Somers explained, "it's gonna save us money in production costs. Instead of sending out a whole lot of stuff wholesale, we get it right to the places that can use it. All of them, and only them. I mean, there's no sense sending out posters to a store that has racks in the middle of the floor, miles away from any wall.

"More to the point, once we've sent it out, we know they're getting it.

No more overproducing stuff that never gets out of the branches. And we can do specialized projects too. Suppose the Cody starts getting country airplay; at that point we can just punch up labels to send stuff to the major country record stores. Finally, the system gives us enormous credibility with our own branches. If somebody says they want twenty-three posters in Cleveland, we can be sure that they're on the way. And the best thing about it—if you can get into this—is that we've really reduced the time for getting an idea—say, a new Cody poster—off the boards and into the record stores. I mean, I don't like to sound like I'm bragging, but it's the best damn system in the business."

The way the system worked on the Airmen's album was that Commander Cody bumper stickers, candy trucks, and in-store posters were shipped as samples to, as Somers's memo put it, "All Regional Marketing Managers, Branch Managers, Sales Managers, Salesmen, Junior Salesmen, Promotion Men, Marketing Coordinators, Regional Artists Relations People, Regional R&B Men and Designated Home Office Executives," during the week of February 7. The following week, posters and candy trucks were shipped in the proper numbers of retail and one-stop outlets and to key radio stations. During that same week the promo men received their bulk supplies of candy trucks and bumper stickers, while each regional marketing manager received ten of the large trucks for in-store displays. For a new band on the label, it was a rather elaborate and expensive merchandising operation, and there was really no way of knowing whether it sold any additional records. "I certainly don't *know* that it does much of anything," said Somers. "It's definitely not as important as airplay, but what it does do is tell all those people out there in the branches that we think this is an important act, otherwise we wouldn't spend this kind of money on them. What that means is that maybe they don't think of this as just another February release, but as *the* February release."

The Airmen received the same kind of push from the company's editorial department, under the leadership of Pete Johnson, a former Los Angeles music critic who had gotten Warner's interested in the Airmen some years earlier. In addition to preparing advertising copy for all local and national ads, the editorial division published a weekly newsletter that was circulated through radio stations, merchants, journalists, and the company itself. *Circular,* which had been rolling along for almost seven years by the time the Airmen's album came out, was subtitled "a weekly news device," and was another offshoot of Cornyn's creative services division. Like the series of newspaper ads that first portrayed Warner's as a company with an ability to laugh at itself (and not-so-incidentally provided alternative exposure for performers like Frank Zappa and the Fugs, whom many radio stations at first shied away from), *Circular* was cheekily irreverent about most aspects of the music business. "I just throw away most of the stuff I get from record companies," said one journalist, "but I always end up actually reading *Circular*." Along with regular features like Ruby Monday's gossip column and Dr. Demento's contest, the February 17 edition had a four-page spread on the Airmen, another signal that the company was solidly behind the band.

The article featured Frayne's coming out of the closet about Kellaway's part in making the album, though his memory of it was perhaps a bit colored by wishfulness: "One track has an unusual story," Frayne told the interviewer. "When the band recorded 'House of Blue Lights,' I was back East on a promotional tour. Since the tune uses a lot of piano, they needed someone to build an arrangement around. So they flew Roger Kellaway up from Los Angeles to help on the work track. I was to come in and redo the piano part later, erasing Roger. I'm pretty lazy, and since all left-handed boogie parts sound pretty much the same, when I came back we wound up just adding my right hand. So on that one tune, I'm playing the right-hand part and Roger Kellaway's is the left hand."

All these activities combined with the single's increasing airplay to fire up the branches, creating a balance between what Cornyn self-deprecatingly described as "sale's 'shove and muscle' style and our effete creative approach. What we're aiming for," he said, "is to get the album to the point where the branches are really on it. They start to smell blood and really go out to kill. They're into saturation . . . tonnage. It's in-and-out stuff, but that's exactly what it should be. You don't want your salesmen to be aesthetes."

Certainly twenty-nine-year-old Russ Thyret, the director of Warner's sales activities, didn't conjure up images of quiet contemplation. Redheaded and modestly paunchy, he always looked as though he were hurrying off to the latest fraternity beer party. The image was enhanced considerably by his office, whose walls were thickly plastered with stickers and posters from scores of Warner's acts, spilling over to cover a huge refrigerator from which he regularly offered beer to his visitors, and by the sounds that emerged from it. Thyret worked in the middle of an almost palpable layer of sound. When he was not playing his special favorite among the latest Warner's records, he was tuned to an AM radio toward which he would shout encouragement every time it had the good taste to play his company's product. At one point, when "Don't Let Go" came on, he started to laugh. "That's amazing, that record is really amazing. I mean, I wouldn't tell this to Joe Kerr, because I'd like him to go on thinking we're as wonderful as we think we are, but we didn't do *anything* on that record. Nothing. It just took off all on its own, and I gotta tell you, it's as hot as any record I've seen since I've been here. With the kind of airplay it's getting, this thing could be a monster. And we really didn't have anything to do with it. It's just that those guys have worked so fucking hard over the years that everybody knows them. They've been on the road *forever,* and all people needed was a little excuse to go on their record. If we can just get it into the stores fast enough, Joe Kerr is going to love us forever."

Getting the product into the stores was Thyret's responsibility, and despite his self-deprecating comments about his work on "Don't Let Go," he was actually using his full range of stick-and-carrot incentives. "You've gotta understand what salesmen are. Salesmen—and promo men too, for that matter—are the last anarchists. They go into the business because they really like to stand on their own two feet. So you can't really tell them what to do, because if they were the kind of people who just followed orders, you wouldn't want them as salesmen to begin with. That means a lot of what we do here is just listen to them. Some people will tell you that they're just delivery men, but that's not true. If there's a record that's got something going for it that we've missed, one of them is going to find it. The thing that makes us different from other companies, I like to think, is that when one of our guys gets movement on a record, we really respond to what he's telling us and support him with time-buys on the radio and anything else that seems useful.

"Also, because these guys are such individualists, we try to play on the individual accomplishment thing. You know, we have lots of contests and prizes and stuff like that. And we have the occasional save-your-job contest too. But it's all out front, and they dig it. Right is right and wrong is wrong, and if you're honest with your people, it's gonna come back to you. If you try and trick them, that'll come back too.

"But still," he went on, "a lot of the motivation talk is just bullshit. Most of the time, our guys sell because they like to. They get off on it. And they know that we'll reward them for chasing a feel when they get it. So most of my time is spent on the phone. On each month's release, for instance, each album must have some plan in every district; 'I didn't get to Emmylou Harris' doesn't cut it. Three weeks after release, I get a detailed report from all the branches, that they've done and what they plan. At that point, we begin the second part of our marketing.

"Most of the national advertising is set up well in advance, and it's not gonna change unless there's really something special. But that's Cornyn's end; we have half the company's advertising budget over here, and we spend it either to push an act that's started to show some response or to help out an account that's giving us good service. It's a day-to-day thing for us. For instance, when Bonnie Bramlett's solo album came out, we began to get a decent response to it. We'd been a little light to begin with, so when the response began to come in, we ran ads—twenty-four or thirty-six spots—on *every* important FM station in the country. Well, with all that money, and all the talk about it, that album would be on fire now if it was going to go anywhere. It isn't.

"Still, there's some response, so you support it where she's touring or where it was going already. You kind of nurture it and wait for the next one. Conversely, if *nothing* happened to it, you'd get off it immediately. There's a lot of intuition in it, and sometimes we guess wrong. Now you take Foghat"—he leafed through a series of computer outputs—"they're the hardest-working English band I've ever seen—most of those guys are just incredibly fucking lazy—and we've spent a fortune on them, but this album has leveled out just where the last one did. Three hundred thousand units and they're done. So I've got to tell their management that we're going off it.

"Sometimes, of course, it works the other way. Maria Muldaur did two albums for us before this one, and both died the day they were released. So this one, we put out maybe eight thousand pieces. Next thing you know, it's 'Midnight at the Oasis' all over the radio, and we're sitting there with no records and no paper to wrap them in. We went *crazy* for a month. But most of the time, that doesn't happen. When you put an album out, you only have one chance to guess wrong; either you do too many or too few. If you're lucky, you can get in trouble twice—once on its release, once when the single hits. Ninety percent of album sales are FM and word-of-mouth, but if you get a single going into top-ten rotation, the whole thing just explodes. The problem is guessing ahead of time what's going to happen. If it hits and you don't have stock, you're in trouble. But if you guess wrong and overship, then you're gonna have returns coming out your ass for the next six months. In some ways, it's easier with a single. The lead time is shorter, mostly because you don't have all that packaging to worry about, and the ratios are clearer. You know almost exactly how many singles to lay out if you go into top-ten rotation at KHJ. It's all mathematics on singles; albums are more gut-level.

"The one thing that bothers me about 'Don't Let Go' is that its sales figures aren't quite as high as I'd expect them to be given the airplay. I think the record is great, and so do most of the people around here, but I have an instinct that it might really be a program director's record, that it appeals to people of our age more than it does to the kids who buy singles. I'm watching the layouts on it pretty carefully, because we're going to have to make a decision on how many albums to press within the next couple of weeks."

Thyret's misgivings may well have been sound, but the next week's charts indicated a steady climb for the record. It was bulleted in all three trades, ranking 79 in *Billboard,* 77 in *Cashbox,* and 56 in *Record World.* The album also appeared bulleted in all three, at 133 in *Billboard,* 152 in *Cashbox,* and 105 in *Record World.* Even more important, given what Thyret had said about the company's listening to its field people, was the report from the Atlanta marketing manager: "WHOO (Orlando) and

WSUN (St. Petersburg), two C&W stations, went on CC. We've also had
C&W response in Nashville and Atlanta to the extent that I feel we should
service the single to C&W stations throughout the market. If we can get
Pop, FM, and Country airplay on this record, we could have a million
seller."

27

EVEN WITH the promise of an unanticipated success with "Don't Let Go," Warner's did not confine its efforts to pushing the single—or even the album. Its artist relations department was looking not only at this particular project, but at the Airmen's longer-term development. "The whole artist relations trip exists," said Ron Goldstein, "because there's a lack of good managers and agents in the industry. What artist relations tries to do is supplement a manager's skills and build a complementary relationship with him.

"With some people it can get pretty hairy, but with a guy who's as solidly established as Kerr is, it really shouldn't be any problem at all. He really knows how we can help him, and he's not uptight about it. He's aware, for instance, that they've got a relatively weak agency booking them. Now they may change— and we're hoping that they do, frankly—but until then, Regehr can really be helpful. He can put together tours and packages in a way that only the really heaviest agents can. And right now, for instance, Joe is looking for TV exposure, but he doesn't have any LA contacts. That's the kind of way that we can help too. It's not that we're taking anybody's authority away or anything like that. It's just that there's a real need."

Another Warner's executive described the role of artist relations in a somewhat less altruistic way: "When we've got a quarter of a million dollars invested in a bunch of high-school kids, do you think we want to watch their management piss it away? Sometimes Regehr is just helpful, that's true, but a lot of times he's protecting acts from their own managers. We'd be crazy to stand by and see a potentially profitable act break up because no one knows what to do when something goes sour."

The second explanation for Warner's taking on the activist role is more persuasive than the first, but many industry observers are bothered by it. "What they're going to do, unless they're careful," said the manager of another Warner's act, "is overturn the whole structure of the business. Traditionally, we've all been independent contractors. We produce records and sell them to the highest bidder, usually on a contract basis. We do concerts on the same basis. Sure there are people we really like to work for, but my job is to send the band where the money is. But what they're trying to do is turn the whole thing around. If they had their way, they'd just put bands on straight salary and move them around like chess pieces. You know, 'Hey, you guys have something going in the Portland market, so we've put you in the Club Horseshit for a week,' and stuff like that. What they don't understand is that a lot of these guys are in this business precisely because they don't want anyone else making their decisions for them."

Doubts about Warner's methods were also expressed by those in the concert end of the music industry. There, though final approval for any act's appearances obviously rests with their manager, day-to-day business is carried out by booking agents and independent promoters. Booking agencies range from large, multicity organizations like International Famous Artists (which handles, among others, America, the Beach Boys, Jefferson Starship, Hot Tuna, Chicago, and Loggins and Messina) to tiny operations that shuffle pickup bands between weddings and bar mitzvahs. Similarly, their clients range from fathers of the bride to the promoters who book major concerts all over the country.

Agents and promoters need each other, and over the years have developed their own ways of working together. An agent seeking to fill a hole on a band's cross-country tour may ask a local promoter to do him a favor and present a band during the middle of the week rather than on the more attractive weekend dates. The promoter may well say yes, if helping the agent out means that he can get another of that agent's acts to fill one of his own weekend holes. Each of them has an interest in making a deal, and if the deal is right, they both will make money. The agent will get 10 percent of the band's fee, and the promoter will pocket the differences between his expenses and his ticket sales.

Both are aware that concerts sell records, but they don't care much. They are also aware that records sell concerts, and they fear that the record companies' invasion of their traditional turf may upset the agent-promoter dialogue that has served them well. "I certainly haven't had any trouble with Warner's," said concert promoter Howard Stein. "They've actually been very helpful in supporting our concerts, but I have heard of them putting pressure on other people, particularly smaller ones. A guy will think he has a deal, then he'll get called back and hear that he's got it only if he agrees to take a specific opening act—or worse yet, if he agrees to do another concert in the future with some totally different group that maybe he's going to get his brains beat out on.

"Now agents do that all the time, but that's different. In the first place, there are only about half a dozen significant agencies in the country, and you're dealing with them all the time anyway. You both sort of sit down knowing what the rules are. When this kind of thing happens—and it hasn't happened to me, mind you—you're not dealing with anyone. The agent can't book without the manager's OK, and the company is leaning on the manager. You're out there trying to put a show together, but there's no one to talk to. Of course packages get put together all the time, but they get put together in negotiations, not when one guy who isn't even in the room—and who doesn't have anything to lose—has a veto over whatever goes on."

Industry misgivings notwithstanding, Warner's approach seems to be the wave of the future, because more and more companies are expanding the traditional hand-holding role of their artist relations departments to include functions that are established routines at Warner's. "It used to be," said a Mercury publicist, "that the typical artist relations guy was someone with a cast-iron stomach and a plastic nose that you'd send out to party with the band when they came into town. As far as I understand, that's one of the roles that David Wynshaw played at CBS before he got busted. But no one can afford to do that anymore. In the first place, there's the grand jury scare, and when those investigators come in, the first place they go is artist relations. But more important than that, the honeymoon is over. We're in the middle of one big recession, and no one can sit still and see an act get fucked behind bad management. Except in some rare cases, a band is usually into its third album before the company begins to see its money coming back. It's just irresponsible for a company not to step in and develop an act on its own when it sees something going wrong."

In the Airmen's case, Joe Kerr was not bothered by fears that the company was taking on too large a role. "I've been waiting for years to see a record company take some interest in this band. These guys have done more for us in three months than Famous did in three years." He paused. "Besides, what have they done for us that we wouldn't have done ourselves if we could? When you've got someone with their kind of power on your side, you go with it. You're a chump if you don't."

Perhaps Kerr was a special case. Even David Berson, who had earlier argued within the company that one reason for withdrawing the offer he'd originally made to the Airmen was their weak management, was moved to admiration. "You know the phrase 'working a building'?" he asked. "Well, Joe Kerr works a building better than anyone else in this business. He doesn't push, or anything like that, just sits around and talks with you for a while, and the next thing you know, you're doing a little something extra for his act. Then he leaves you and goes and does the same thing in the next office. Everybody talks about the power of the record companies, but let me tell you something. Kerr might as well be chairman of the board here. He's got this whole fucking place working their asses off for him. And I still haven't quite figured out how he does it."

Another manager put Berson's remarks in perspective: "Kerr's good, all right, but you've gotta realize that Berson's gonna be saying nothing but marvelous things about Kerr. Kerr's got a hot act, and Berson fucked him. If this record keeps going the way it has, guess who's gonna be in a position to get even.

"Besides, every manager who's not crazy works the building. You don't go into your company with any kind of formal agenda up front, because then you're negotiating. And if they think you're negotiating, then they've gotta play tough. But if you're just kind of wandering around and asking for a little bit here, a little bit there . . . shit, they've gotta give you *some-thing*."

Typical or not (and inappropriate as it might have been during the Airmen's tense moments with ABC), Kerr's relaxed approach seemed perfect for Warner's. The artist relations department was working hard for the Airmen. Regehr had assigned primary responsibility for their first post-signing tour to George Gerrity, an amiable hippie who had fled CBS because of its "unlovely traits" to join the more congenial environment at Warner Brothers. In many ways, he was the perfect choice. Kerr and Hessenius had spent a great deal of time in Burbank and had grown familiar with the company, but the Airmen themselves had been exposed only to Berson, whom they most emphatically did not like. Gerrity was another story. "He doesn't seem LA at all," said Bruce Barlow.

Had their first serious Warner's contact been a platform-shoed hustler, their relationship with the company would have started on—well, the wrong foot. Hence, after a successful "tryout" in Sausalito, Regehr pulled Gerrity off his regular West Coast beat early in February and dispatched him to join the band in Texas.

The initial contact had taken place at the Sausalito Record Plant, where the band responded to Warner's request to record a "live" concert for KSAN, a Metromedia station that was San Francisco's major progressive rock outlet. KSAN did a regular weekly series of such broadcasts, generally featuring a group that was on tour in the area, but the Airmen, as perennial local favorites, were also made to order for the station. The "live" concert gimmick had begun some years earlier, and was firmly established as a staple of progressive programming. It further distinguished the FM stations from their tight-playlist competitors on the AM band, and in multi-station listening areas it provided an edge to the station that was able to present the most interesting packages. It was also, from the record companies' perspective, a solid hour's exposure to bands with new product. At Warner's, responsibility for all radio and TV specials, as distinct from regular airplay, was the province of artist relations.

"This one was real easy to do," said Gerrity. "Everyone up there knows and likes them, and the band is at least as good live as it is on most of its records. There are lots of times when you want a band to do something like this, but you don't quite trust them not to screw it up, or not to sound just plain lousy compared to what they can do in the studio. But this was great. And besides giving it to KSAN, we were able to distribute copies of the tapes—after their broadcast—to about twenty other smaller stations. And most of them gobbled it up, too."

The local "live" tape gimmick, with all its free promotional advantages, was beginning to wear thin, because several national syndicators were providing similar programs, and some stations were choosing these over locally generated programming. The nationals had several advantages, including wide distribution, which allowed them to get big-name groups that were unlikely to submit to repeated live tapings across the country; such bands consequently could be sold to the stations as rating boosters. Perhaps even more important, many of the syndicated shows came with presold sponsorship. The 3M company (for its Scotch brand recording tape) and Clairol shampoos regularly sponsored the King Biscuit Flower Hour, a concert show that ran every other week on more than a hundred FM stations, and Toyota underwrote an interview-cum-record show called "Innervisions" for ninety minutes each week. In addition, of course, local commercials could be fit in around station breaks. "We took the Cody," said the manager of a northern California station, "because they perform around here a lot, and they've got a decent following. Besides, they're kind of outrageous live, and that's the image we like to project. But for every one of those tapes we use from a record company, we get maybe five or six. The same week that we got the Cody, some promo man was beating the shit out of me to put on a Golden Earring show. Golden Earring, for Chrissake. We play their single a lot, but nothing else they do sounds anything like it. If I put on an hour of them, I'd have everybody in the market watching reruns of 'Hawaii Five-O.' But those guys don't understand that. They're giving you a chance to alienate half your audience, and they come on like they're goddamn Santa Claus. They're more like Typhoid Mary." But despite the radio stations' increasing leeriness about being "used," Gerrity's travels on the first part of the Airmen's promotional tour brought a live simulcast of one of their concerts from Houston, as well as a handful of interviews. Three important Texas stations broadcast the KSAN "live" tape just after the Airmen's Texas swing.

After a week in Texas, the band had a night off, then worked for two nights in Arizona before taking a day to travel to the most important stop on the first leg of the tour, a four-night stand at the Troubadour. It was also the only stop on the tour that they didn't want to make. "Those people suck," said Frayne succinctly.

"Right," Kirchen agreed, "their idea of gettin' real funky is prewashed denim from Paris." The people of whom they were talking, however, were the West Coast music industry. The Troubadour was theoretically a night club like any other, but it essentially belonged to the music industry. Acts that could have played in larger halls performed there regularly, showcasing their latest work for audiences dominated by music-business figures. The Troubadour was the "in" place. Its owner, Doug Weston, reported that on an average night, as much as half the audience were there as guests of whatever record company owned the headline act.

"Of *course* it's a terrible place," said Gerrity, "but do you think you're going to get Elton John to drop by and see you at a giant place like the Forum? He'd get mobbed. The thing about the Troubadour is that it feels like a private club. We put Randy Newman and Wendy Waldman there and it was great. It really felt like home. Of course Newman really gets off on a quiet audience that's part of all the in jokes and stuff like that. Cody is different. The drunker and crazier the audience gets, the better they get. I think they're gonna do all right here, but it's a risk. Everybody says, 'They've *got* to play the Troub',' but I would've put them out in the Palomino with Emmylou and let people who really wanted to hear them take their chances."

To some extent, the Airmen felt the same way. "There are two things wrong with the Troubadour," said Frayne. "First of all, Weston's a prick. He's making money like crazy from the record companies, and his dressing rooms are still pieces of shit. But the other thing is the audience. They don't come to hear *us*. They come because it's the Troubadour. So we just go out and give our show, and even if we're good—which we sometimes are—and they get off on us, they're embarrassed. They don't think they should *like* the music; they think they should just kind of be cool and watch it. The last time we were here, man, the record company wasn't doing much for us, and some people snuck in who came to hear the music, and the show was great. Everybody was up and screaming, you know. So the next day the *Los Angeles Times* came out and said we were a crude and revolting bunch of drunks. Los Angeles is the worst place in the whole fucking world." Nevertheless, the Airmen desperately wanted to be good when they played there.

Partly, of course, the band simply felt the need to prove themselves to an audience they'd never reached. As Farlow put it, "There's a whole bunch of people who think that you've gotta have dry ice and glitter and all that shit to be a band. Well, we don't use any of that crap, and we're just gonna be the best band they ever heard anyway." But their desire was also rooted in their recognition of commercial reality. There may be bands of such stature that they can go over the heads of the industry and the critics to reach their audiences directly, but the Airmen were emphatically not on that level. "It pisses me off," said Frayne, "to know that we could play for all our lives in bars, really getting people off on what we do, but unless we come in here and play LA to the LA folks, we might as well not exist."

And so they had prepared for the Troubadour shows very carefully. Farlow, whose voice had ranged from scratchy to nonexistent during the latter part of the Texas and Arizona tours, had simply not sung on those dates, instead saving his voice for the Troubadour. "I probably could've sung, you know, even at kind of half-strength, but I wouldn't have had anything left for these shows." Gerrity, who had been traveling with the band, had called ahead to the Burbank offices to make sure that one of Los Angeles' best throat doctors was available to see Farlow as soon as the Airmen arrived.

"That's part of what you do," he explained. "I didn't know if he'd really need a doctor or not, but I knew for sure that someone in the office would know exactly who the best doctor was and have enough clout to make sure that he gave Billy an appointment. We can do that sort of thing for our acts. There's certainly no way you could expect a typical road manager to know the best throat doctor in Duluth, but we do." The artist relations department knew a lot more than that about Duluth. It had prepared a guide (originally for Warner's acts only, but later for general publication) called Book of the Road, which in addition to such vital information about concert halls as the dimensions of their electric power and loading doors, listed selected restaurants, hotels, musical instrument shops, and local entertainment for cities all over the world. A brief measure of what life on the road is like is that it also listed V.D. clinics and the office of the local Civil Liberties Union.

In addition to his clearly functional activities, Gerrity was also charged with holding the band's collective hand during their preshow nervousness. From the time the Airmen arrived at the Ramada Inn on Sunset Boulevard, Gerrity was with them. Never ostentatious, he was simply there. "It's really a kind of silly job sometimes," he said. "Particularly with a bunch of guys like this. I mean, they've been around for a lot longer than I have, and they're pretty relaxed. They're not your typical high-school band.

"But sometimes it's almost like they know too much. It's only because they have been around that they understand what the Troub' is like. You'd get other people who aren't as smart or experienced just wandering in there like it was just another gig. But not these guys. I mean, I don't know

George that well or anything, but I've never seen him this nervous about anything. So mostly I just sit around and get loaded with them and tell them that everything will be all right. Which it will, because I also told them that we've bought up almost all the tickets for opening night anyway."

Nevertheless, opening night was as tense as the opening night of a Broadway show. On the face of it, it seemed ridiculous that performers who worked more than two hundred nights a year in towns all over the country could have an "opening night," but performances in Los Angeles and New York invariably take on that aura.

Before the show, as the band gathered backstage at the Troubadour, Kerr was the host (or tried to be, because Warner Brothers ended up covering the check) of a dinner at the Italian restaurant next door to the club. On nights like this, the restaurant was itself an extension of the private-club ambience, and throughout the dinner people patted Kerr's back and muttered good wishes as they passed his table. Producers, company presidents, publicists—all stopped to say something, and all of them made Kerr increasingly nervous. He responded by talking constantly, and he and Magna Artists' Ron Rainey manically swapped reminiscences of various disasters and high points in the Airmen's history. Across the table from Rainey, Ron Goldstein was polite but little more, for he had been urging Kerr to switch booking agencies. Hessenius too was nervous, and spent a fair amount of time bouncing up and down to go to the men's room. As show time came closer the conversation became more intense, drawing Boylan, Hunt, and Faralla into the maelstrom. Finally, after a brief flurry of attempted check paying a few minutes before the show was to start, the table adjourned and moved next door.

The Troubadour was hot, smoky, and packed, with a line for the second show's few remaining tickets already forming before the first had started. Kerr and his entourage slipped in a side door and passed through the crowded bar in relative anonymity. Although various people nodded greetings to Kerr and Goldstein, the supportive comments were mostly directed at Boylan, because this was much more his territory than Kerr's. Despite the Troubadour's flash, many of the people who stopped him to talk seemed genuinely glad to see him and truly delighted over his success with the Airmen.

Boylan probably needed the lift. His producing skills had taken a public beating during the past month. In addition to producing Linda Ronstadt's early solo albums, Boylan had been her lover and manager as well. When her most recent album took off, any number of reviewers had commented that she "at last" had a producer instead of a boy friend at the console, and credited her success at least partly to that change. Boylan was stung by the implied criticism, and if prompted was quick to point out that he had been a producer long before he'd met her, but such statements sounded like sour grapes, especially when Ronstadt herself repeated the charge to several interviewers. To hear "Don't Let Go" booming over his car radio was a tonic for Boylan. It proved that he could take an act that had failed under other producers and put it on the charts. At least some of the music-business figures at the Troubadour that night were there in tacit support of Boylan.

Most of them, however, were there because they smelled success. As a result of the KHJ play, "Don't Let Go" was already on the move in LA and seemed on its way to national top-ten status, so the hangers-on who might otherwise have skipped the Airmen's engagement felt obliged to show up. If the band had still been struggling along without record-company support and without a single on the charts, the success followers either would not have been there or would have been coolly cynical, but this crowd was eager to share in the Airmen's success. They were not just another band; they were—implausibly enough, but there it was on the charts—the latest hot band, and the prewashed denims had turned out to pay homage. Success, after all, is no less worshiped in the music industry than in politics, sports, or any other American pastime.

The Airmen's dressing room was crowded with well-wishers bearing powdered offerings, and when the band reached the stage, the opening applause was much more enthusiastic than the merely polite reception they'd anticipated. Throughout the set the crowd's response built, fired by a guest appearance by Emmylou Harris and the arrival of Renée Armand and Ronee Blakley (of *Nashville* fame) as backup singers on "Don't Let Go." But it was at best only an average performance. Farlow, whose voice was still off form, essayed only a couple of tunes, and to people familiar with the band, Hagar seemed to be having an off night.

When the Airmen returned to the dressing room they were at once relieved, disappointed, and somewhat contemptuous. As he stood in the crowded dressing room, Frayne said, "These people don't care what we play. They just care that we're hot, that's all. If we didn't have all the hype going for us right now they wouldn't even be here. They would've been throwing things at us if we'd played like this at the Armadillo. And hit or no hit, they would've been right. That's why I hate playing in LA, man. If they think they should stand up and scream 'Boogie,' they'll do it whether you're playing shitty or not. There's about as much honesty here as there is meat in a burrito."

The backstage hubbub rolled on as before, and strangers as well as old friends dropped by to say, "Great set," before disappearing. (A few stayed longer, and when a Troubadour employee poked his head in the door to ask Higginbotham if all these people were all right with him, Higginbotham said, 'Sure.' After a quick head count, the employee disappeared downstairs, but the people he'd counted were all charged admission for the second show and the total deducted from the Airmen's check at the end of their Troubadour engagement.)

The second set was somewhat better and certainly more relaxed, with Frayne screaming out his "Commie. . . . pinko . . . butt-fucker" introduction to "Hot Rod Lincoln." It got an even stronger audience response, but the Airmen were still not happy. "It's something in the air," said Barlow. "We're allergic to this place."

The next day, however, as they stumbled off their bus into the middle of a nineteenth-century town, the band had what they agreed was their first pleasant Los Angeles experience in a half-dozen years of touring. Goldstein and Gerrity had come up with the idea of introducing the Airmen to the Warner's office staff by having a picnic in their honor. The party, nineteenth-century town and all, was staged in a back lot of the Warner's film studios. It brought together the Airmen's traveling circus and the hitherto faceless collection of record company figures who were pushing their album. "What does it cost?" asked Goldstein rhetorically. "Three hundred bucks for beer and pizza? That's cheap, and no one does anything around here on Friday afternoon anyway."

The high spot of the event was supposed to be a volleyball game between the Airmen ("Commander Cody's Fists of Fury," as Kirchen modestly named them) and a Warner's team, but the activity around the volleyball net, which the merchandising department had mysteriously procured from somewhere, either degenerated or escalated into a cheerful pickup match with people playing on no particular side. It was a metaphor for the relationship between the company and the band; whatever happened to the record was so intertwined that neither group could take responsibility for it alone.

As the Warner's staff gradually drifted back to their offices, burping contentedly, the Airmen wandered through the remaining film sets, spending most of their time in Shangri-La. "We came here for the pizza and ended up in paradise," said Kirchen. Then, with a grin, "Now talk about your metaphors . . ."

28

Standing in the midst of a glorious "lost city," Kirchen and the others were entitled to their enthusiasm, but Los Angeles was not a land of milk and honey for the Airmen. Pushing the record required work, not only the two-shows-a-night grind at the Troubadour but, for Frayne, visits to radio stations to chat with disc jockeys and program directors. The exhausting routine, which for most of the band routinely included too much drinking, was followed by afternoons of generally boring recuperation. Some of the Airmen had taken advantage of Los Angeles' proximity to Marin and the rare chance to stay in one place for four days at a stretch to bring their wives down, but generally the motel in Los Angeles was indistinguishable from any of the hundreds of other motels they'd collapsed in during their years of touring. Tichy spent his afternoons sitting by the pool and studying a mathematics text. "I always have a project to work on during a tour," he explained. "Otherwise I'd get crazy." But many of the Airmen hung out in their rooms, watching afternoon movies on television and smoking dope.

On one such afternoon, Frayne wandered into Higginbotham's to look for a newspaper and found three or four Airmen sitting complacently wrecked in front of an old war movie. Gerrity, who seemed to have an endless supply with him, had provided enough dope to render everyone pleasantly comatose, and no one had the energy to do much more than nod at Frayne, "Jesus," he said, looking around at the bodies, "I thought *my* room was the boring room."

The first review of the Troubadour appearance had not done much to energize the band. The *Los Angeles Times* had sent its second-string critic, who had panned the Airmen's last appearance viciously. This time, though the review was basically favorable, the overall tone was grudging, as reflected in its opening paragraph: "Possibly because it's simply becoming a tighter, more confident musical aggregation, perhaps because the Troubadour engagement allows it the opportunity to emphasize aspects other than the crude and raucous, Commander Cody and the Lost Planet Airmen seemed more interested in musical credibility than in clowning around during its opening set on Thursday."

Frayne skimmed the review and said, "Tremendous, I'll have him send my mother a note that I've stopped chewing with my mouth open."

As the Airmen heaved their equipment into the bus for the drive to the Montana engagement that would end the first phase of the promotional tour, there was a stronger spot of good news: the Warner's promo department reported the first signs of East Coast movement for "Don't Let Go." It looked as though their East Coast swing would be perfectly timed.

The new album and the new company had gone a long way toward making it easier for the band to get bookings, and for the first time in six months there were no awkward zig zags or low-priced fill-ins on the swing. Though the concert business was still reeling from the effects of the recession, the Airmen, at least for the duration of "Don't Let Go," were a hot attraction. Their success had come along none too soon, for the bottom had fallen out of the concert business during the fall of 1974. Hundred-dollar-a-night bar bands could find work, and superstar concerts were still obligatory events that sold out as regularly as ever. But middle-level bands like the Airmen were in trouble. The record industry, partly because of a one-dollar hike in retail album prices, seemed to be weathering the economic storm, but the live performance market was weak. Even a hit record was no guarantee of success for mid-level performers. At a time when Billy Joel's second CBS album was winging up the charts, he drew only 739 people to a 7000-seat auditorium in Nebraska and only 400 to a 3400-seat hall in Minneapolis two days later. Even traditionally strong concert markets like Boston, with its large concentration of college students, were hurting. The Souther, Hillman, Furay Band, with a top-three album, grossed only $6,000 of a possible $18,000 at Boston's Orpheum, leaving the promoter at least that much in the red.

"You have to understand," said Howard Stein, who books acts in a score of cities, including New York, "we're the last entrepreneurs. When I make a deal with an agent for $20,000 for some band, that band *knows* it's gonna make twenty. And when the agent hangs up the phone, he knows he's made two. And the manager knows he's made *his* two, or maybe four. The people who run the hall know what they're gonna get. The sound companies, the unions, they *all* know. Everybody knows but me. I gotta go out there and sell the tickets. If I sell 'em, I make a little money.

I make good money. But if I guess wrong, there's no limit to what I can lose."

Stein and other promoters were also suffering a massive hangover from a two- or three-year spree. Ron Delsener, Stein's chief New York competitor, noted that "there really seemed like a time when a concert was a license to print money. It was a ritual to go to the Fillmore or one of those places on a Saturday night, and every town had its Fillmore equivalent. You could book *anyone* and it would sell out." Promoters had spent more time struggling to get bands to appear at all then they had negotiating fees.

"It's all been crazy," said Stein, "a totally lopsided sellers' market. For the last two years I hardly negotiated a contract at all. I was offered a package and either I took it or I watched one of my competitors take it. So I gave $10,000 more than I should have to a band. Or I threw in five limos and some Dom Perignon for them and made $500 less. I was still doing all right. But that's over. I'm no longer a livery stable. I'm no longer a caterer. I'm back in the business of producing concerts."

Stein's bitter references to catering and livery service were echoed by promoters all across the country. They were tired of being involved in what they saw as simply the competitive ego-tripping of artists. The ego-tripping showed most clearly in performers' "riders," clauses added to the standard booking contract that incorporated the necessary union and legal boilerplate. Performers' riders began when barnstorming bands wanted to protect themselves from working in halls with substandard sound, wiring, or lighting facilities. "The kind of rider that makes sure that some junior college in Iowa isn't going to expect a band to perform over the PA system they use for pep rallies," said Stein, "makes sense to me. That's acceptable. But a lot of this crap—flowers and brandy—is insulting. It's eighteen-year-old kids acting like they're princes."

Stein rapidly fired off a few examples of "insulting" riders: Deep Purple demanded white limousines for each member of the group, plus a black one for the road crew; the Grateful Dead required fifty meals—forty-nine steaks, and for their lighting person, who ate no meat, one lobster; others demanded a bewildering variety of exotic beverages. "Superstars get superstar treatment," said Stein. "That's fair. But with everyone else, I'm just crossing out anything I consider insulting. If they don't want to work in my concerts, that's up to them. But from now on, especially when I'm dealing with artists who are artists only because that's the word used in the contracts, I'm calling the shots."

By the standards of the riders that Stein found insulting, the Airmen's was disarmingly modest. In addition to three or four pages of technical specifications, its one exoticism was a diffident plea, inserted at the request of sound man Neil Fink, that the sandwiches for the crew contain "no processed meat or cheese, please." The Airmen's modest eating and drinking desires, however, had little effect on their ability to get bookings. That was conditioned by a number of variables, only a few within their control.

"When I'm thinking about bringing a band in here for a weekend," said an Atlanta club owner, "there are three or four factors I consider. One, of course, is whether the band has played here before and what kind of a show they did. Even if they didn't draw, but put on a good show, I'll give them a second or third shot and hope that the word of mouth brings more people in. Another thing is just the way they feel—one of the nicest things about Cody is that their road crew doesn't come on like they're king shit and you better just hop to and do whatever they say. And then there's whether they've got new product, whether their company is supporting the tour, how much money I've got to spend at any given point, and what else is going on in town that weekend."

On the factors they could control—the show they put on and the way they and their crew worked with the local promoter—the Airmen had managed to earn a living even without significant recording success. But as the money market tightened, even they had found themselves scrabbling for bookings. The college circuit, which had been a mainstay for touring acts ever since the early sixties, was feeling the pinch especially hard, as declining enrollments and straitened budgets reduced both the number of concerts any campus might have and the budget for each. Thus each tour was laboriously assembled, balancing the Airmen's need to play any given region frequently enough to keep in touch with their fans, the amount of travel required, and the fee.

This tour was different. "What Warner's did," Kerr explained, "was tell us the markets we needed to get into on this swing: Boston, New York, Philadelphia, Chicago, and Detroit. Anyplace that we couldn't set something up, they stepped in and got a booking, so that all we had to do was fill in the travel dates. I know they aren't gonna do this for us all the time, but when they do, it makes things real easy. The only thing they wanted that I wasn't all that hot for was for us to go back to New York. I thought it was a little too soon after the Academy date, but they say New York is key for the media, and they're absolutely right. So we agreed to a two-night showcase thing at the Bottom Line, which is already selling fantastically. The band isn't so hot for that gig either—they figure it'll be just like the Troubadour—but they know what they've gotta do."

Before they reached New York the band was scheduled to take their bus on what Frayne dryly called "Commander Cody's Ivy League Express," playing dates in Ithaca, Cambridge, and New Haven. When they reached Boston they were met by the East Coast artist relations representative, Alan Rosenberg. "Rosenberg is really different from Gerrity," said Frayne. "We got on really great with George, you know. He's a sloppy hippie and everything, but he's got his shit absolutely together.

Alan is kind of this sophisticated New York type. Museums and every-thing, right? So he's just the opposite of Gerrity—an older straight guy, but with a couple of bolts loose."

Notwithstanding any loose bolts—or perhaps because of them—Rosen-berg and the Boston promotion staff had things solidly lined up for the Airmen's Cambridge appearance. The windows of the Harvard Coop featured a full display of the album built around the posters and model truck that Somers had supplied. They had even set up an autographing party for Frayne inside, but he turned it down with a firm "No geek shows. I ain't Bo Donaldson, after all." Aside from that momentary dis-appointment, the first part of the tour went well. The Boston FM stations were playing the album fairly regularly, and WRKO, the area's major AM rocker, committed itself to add "Don't Let Go" if the record showed chart movement for two more weeks. At the end of the first week, as the Airmen were on their way to tape a concert at a large college on Long Island, it had jumped another notch, holding its bullet and reaching 67 in *Billboard,* 63 in *Cashbox,* and 44 in *Record World.* "One more week," promotion man Mike Symonds had assured them, "and we'll be on WRKO." If they broke into a major station in an eastern market, the record's momentum would continue to build. With that one more surge in the charts, they would be on their way to top ten.

Though the promotion was going well, neither Frayne nor any of the other Airmen were particularly happy about the quality of the music they were making. In particular, some of them felt that Hagar was simply coasting along, recycling old licks rather than driving himself to take on a more inventive role. "It's the first time Ernie's actually been in a touring band in his life," said Frayne. "All the other stuff he did before was studio work or house band stuff, where you play different things all the time. In any show we do, though, there's a certain amount of stuff that we have to do because our audience has come out to hear it. It gets pretty repeti-tive, and unless you keep working to make it new for you, the edge goes right off your playing."

Just before their New York date, Frayne took Hagar aside and gave him a combination pep talk and tongue-lashing. "I reminded him that Bobby Black was back in California looking for work." Black was the Airmen's previous steel player, and annually among the top vote-getters in the highly respected *Guitar Player* poll. "That's a tough thing to lay on anyone, but Ernie's very security conscious, and I figured maybe that was the best way to get to him. Whatever it is, though, he's got to get his ass in gear and start playing. I don't like to fuck up any gig, particularly now when we're playing tighter than we ever have before, but I certainly don't want to blow the Bottom Line."

The Airmen had never played the Bottom Line before, and had played no Manhattan club dates in years. Most clubs simply couldn't take in enough money in an evening to afford the band. The Bottom Line, like the Troubadour, was an exception. Though it had been open only about a year when the Airmen played it, the Bottom Line was the showcase for New York media. Record companies that wanted their higher-priced acts to appear there supplemented the club's payments with payments of their own and also subsidized the club directly, buying large numbers of tickets and paying tabs for dozens of invited guests. During the Airmen's four shows at the Bottom Line early in March, Warner's picked up the five-dollar admission charge and free drinks for more than two hundred critics, disc jockeys, program directors, retailers, and distributors, each of whom was entitled to bring a guest. The Airmen were pleased to see the company spending that kind of money on them, but they sensed that they would be facing another coldly cynical music-business audience rather than people who'd come out to see the band because they *wanted* to. As a result, their preparations were a little more intense than usual.

The first show was not to begin until four hours later, but they met at the Bottom Line at four in the afternoon, drifting down to the Village from their day's pursuits. Kirchen, who had been haunting the city's discount record shops, came in with a stack of out-of-print country and rockabilly records that he passed around while he traded shopping locations with Farlow and Barlow. With a self-deprecating grin, he reported that every store he went into seemed to have a large supply of the Airmen's second album selling for $1.99. Though their contract with Famous had specifically forbidden the company to sell any of their albums at low-budget prices without changing the packaging, the company had over-pressed the second album and had dumped large quantities of it on the market at near give-away wholesale prices. The resulting glut of $1.99 Airmen albums (for which the band received no royalties) had presumably hurt the sales of their regular-priced albums, but by the time Kerr discovered the breach, it had been too late to do anything. Famous had given up control over the albums when they'd sold them off. "If you think there are a lot of them around *now*," said Kerr, "just wait till ABC dumps its inventory."

He didn't seem disturbed by the prospect; ABC was unlikely to dump its inventory until after the Airmen's rerecorded "best of" album appeared (until then, any renewed spark of commercial interest in the band would help them sell off what remained in the catalog at regular prices). The conversation trailed away as Frayne arrived from his parents' Long Island home, and work on the sound check began.

The sound check, a ritual for many rock bands, was a departure for the Airmen. Fink had been struggling for years to get them into the habit of afternoon run-throughs but had not succeeded, primarily because their intensive traveling schedule had generally left them too tired to do much more than sleep during the afternoons. The infusion of money from Warner's, however, had enabled the Airmen to buy a slightly larger van for the road crew, which had previously needed to pack the equipment in the band's bus. The band no longer had to travel along with the equipment, and could occasionally get an extra night in a motel rather than trying to sleep in the jouncing bus. More or less as a price for the extra strain such traveling put on the road crew, Fink had exacted a promise from the Airmen that they would be available for sound checks any time they played a new hall. Since the Bottom Line was the most important stop on the East Coast tour, Fink had had no trouble convincing them that an hour's work in the afternoon would pay dividends at night. As they assembled onstage, he climbed the ladder leading to the mixing platform, and the sound check began.

As the Airmen loosened up with a couple of country instrumentals, Fink worked with the general sound balance and level, making sure that all the equipment was in working order—especially the monitors, the small speakers beamed back toward the stage on which the Airmen would hear themselves. "OK," he called down after a while, "let's have a vocal," and Kirchen, who was usually the first vocalist to warm up, stepped to the mike to begin "California Okie."

A few bars into it, he stopped. "Hey, Neil, I think it's too loud. Especially for a club."

"Right," Stein agreed, "you gotta be quiet enough so that people can talk over you without being disturbed."

After checking with a Bottom Line staff member who assured him that their audiences generally *liked* it loud, Fink lowered the volume only slightly. It was then Farlow's turn to try his mike, and he did a quick run-through of "Keep on Lovin' Her." As he sang, the other roadies moved around the room, checking for dead spots or speaker imbalance. They found none.

"I didn't think they would," said Fink, "but it's something you always have to check, even though you can usually tell just from looking at the equipment whether the sound is going to be any good or not. The stuff at the Troubadour, for instance, is really cheesy compared to this. The only problem in the house system here is with the monitors, and I was warned about that ahead of time and rented our own set."

By club standards the Bottom Line was luxurious. When its owners, Alan Pepper and Stanley Snadowsky, took over the former banjo bar, they had decided to spare no expense to make it the best performing room in the city. The sound system was a fifty-thousand-dollar package that included eight separate speakers and a mixing board with twelve outputs. The owners had also soundproofed the performers' dressing rooms, installed a full system of theater lights, carpeted the room, covered its wall with acoustic fabric, and installed cash registers that slid open and closed silently, so that the important business of selling drinks would not interfere with the performance any more than absolutely necessary. The expenditures had paid off, for record companies and performers practically lined up for the opportunity to play there. Despite weekly expenses of $16,000, excluding performer's fees, the Bottom Line was a highly profitable enterprise. Because it was far larger than any of its competitors—with more than four hundred seats, it held nearly twice as many paying customers as the Troubadour—it could afford to offer such amenities. A week before the Airmen's performance, Pepper and Snadowsky already had enough cash on hand from advance sales to pay for the band and cover all the club's salary and overhead expenses. The markup on food and drink (a two-drink minimum of three dollars was in force) from eight hundred people a night was clear profit. "Cody brings in a good drinking crowd, too," said Pepper.

They certainly brought in a large crowd, and even at the higher-than-usual midweek admission price of five dollars, the sixteen hundred tickets were sold out a full week before the band arrived. An unanticipated side effect of the Bottom Line's large capacity was that, despite Warner Brothers' largess, no audience was entirely a music-business one. Even the opening show, which most of the industry guests attended, was fully half hard-core Cody fans. When the band returned from their dinner break and passed, largely anonymously, through the crowd at the bar to their dressing room, they noticed it immediately.

"Listen to the *noise* out there," said Farlow as he shared a backstage joint with a couple of New York friends. "Now that's what I call a Cody crowd. None of this LA shit, man, these people are here to have a good time and hear some music. This is going to be all right." He was under-stating. *Good Times* reviewer Mitch Schneider summed up the evening by reporting that the Airmen brought the sophisticated New York audience to a "hooting, clamoring and stomping frenzy."

A more restrained appraisal, typical of the somewhat more practical attitude of the paper in which it appeared, was provided by *Variety*'s Fred Kirby, who noted that the Airmen were "dishing out exuberant cracker-jack rock, boogie and country music with a seeming casualness that has drawn a loyal coterie of young fans." He went on to issue a mild warning to club owners: "These enthusiastic youths are jamming this Greenwich Village café, even jamming aisles and affecting sightlines by the end of the lengthy set," but concluded with a silver lining: "Cody's fans are good drinkers, which makes this act most welcome in major rock bistros."

From their different perspectives, both reviewers captured the spirit of the Bottom Line appearances. The nervous tension of a major New York media booking combined with the receptive audience to spark the finest performances the Airmen had given in weeks. *Variety*'s observation that sightlines were occasionally blocked really failed to do justice to the occasion; sightlines may have been blocked by the first standees clogging the aisles, but they didn't stay that way long, for soon everyone rose. With a full half-hour still to go in the Airmen's opening set, it seemed that the entire audience was on its feet and bouncing back and forth. By the time they got offstage, after a second encore, the Airmen were floating, and the dressing room had more smacked palms than the winner's locker room at the World Series.

Hagar in particular was singled out as one by one the other Airmen praised his performance. "Ernie really came alive tonight," said Fink, "and he picked the perfect place to do it." Hagar himself was a little mystified by what had happened. "I don't know," he drawled softly. "It seems to me that I was playing the same as always, but I know it sounded different. Sometimes, especially when it's a song we've played every night for six months, I'll kind of find my attention wandering when I'm just doing background fills. But tonight, somehow, I was really there for every note in every song. It's all just a matter of concentration, I guess, and it's hard to get it up all the time. But when you're doing a show like this one, it all just comes without any real effort."

The between-sets dressing room scene was confident and somehow special. It was as jammed with well-wishers as the Troubadour had been, but it was refreshingly free from show-biz heartiness, and after a very few requisite handshakes and hugs, the crowd thinned out enough so that the Airmen could relax. Because every one of the Airmen's New York admirers seemed to have brought some sort of offering to be burned, there was a possibility that relaxation would soon slide into catatonia, but the ripples of energy around the room seemed to intensify rather than dissipate. By the time the club had emptied out and the next round of customers was seated and their first drink orders filled, the Airmen were ready to go again. "Sometimes," said Frayne as he lumbered from the dressing room, "it's really good not to have an opening act. When you've got something going, you just want to ride it."

The second set was, if possible, even better than the first. There were occasional mishaps (Stein broke a string just before the major fiddle solo of the evening, and Hagar had to improvise a steel blues while it was replaced), but for the first time the set combined the precision that the band had developed in the studio with its lengendary performing bravado. The result was extraordinary, and so was its effect on the audience. For nearly the first half of the set, everyone sat spellbound, and the occasional applause seemed almost as out of place as shouts of "right on" after an Episcopalian sermon. As the set built in its usual carefully structured fashion, there was clearly a period when people wanted to stand up and rush toward the stage but were held back by the sense that they were witnessing something special. Then, as Frayne finished a particularly rococo piano solo, someone at a rear table let forth a rebel yell, which instantly freed the rest of the audience to shout, stand, and dance. In one moment the aisles went from empty to full, and the suppressed excitement that had been building through the set finally burst out and washed across the stage in waves. As the band returned to the dressing room to await an encore, Kirchen said, "I've never felt anything like that before. The first part of that second set, man, it was so good it scared me."

Before they went out to play an encore, each was offered a couple of snorts from the knife of an old friend who'd once promoted them in a series of concerts. The coke had been a gift. "I was up in Canada when ten pounds, *ten pounds,* arrived, and my friends just offered me a bag. I didn't even have time to cut it yet."

Clearly not. When it combined with their exhilaration at their performance, it made the night seem even more special. Even after their third encore had not entirely quieted the appeals from the crowd, a large part of which continued to call for more even though it was by then two o'clock on a Monday morning, the Airmen were ready to go back. The owners, however, finally raised the house lights and ended the applause, and the Airmen unwound by sitting around the dressing room and singing rock'n'-roll tunes from the fifties. One by one, as fast as someone could remember the words, the songs came tumbling out, with Stein quietly playing sax fills and Barlow setting perfect time with his bass. At last the record company personnel drifted away, and the Airmen were left in their dressing room doing what they liked best—making the music they'd grown up on.

The next day, when Alan Rosenberg telephoned his daily minutes into the tape recorder at Warner's Burbank headquarters, the transcription read, "Commander Cody opened last night at the Bottom Line. It was truly an Event, such as New York rarely sees, or hears. The place was packed, people were boogeying in the aisles, and everything was just incredible. CC was happy, the Lost Planet Airmen were happy, The Bottom Line was happy, Joe Kerr was happy, and I was happy, which is more incredible still."

The second night's performance was not quite up to the standards of the first (it is difficult to imagine how it could have been), but much of the pandemonium was repeated: long lines outside; drinking, shouting and dancing inside. Rosenberg was more than happy. Mixing qualitative and quantitative distinctions in a way typical of the music industry, he sent the following message to the home office: "CC's performance at the Bottom Line was sensational; they could easily fill the Felt Forum or the Coliseum. Their appearance here was definitely a help to them in all avenues other than radio."

29

WARNER BROTHERS HAD DEMONSTRATED that there were other ways of selling albums—though FM was an important part of that marketing picture—but there simply is no marketing plan for singles that doesn't depend on AM play. The Airmen had gotten an enormous break when KHJ went on "Don't Let Go" without waiting for the record to work its way up through the secondary stations, but KHJ's blessing could be viewed as a curse in disguise. Despite the content of what it sells, the record business itself is rather conservative; record companies, radio stations, and concert promoters all follow established patterns quite closely. "Don't Let Go" fit none of those patterns.

By the time it had been on KHJ for six weeks, a single record would normally show a certain pattern of national sales. "Don't Let Go" did not —for one very important reason. Ordinarily, KHJ didn't even start to play a record until it had sold a certain number of copies—roughly 40,000. The Airmen's single hadn't reached that number until their Bottom Line appearance—a full six weeks after KHJ went on it. In a business less fond of patterns than the music industry, such an anomaly would cause no problem, but "Don't Let Go" ran into trouble.

The first hint came from the Warner's observers assigned to follow the workings of the chart makers. Having weathered a few scandals of their own in the past, the trade publications were scrupulously concerned that their charts be above suspicion. And they were very nervous about "Don't Let Go." It was getting strong radio play, but sales were geographically spotty. In terms of sales, it was doing quite well for a record six weeks off release; but it was not doing well for a record with six weeks on KHJ. Although Los Angeles sales were almost exactly on target, the rest of the country was lagging. At the same time, no major station other than KHJ had yet started to play it; its sales figures *were* reasonable reflections of the play that it was receiving on secondary stations. It didn't fit the pattern.

The chart makers were apparently afraid they might have been beguiled by KHJ's play and gone out on a limb with "Don't Let Go," pushing it up the charts too fast. They were not going to drop the record, but in the absence of any substantial upsurge in their measurements (such as WRKO's adding it to its playlist), they were going to soft-pedal the record for a week. It would continue to show modest upward movement, but it was going to lose its bullet until they figured out what was going on.

The problem seemed manageable to Warner's. The Boston promotion man was convinced that he had WRKO locked up, and even if the record lost its bullet for a week, WRKO's going on it would restore the bullet the following week. That week's jump would easily let their promotion men in other parts of the country explain the previous week's slowdown, and would also bring the record high enough on the national charts to aid their campaign with major stations in the other seven marketing areas.

As expected, seven weeks after it had first made the charts, "Don't Let Go" moved up one place in *Billboard* and *Record World,* and two in *Cashbox,* but it had lost its bullets. It was disappointing, of course, but hardly disastrous. Unfortunately, disaster followed rapidly. KHJ, faring poorly in a major LA ratings battle, brought in a new program director, and one of his first moves was to drop "Don't Let Go" from the station's playlist. It wasn't selling well enough, he said.

"That's bullshit," said Russ Thyret. "You can look at our layout sheets and our returns, and we were right on target with that one in LA. We'd done a little over 37,000 pieces when they dropped it, and it wasn't even in their top twenty yet. There's no way that record wasn't selling in their market." He and others at Warner's felt that the decision was simply political, a way for the new man to signal his differences from Peterson, the old program director, by pulling off the record that had been his predecessor's personal favorite as well as his "pick hit." At any rate, Warner's brandishing of sales figures was not enough to change KHJ's mind. Whatever chance "Don't Let Go" might have had to become a national hit vanished.

"You gotta understand," said a Baltimore program director, "most of this business is *looking,* not listening. We listen to everything that comes in, and sometimes something will be so outrageous we'll go on it right away. But that's what, once or twice a year? Most of the time it's looking. I read the trades, the tip sheets, look at the charts. I could see that Cody record moving up. We listened to it, and we all liked it—of course we're a little older than our listeners, which is one reason we don't only trust our ears—and it was beginning to look right for an add-on.

"Well, all of a sudden you've got KHJ going off it and firing their PD. I don't know *what* that means. But I know this: I'm not gonna go on that record until I find out. I mean, suppose they paid some guy to get it on KHJ and there's a big investigation. They're gonna have grand juries wandering around every station that went on 'Don't Let Go.' What am I, crazy? That's what I am if I go on that record."

Apart from the caution (or paranoia, or defensiveness) of some program directors, others stopped playing "Don't Let Go" simply because the loss of the major LA station meant that there was no way it could become a national hit. They interpreted the move to mean that "Don't Let Go" hadn't found a strong response on the station that had been playing it longest. The more skittish program directors dropped "Don't Let Go" as fast as they had added it. KHJ had almost made "Don't Let Go" a hit; just as quickly they had made it a certain miss.

The following week, the single held steady at number 53 in *Cashbox*, and dropped three points to 46 in *Record World*, but in *Billboard*, by far the most important of the three, it plunged into oblivion. The week before it had been 56; this week it was completely unlisted, officially signaling the single's demise. The same week's charts showed the pattern for the album that they'd shown a week earlier for the single: modest gains coupled with the loss of its bullet.

30

THOUGH THE SINGLE WAS evidently dead, it had been something of a bonus anyway. "Unless you've got a Doobie Brothers or an America," said Goldstein, "you can't really plan on a single. If it happens, great. But if it doesn't, we're still really in the business of selling albums." For album sales, the crucial stimuli were FM airplay and reviews in the key rock-oriented publications. FM airplay remained strong on the Airmen's album, and in spite of what had happened to the single, the album could still be rescued. "Finally, what happens to the album will depend on the reviews," said Goldstein.

At Warner's, responsibility for printed media was lodged within the publicity department, a ten-person division centered in New York. "When we were wooing Billie Wallington to run our publicity," said West Coast publicity director Gary George, "the deal was that she could stay in New York and open up the town-house operation there. In general it makes sense, because that's really the media capital. Occasionally things slip through the cracks because of the distance, but not often. I'm on the phone with them every day.

"You won't see the results of what we do for this record as quickly as you see results from radio," he continued, "because it takes so much longer to get print stuff set up, but if we can get strong favorable reviews in *Rolling Stone* and the *Voice* it makes a measurable difference in sales. Those papers not only sell records on their own, they influence every other review in the country. It doesn't mean that other papers are just going to repeat what *Stone* says, but it does mean that if you get a lead review in *Stone,* it guarantees that other papers will have to review the album. And that means that the FM stations will give it a shot.

"That's one of the things that made a real difference on Maria Muldaur's first album. The single is what really took it over the top, but we were getting solid sales on it long before the single broke. It was the *Rolling Stone* review that started it off."

The review, a long rave by the magazine's most prominent critic, Jon Landau, had been a surprise. Muldaur had been something of a cult figure over the years, but she was relatively unknown to the general public and her first two albums for Warner's had not sold well. Wasn't it unusual for *Stone* to give such prominence to a virtual unknown? "Sure," said George, "that's what made it such an important review for us. I knew that Landau knew her from Boston, when she was with the Jug Band, so I got the album out to him in an advance pressing and gave him time to get used to it. We all thought the album was pretty good, so there wasn't much of a gamble involved, and there was always a chance that it could pay off big. Which it did. A lot of this business is just knowing who likes what kind of performer and making sure that those people get first crack at their albums. John Rockwell at the *Times,* for instance, is really into female vocalists, so we got Emmylou out to him early and he gave it a good shot in his column. But I wouldn't expect Christgau at the *Voice* to go for her in any big way."

In addition to the relatively small number of staff writers and editors who have guaranteed access to print, the Warner's publicity department keeps tabs on a farflung network of free-lancers who provide the bulk of record reviews for publications like *Creem, Crawdaddy, Country Music,* and a host of local "underground" papers. "We have a mailing list," said George, "of about a thousand people who regularly get Warner's product. Some of them are staff writers, but most are free-lancers who get stuff published often enough so that it's worthwhile to send them free records. Right now there's a lot of pressure to save money, so we've been looking at our lists pretty hard and have dropped people who just weren't productive enough, but I think there's a limit on how much you can really save. Suppose, for instance, that I'm trying to get something done on the Doobies; I can't just send out all five albums to someone and expect him to listen to them overnight. The process has to be gradual."

As sensible as what George said was, his assumption that he could or should have been looking for someone to do something on the Doobies raises a significant issue. Wouldn't readers who base their record buying on magazine articles be a little disturbed if they knew that the author of a rave review of Warner Brothers' latest product had been chosen, not by an independent editor, but by the company that stood to profit from any sales the review generated? Such occurrences are more usual than not in the record industry, partly because the bulk of fan magazines are underedited and understaffed. They depend on free-lancers, whom they pay very little, for most of their stories, and there is no free-lancer of any consequence who has not been called by record company publicists with inducements to write about a particular act. Frequently the inducement is a spot of traveling.

"I remember when I first started writing regularly about music," said one journalist. "I'd had a few pieces in the *Voice,* and even one in *Oui,* but mostly I was feeding stuff to *Zoo World.* One day I got a call from Atlantic Records; it was a woman I'd met at one or two concerts and she said, 'How'd you like to go to Chicago to see Genesis?' Well, I was naïve then, and I guess I was a little stunned, so I just said something like 'Huh?'

"Right away, she figured I was trying to hold her up. I guess it never occurred to her that I might really not have understood what she was talking about, so she just started raising the bid, you know. If I would agree to write about Genesis, they would fly me out to Chicago from New York, put me up in the hotel with the band, cover all my expenses, bring me backstage at the concert—the whole thing. 'And,' she said, 'if you've got friends you want to see in Chicago or something and you want to stay out for a couple of extra days, that's all right with us.'

"I couldn't believe it. Here *Zoo World* was paying me something like forty bucks for a thousand-word article, and Atlantic was going to spend ten times that flying me around and feeding me so I could write it. But like I said, I was naïve then, and I said something like 'How do I know the magazine will want it?' and she just laughed and laughed."

A refugee from the now-defunct *Zoo World* confirmed the story in outline: "I don't remember that one in particular, but stuff like that used to happen all the time. Back when Cody was on Paramount, they flew a whole bunch of people down to the Armadillo for a weekend when the band was doing a live album. We sent someone on that. Why not? It was a legitimate story. Besides, we didn't pay our writers shit; we couldn't afford it. I mean, if we were making money, we wouldn't have gone out of business. So if a record company wants to spend some money and you've got a chance to give a break to someone who's been turning stuff out for you at thirty dollars a ream, why not let him do it? A lot of those people who wrote for us only ate decent meals when record companies were buying."

The net effect is that magazines like *Zoo World* run the risk of becoming record-company house organs. Their advertising comes almost totally from record companies, and their meager writers' fees are supplemented by company largess. Broadcasters can at least meet the record industry's attempts to influence them on an equal footing, but the marginal music magazines and fledgling journalists who write for them are much more malleable. "*Zoo World* was ridiculous," said George, "absolutely exploitative. But at least they were straightforwardly for sale. If you bought enough ads, you could pretty well guarantee a particular story. The sad part is that they were just beginning to get solidly enough established so that they could show some independence when they folded.

"I don't mind it when a writer who's hard up for money sells off the albums we send him. It's in the nature of a subsidy, and I spent enough time as a starving actor that I'm not about to criticize anyone for that, but there are some people who are totally rip-off oriented. *Zoo World* was one example, but that was straight business. What are you going to do about a Lisa Robinson, who comes at you with all this peer pressure? There the social problems are much more interesting."

Lisa Robinson is the editor of *Hit Parader,* a teen-oriented music publication. Along with her husband, Richard, she is at the core of a tightly knit group of friends who move back and forth among writing, editing, and publicity work. She has apparently ended *Hit Parader's* longtime policy of printing pieces written by record company personnel as though they were by independent authors, but the magazine still tends to reflect the predilections (and clients) of her friends. "I don't know what the circulation of that thing is," said George, "but she comes on like it's the most important thing in the world, and a lot of people find it hard to say no to her. I don't mind buying an article by underwriting a trip for a writer, but when you deal with her you're also contributing to her little fund of personal power. But you don't want to offend anyone, and even in her case what it all finally comes down to, unless the request is totally outlandish, is 'yes' if you have the money, 'no' if you don't."

For the Airmen, Warner's had the money.

One of the early interoffice memos about the Airmen was a note that Dave Hickey of *Country Music* magazine would be attending the band's Austin appearance, at which—courtesy of Warner's artist relations department working on behalf of Emmylou Harris—Harris was to be the opening act. Hickey's air fare and expenses were covered by the record company. Patrick Carr, the editor of *Country Music,* recalled the incident: "It's funny that there should be a Cody memo on that," he said, "because Cody was incidental in the whole affair. How that article came about is that I thought up articles Hickey could do for us. He's a good writer, and has the Austin scene down fairly well. So when I heard that Emmylou— whom we clearly wanted an article on—was going to be in Austin, it seemed like a natural. We were really looking for an attempt at the definitive piece on her. I've known her work, of course, and it was clear from what Warner's said that they were geting ready for a major push. If we could get in with an early piece, it would be very good for us. As far as Cody is concerned, we'll review their albums and so on, but they aren't a feature for us unless they really go out on the country circuit sometime.

"Somewhere along the line, however, and I don't recall exactly how it happened, it turned out that Hickey really couldn't come up with the definitive Emmylou Harris piece, and the story was converted to a 'one weekend in Austin' type of thing—which was still a quite fine story.

"Now, Warner Brothers did indeed pay for the plane fare on that, but I don't think it influenced the story at all. Unlike some of our sister publications in the rock field, we are sensitive to the implications of taking record company money, so I really am very careful about that sort of thing. If I've decided on an article I think we ought to do, and if that article involves some traveling, and if I know that the record company is cool and does that sort of thing anyway, I'll certainly call and try to get them to cover our writer's expenses. But whether I do that or not depends both on my history with that company and my mood at any given moment. Right now, as it happens, I'm feeling fiercely independent, but that doesn't mean that there aren't record companies I'd feel quite free to hit up for a plane ticket.

"On the other hand, there are a few that I just don't think we can afford to ask for anything, because they suddenly think they've bought you for the price of a plane ticket. In some cases, letting the company pay leads to too many scenes and hassles. I called up ABC one day, in fact, and told them that from now on *Country Music* pays for everything. Everyone else—well, almost everyone else, actually—is fairly cool about things, but ABC is, well, how shall I say, a little heavy-handed.

"It actually goes back a ways, to just when I came in here, but they used to advertise in *Country Music,* then stopped and made rather a big point of it. It seems that Peter McCabe went out to Las Vegas on their money and did a piece about Diana Trask that they didn't like at all. And there was also in the same issue a review of a Roy Clark album that was a little less than ecstatic. That's all it was: less than ecstatic, but on the whole quite sympathetic.

"Well, they're still not advertising. The advertising guy says it's cool, and that they just don't believe in print for country product, but the fact is that they're punishing us. Now, my position is that if I want to cover ABC artists, I'll go ahead. I'm not going to put a performer at a disadvantage just because his record company is crazy. But I'm in a rather special position; as far as country music print is concerned, we're it. We sell now about two hundred thousand copies, and we're all there is. But if we were still struggling, or if we were struggling in a more competitive arena, all these positions I'm taking would be a lot harder."

So there were no ways in which advertising or company subsidies influenced *Country Music*'s coverage? "Well, not quite. There was a situation—which also involved ABC, as it happens—back when we were starting the syndicated radio show. Our advertising guy came up to me and said he'd found a sponsor, Suzuki, but that one of the terms was that we would find a way to get a Suzuki motorcycle on the cover.

"It turned out that the request was manageable, though it bothered me some, because we had a piece already in the house on Billy 'Crash' Craddock, who was also an ABC artist. ABC knew we had the piece in— and I don't know precisely how they knew, but there are no secrets in this business—and were pressing me about putting him on the cover. Suddenly the two things just came together in a way that didn't leave me with a bad taste. Craddock is a racer who does occasionally drive a motorcycle, and I reckoned we could shoot him on top of a Suzuki and be done with it.

"Well, everything went wrong. The motorcycle that the local dealership sent over as a prop was about four hundred miles high. We put Craddock on it and he ended up photographing like a dwarf. We couldn't use any of the pictures. I called ABC and explained about it, and it all seemed very reasonable, but our advertising guy says they think for sure that I was getting even with them for not buying ads. This, I like to think, is an honest publication, but the whole business is so corrupt that they put their own interpretations on top of everything. Next to them—in fact, absolutely—Warner's has never asked for anything back at all."

A woman who worked in the Warner's publicity office at the time the arrangement with *Country Music* was struck remembers things in a slightly different light. "The first call we got about it was, I think, from Hickey, who was checking out Emmylou's schedule. We obviously wanted *Country Music* to do a story on Emmylou, because we were trying to break her country as well as pop. But we also knew that the West Coast had gone to some effort to get her on a couple of Texas bills with Cody. We're not that strong in country, and I guess they'd figured they could use Cody to piggyback her to certain audiences. What we figured was that if we were going to put our money into flying a writer down to Texas, we should get two acts rather than just one. So we suggested the 'weekend in Austin' thing. Just a suggestion, but we could see that it kind of interested him.

"That's really all we had to go on, but when Paddy called up to see whether we'd go for a writer's expenses on the story, we said sure, but we also pushed the Austin-Cody-Emmylou thing with him. We didn't know what it was going to be until the issue came out, but we like to think that we are responsible for the way the article turned out. For her, at this stage of her career, a shared article in *Country Music* is enough to make her management more than happy, and if we could get Cody in too, well, then it's a real plus for us. But none of that is any big deal. I think it helped Emmylou and all that, but features don't really make a difference unless you're hitting *Time*. As far as selling records goes, it's the reviews that count."

The reviews of the Airmen's album were disastrous, or, more accurately, the band considered them disastrous. Raves from *High Fidelity* ("Commander Cody's debut LP for Warner Bros. is his best ever"), *The Aquarian* ("a fine album, one that gets better with repeated listenings . . . a good addition to your record collection"), Baltimore's *Forecast* ("their best album"), *Boston Phoenix* ("for the first time, they sound like the cookin' pros they are"), and *Crawdaddy* ("an entertaining and enjoyable romp") paled beside detailed critical notices in *Rolling Stone* and the *Voice*.

Both of those reviews, written by people who obviously loved the band, were condemnations in the more-in-sorrow-than-in-anger style, and both emphasized the Los Angeles–San Francisco dichotomy that dogged the album:

Rolling Stone—May 8, 1975
COMMANDER CODY AND HIS LOST PLANET AIRMEN
WARNER BROS.   BS 2847
by Dave Marsh

In 1971, Commander Cody and His Lost Planet Airmen, already a legend in such disparate climes as San Francisco and Detroit, finally reached a recording agreement. Quite self-consciously, they chose Paramount Records, undistinguished for its pop product but with a leading reputation—through its Dot subsidiary—in the country market. It was Cody's plan to exploit their natural abilities as country songwriters and musicians, and to become the first of the long-hair C&W acts to reach full acceptance in the C&W market.

It was a flawed decision. Cody did, indeed, have some fine country songs—particularly "Seeds and Stems (Again)"—but as a live act, which is what sold them, their principal attraction was their wild rockabilly music. In Billy C. Farlow, the group had one of those crazy, twitchy kids who didn't just know how to sing like Jerry Lee Lewis but had the manic presence that went with the vocal mannerisms. As country players, Cody were competent and more, but they were great as a rockabilly band. If their root desires were to play straight country and western swing, to be a unifying influence between rock and country customers, that didn't change the facts.

And it hardly detracted from the spaced-out hillbilly persona they were trying to build. On the contrary, it enhanced it, just as the Rolling Stones' early success with rock enhanced their passion for the blues. Certainly, it didn't place them in the phony, soft-country league of Poco and the New Riders of the Purple Sage. Instead Cody stood with the various Gram Parsons–led groups and Asleep at the Wheel as one of the few country-rock bands whose passions and proficiency seemed legitimate. That they did not realize those farfetched ambitions of audience unification had as much to do with the reluctance of their listeners to be brought together as with any musical failure on Cody's part.

But a fluke hit, "Hot Rod Lincoln," a sort of prerockabilly novelty song, intervened. Now Cody, sadder but wiser, have opted—equally self-consciously, no doubt—for the home of the very safe and slick soft country music they originally repudiated by definition. The move to Warner's says much more about the band than the label—which just recognized a piece of talent and picked it up—but it does not necessarily bode well for Cody continuing to be so far-ranging in their attempts.

Commander Cody and His Lost Planet Airmen is a safe record. It exploits everything Cody fans take for granted, without making a nod in any direction which might expand that basic listenership. There is only one thing Cody fans are not offered here—surprises. Farlow's wildness, toned down because it has become a commonplace, is now dominated by John Tichy's more conventional country vocal style. The most distinctive track is another novelty track sung by the Commander (à la "Hot Rod Lincoln") called "That's What I Like About the South." Symptomatically, it is a recitation of clichés about the region—the very clichés Cody originally sought to explode. The effect is something like Mick Jagger, rather than Curtis Mayfield, singing "Choice of Colors."

Similarly, the group which was once audacious enough to dominate its second album with truck driving songs now delves into the shallowness of the L.A. rhinestone cowpoke scene for Lowell George's hackneyed "Willin'." Only on "Keep on Lovin' Her," "Four or Five Times," and the masterful "Don't Let Go" do Cody really recall the promise they once held. Significantly, all of those cuts are closer to upbeat Fifties rock than to weepy country.

I still think Commander Cody and his gang would sound great at the top. But I doubt if they are going to accomplish their goals by becoming Commander Coy and His Long-Haired Sidemen. When, as on "Don't Let Go," Farlow cuts loose with his slice-of-Elvis voice and Lance Dickerson recalls that his original background as a drummer was in blues and R&B bands and Andy Stein is allowed to wail on the sax, Cody are everything their fans ever believed they could be. But regardless of style, I just wish they would offer us their best ideas more often, rather than merely their most convenient.

Village Voice—March 24, 1975
COMMANDER CODY COCAINE COWBOY?
by Ed Ward

When one is close to a band, has been following it for years, and has had one's share of good times and get-downs with them, one finds oneself in a peculiar position when it comes to critical evaluation of the band's recorded product. What that stiff sentence means, in this case, is that I feel funny about the new Commander Cody album (audaciously entitled "Commander Cody and His Lost Planet Airmen"). I mean, I know these guys, personally. I've gotten loaded with them, at their homes and mine. I've spent hours talking with their manager, Joe Kerr, about the problems they've had over the years. And that's another reason "CC & His LPA" has me up against the wall.

With the exception of their last live album, Cody and the boys have never put out an LP that communicated the rowdy flavor of their live performance at its best. Sloppy recording, stiff vocals, and dull production marred too many songs; hideous promotion by their last label, Paramount, hurt their chances even more. But the band, torn between the stringent requirements of a country music career and the fact that most of their gigs were on the boogie circuit, may have equivocated themselves into a sort of professional limbo. Neither the old-timey rock'n'roll band they once were nor the purveyors of mutant Western Swing they wanted to be, shackled—still!—by their freak hit, "Hot Rod Lincoln," CC & His LPA show signs of intense uneasiness at the prospect of slogging along like this forever.

On the other hand, this would hardly be the time to give up. "CC & His LPA" is a new start on a new label and, while it's not a great Commander Cody record, it's still head and shoulders above the run-of-the-mill country-rock band's record. Because that's where it looks like Cody's going now; the Poco/Eagles/New Riders (Joe manages them too) audience. Proof? Cut one is "Southbound," a Hoyt Axton song, for chrissakes, and they've even sold out so far as to include that stereotyped misapprehension of truckdriving, "Willin'." (You guys coulda found a better truckdriving song than that—Tichy knows 'em, and so do I.) They'll get airplay with this stuff, and they'll sell records.

And who knows? They might even get a hit—"Don't Let Go" is a catchy little number, and Billy C doesn't say "Aw, shit" once in it, like he does on stage. One senses that Warner's will try to break the single, something Paramount never did such a hot job of doing.

Besides the single, there are some commendable cuts: "Hawaii Blues," "Four or Five Times," and Cody's ridiculous reading of "That's What I Like About the South." On the other hand, there's never been so much filler on a Cody album before, and even Blackie Farrell's one contribution, "California Okie," isn't up to his high standards of straight-ahead country or loving caricature.

I don't know. "CC & His LPA" is produced with a certain sensitivity, blessed with a neat Chris Frayne cover, and doesn't sound like it was recorded in the La Brea tar pits. What's on the inside, on the other hand, is thin enough to make me wonder how interested in staying together the boys really are. If the album sells at all well, their spirits may revive. And even if they are going country-rock, I'd hate to see them bust up and leave the field to what passes for their competition—the cocaine cowboys. It may not show here, but at least Cody and the boys have roots.

The reviews, though aesthetically contradictory, were commercially devastating. To have the two most prestigious music publications in the country simultaneously coming down on the record not only prompted FM program directors to ease up playing it, it gave people at Warner Brothers second thoughts about how hard they should try to push it. In their own way, the reviews also captured the Airmen's problem perfectly. The Airmen had felt that their survival and growth meant that they had to change what they'd been doing. Marsh and Ward wanted them to remain what they'd always been.

"What they'd always been" was, unfortunately for the Airmen, different for each reviewer. Marsh, who remembered the band (and Billy C.) from his own days in Detroit, wanted them to be a basic rock'n'roll band; Ward, reflecting his own Bay Area sensibility, wanted them to go back to western swing (hence Ward dismissed "Don't Let Go" as "a catchy little number," while Marsh singled it out as "masterful").

Both reviewers made a point of blaming "Hot Rod Lincoln" for whatever had gone wrong with (their own versions of) the Airmen's career. Yet that record had been the one moment of wide popular acceptance in the Airmen's history. And it is reasonable to argue that their attempt to recapture that success without simply seeking out another fast-talking novelty—while retaining enough of both their country and rock'n'roll roots to frustrate reviewers who wanted them to be one way or another— was a genuinely noble effort.

But it was undeniably a futile one. When the reviews were added onto the loss of morale that the Warner's staff had already suffered after the precipitous decline of "Don't Let Go," they signaled the end of the album. "Warner's has real virtues," said Hessenius. "If a record has a handle, they can pick it up and go with it, but they're a new organization. They don't have the machine that CBS does, and they don't have the kind of control over WEA that CBS has over its salesman. They run on enthusiasm. And when the single died, there was no way they could get the enthusiasm going again. How are you gonna get a promo man who's been hyped to think of Cody as the second coming to trudge around to secondary FMs trying to scare up a little album play? Once the single died, there was no way that the album was gonna happen." Finally, the album receded slowly down the charts, and sales leveled out at about 100,000, just about what the last three had done—and far worse than the Airmen or their record company had hoped.

31

LIKE A HANGOVER, a divorce, or any other unwelcome souvenir of a broken dream, the aftermath had its quota of bitterness. The band, the company, Boylan, Kerr—all were forced to ask that most uncomfortable of questions: "Where did we go wrong?"

The question came hardest to the band. Warner's had at most to deal with having made a bad business decision, Boylan was already in the middle of his next project, and Kerr had had little to do with the album proper. The Airmen had no such comfortable distance between them and their disappointment. They began to think maybe they just weren't a very good band.

"Of course that's the kind of thing you think," said Frayne. "But it's also the kind of thing you can't let yourself go on thinking for too long, because then you start to play as if you thought you weren't any good. And when that happens, you aren't."

But there was no magical way to overcome the disappointment, particularly because when their first flush of enthusiasm was so suddenly dampened, the record somehow stopped sounding good to them. And to some extent they were right. Boylan had done exactly what had been asked of him, but it had turned out to be a mistake. The Airmen were not the Eagles, and the attempt to make them sound that way on a record had been misconceived. Live, when they were able to fuse the precision that Boylan had instilled with their natural performing exuberance, they reached the extraordinary heights of their Bottom Line show. The record, by contrast, sounded emotionally flat; it just didn't work. Instead of being unique, if perhaps not commercial, they had become imitators of a style that was alien to them. And because it was alien, they had remained not commercial.

"The only thing worse than selling out," Frayne joked halfheartedly, "is selling out and not getting bought."

Frayne's hopes were unquestionably shattered, but perhaps he was being too pessimistic. Several of the album's cuts had been in the Airmen's traditional vein, and in areas where his vision had merely refined rather than replaced theirs, Boylan had undoubtedly made them into a tighter and more relentlessly swinging band. And the Album *had* sold a hundred thousand copies. Even considering the cost of the ABC buyout, Warner's had not lost an unprecedented amount. The relatively heavy promotion had increased costs, but a very conservative estimate of preroyalty profits (based on the $300,000 sales to distributors) was $75,000. Add to that earnings from the single of approximately $20,000 and the WEA net of some $10,000 from the distributor's margin, and Warner's was back in the ball park. If the next album hit, sales of this one from the catalog might even make it profitable.

"I think the deal was steep; I thought that to begin with," said Mary Martin. "But I can't imagine us giving up on this band. They're just too good for that to happen. And this company has never walked away from an act whose music we believed in."

The Airmen couldn't know that, however. Warner Brothers was used to hits, flops, and everything in between, and though the Airmen felt that their album was a flop, for Warner's it was at worst a high in-between. While the Airmen were still reeling in pain, Warner's was gearing for the next album. This time, said Ed Rosenblatt, they would push the album first: "We'll wait for the reaction before we pick a single." If the company felt it had made a mistake, it had at least been one they could learn from.

In addition, Warner's had the resilience characteristic of bureaucracies. The Airmen, individuals as well as individualists, had no such emotional cushion. They could, and did, lean on each other for support, but at least for a while, they would have to live with failure. For the first time, they had made a money-losing record. In the face of that reality, their decision to gamble with the short-term Warner's contract suddenly looked like a mistake. They believed that if their next album didn't do appreciably better than this one, Warner's would probably not pick up their option.

"Behind that," said Kerr, "they just freaked out."

The band certainly proceeded to make changes. Hagar was the first to go. "But that didn't really have much to do with the record," said Frayne. "That was starting to happen even when we thought we had a hit. I suppose it might not have happened if the record had been a real monster, but I'm not so sure."

No one can be, but it is likely that Hagar's sensibility and life style differed so sharply from the rest of the Airmen's that only the external force of a hit record could have kept him with them much longer, especially when the former Airman, Bobby Black, was looking for a chance to rejoin them. The parting was amicable, and while the Airmen were on the road giving concerts and gradually trying to develop songs for the next album, Hagar, who remained under contract to Warner's, was in Los Angeles organizing his own country-oriented band.

Boylan was next. "I think they really took those reviews, particularly the one in *Rolling Stone*, to heart," said Mary Martin. "After that they were looking for someone who was into basic rock'n'roll, and when Hoyt said he was interested in working with them, it just sounded so right that they all jumped at the idea."

Hoyt Axton, though he was hardly a proven quantity as a producer, was both a good friend of the band and the possessor of very shrewd commercial instincts. For safety, however, Warner's, which had the contractual right to approve producers, insisted that he be paired with an engineer of their choice. "I had several long chats with Joe about it," said Mary Martin, "and it seemed to me to be a really good balance of a creative mind with a practical application. I was all for that."

And so in July, less than a week before he was to return to the Record Plant to begin working on the second album the Airmen owed Warner's, Boylan learned that he had been replaced.

"I understand why they did it," he said, "though of course I think they made a mistake. I think it was just one of those things where you sort of jettison everything you can and hope that you somehow manage to throw out whatever it was that went wrong."

For Boylan, whatever went wrong was not simply a matter of failures to be found in the grooves of the record: "The common thing for an independent producer to do is blame it on the record company, so I might as well remain true to form: they lost it.

"Look at the LA sales; there's your clue. When a record is released, there are maybe three things that can happen to it. One is that nobody plays it, which means it doesn't sell. Now that might be the record company's problem, in that they didn't know how to get any program directors to listen to it, or it might be yours. Everybody who listened to it might have hated it. So when that happens, you can't tell where the problem was.

"The second is that it gets lots of airplay but nobody buys it. In that case it's clear that the record company did its job just fine, and that there was something wrong with the record.

"The third possibility—which is what happened with this record—is that when it gets airplay, it gets sales. 'Don't Let Go' was a solid regional hit, and they couldn't spread it across the country. That's the record company's fault. It was also," he continued, *"that* close. If KHJ had stayed with it one more week, RKO in Boston would have gone on it and it would have been all over. That's not saying that there weren't problems with the album—I can list a whole lot of them, and I like to think I would have corrected them on the second one—but when a record gets as close as that one did, the company should be able to push it over."

An examination of the sales figures seems to bear out Boylan's contention. As of mid-April, when "Don't Let Go" fell off the charts, its Los Angeles sales totaled more than 41,000 units. In New York, where Warner's had been unable to crack the AM radio barrier, the single had sold less than 3,000 copies, and the album had actually outsold it by more than a two-to-one ratio. The same pattern was repeated nationwide; in those cities where the single had gotten AM play, it sold quite respectably—14,000 in Cleveland, 9,700 in Atlanta—but in every other market except Boston, it actually sold fewer copies than the album. "You can't get around it," said Boylan. "Warner's just didn't do the job."

Predictably, Warner Brothers' Ed Rosenblatt had a different explanation: "The ultimate thing that went wrong is what the Commander put on that album. Any other thing that somebody says is just an intellectual jerk-off. Sure, we had the single going for a while—had five or six weeks of everybody jumping up and down—but if the business is a crap-shoot, singles are the crap-shoot of crap-shoots. Out of four thousand singles that come out every year, how many hit top ten? Fifty? Seventy-five at most.

"The thing is, we've had lots of success with albums where the single has gone down the toilet. And that didn't happen with the Commander. If we were a company that depended on singles to break our albums, I'd have to say that maybe we did blow this one. But we're not. We never have been, and if it's in the product, we'll bring it home. This album got a lot of FM play—not massive, but a lot—but it didn't move out of the stores. And that's not our fault."

Kerr tended to agree with Rosenblatt. "I don't think Warner Brothers was remiss; I don't think the band was remiss. The single was out there, the band was out there touring, the album was in the stores. . . . People just didn't buy it. I think Warner Brothers treated the band righteous on the whole.

"I also don't think that what happened was any real kind of disaster. That album got higher on the charts than anything they've ever done before, including the first one. It didn't sell as many copies, but some of that is just the economy. The Jefferson Starship just had a number-one album, and it was number one for almost two weeks before it went gold. It used to be a couple of years ago that every album in the top ten was gold. Sure, the record company lost money on it, but that was partly because the deal was steep. If they sell a hundred thousand albums and a hundred thousand singles and *still* lose money, all that means is I made a good deal for the band."

Kerr was one of the few principals on whom the failure of the record could not be blamed, but he was nonetheless the next to go. At a stormy midsummer meeting six months after the album had been released, the Airmen overcame arguments from Higginbotham, Fink, and Hessenius and voted unanimously to leave Kerr. Their decision had little to do with the record—though Hessenius pointed out that they probably wouldn't have had the incentive to change if they'd been on the top—but a great deal with their feeling that Kerr had grown personally distant from them.

"I think," said Higginbotham, "they just didn't know what Joe was doing. They knew we'd gotten all this money from Warner's, and they knew they were out working almost every night. Yet by June we had started skipping salary checks again. There were some reasons for that. One was that concert business always gets slow in the summer. But the big thing was that we hadn't planned on signing the kind of deal we did with Warner's. All of a sudden, we were a profitable corporation and had to pay taxes. But that record started off looking like such a monster that we just miscalculated and didn't set enough money aside for taxes. I think Joe could have explained that to them. All they wanted to know was *why*. But he never got around to telling them."

Hessenius theorized, "Joe just forgot who his client was. He knew he was working for the band, that they were his employers, but he got so wrapped up in wrestling with the record companies and the bookers that he didn't apply what he knew." In this view, Kerr had become like the character in *Catch-22* who got so caught up in the mechanics of cornering the Egyptian cotton market that he ended up bombing his own troops. Only in this case they bombed him.

They wounded Kerr so badly that he thought of suing them for breach of contract. But there was no contract. When they began, they had been a family; imperceptibly, as Kerr's thoughts of litigation indicated, they had become a business. Yet the Airmen hadn't forgotten their past, and, his pain eased by a promised cash settlement that the band was under no legal obligation to provide, Kerr was finally fatalistic: "It's one of those things that just happens. It's like baseball: when you're losing, you fire the manager."

But firing the manager can be as much a cosmetic gesture in music as it is in baseball, and Kerr spoke pessimistically of the Airmen's future. "The hard-core bought that album, like they always do, but what the band has to face is that maybe that's it. They were in the vanguard, and somehow the whole thing just passed them by. They used to be '*the* long-haired country band,' and now, unless this next album really takes off, they're just the old guys who started it all."

For the Airmen, just being the "old guys" was obviously not enough. The convulsive purges in their organization would be meaningless unless they somehow managed to fight through their disappointment and pain to find themselves musically. And they worked at it.

"One of the things that really helped to get us back up was touring," said Frayne. "Warner's was great, man, because even when the album did its turkey number, they didn't back off. We did a whole bunch of colleges in the spring, and they organized beer parties and contests and stuff like that on every campus we hit. It sort of showed that they still believed in us. And by then, too, we were starting to work on new stuff for the next album, and that's always kind of a good time. You get to try stuff out cold and see how people respond. It's one thing to stand up and do 'Hot Rod Lincoln,' but when you can get people going with stuff they haven't heard before, that's really great."

Even more important than working on material for the new album was the kind of music they chose. Systematically, they dropped the previous album's smoothest songs—"Southbound" among them—from their act and began replacing them with the eclectic mix of rockabilly and country that had always been their long suit. They knew that they might have only one more album to make: they wanted it to be theirs. If Warner's ended up dropping them at the end of the option period, they would at least go out with their heads high. If the business hadn't made them stars, neither had it made them sycophants. But it had been close. The "star-making machinery" that had turned them into a product had almost succeeded in grinding them up.

INDEX

ABOUT THE AUTHOR

GEOFFREY STOKES is on the staff of *The Village Voice,* where he writes regularly about music and politics. He has also contributed to *Harper's, Ms., Oui* and other publications. In 1976 he won the New York State Bar Association's media award for outstanding reporting of legal issues.

VINTAGE POLITICAL SCIENCE AND SOCIAL CRITICISM